El Salvador

A Country Guide

El Salvador
A Country Guide

Tom Barry

The Inter-Hemispheric Education Resource Center

Albuquerque, New Mexico

First edition, February 1990
Second edition, January 1991
Production by Jenny Beatty / The Resource Center
Cover design by TypArt

Published by The Inter-Hemispheric Education Resource Center

ISBN: 0-911213-30-9

Library of Congress Catalog Card Number: 89-82375

.

The Inter-Hemispheric Education Resource Center
Box 4506 * Albuquerque, New Mexico * 87196

Acknowledgments

El Salvador: A Country Guide, like the other books in this series, represents the contributions of many Resource Center staff members. I thank Jenny Beatty, Joan MacLean, Felipe Montoya, Debra Preusch, and Thomas Weiss for their research assistance; Connie Adler and Jenny Beatty for editing and proofreading the manuscript; and Jenny Beatty also formatted the book and otherwise prepared it for publication. Martin C. Needler contributed portions of the manuscript and compiled the chronology. I greatly appreciated the comments on the manuscript offered by Roberto Codas, Charles Kernigan, Thomas Quigley, and Mike Zielinski. I relied extensively on the excellent publications of the University of Central America in San Salvador.

Table of Contents

The Resource Center

The Inter-Hemispheric Education Resource Center is a private non-profit research and policy institute located in Albuquerque, New Mexico. Founded in 1979, the Resource Center produces books, policy reports, and audiovisuals about U.S. foreign relations with third world countries. Among its most popular materials are *The Central America Fact Book* and the quarterly *Bulletin* mailed to subscribers for $5 annually ($7.50 outside the United States). For a catalogue of publications, please write to: The Resource Center, Box 4506, Albuquerque, NM 87196.

Board of Directors

El Salvador

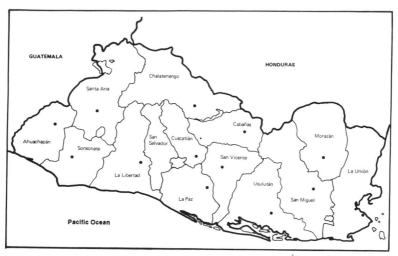

GUATEMALA

HONDURAS

Chalatenango

Santa Ana

Cabañas

Morazán

Ahuachapán

San
Salvador

Cuscatlán

Sonsonate

San Vicente

La Libertad

La Unión

Usulután

La Paz

San Miguel

Pacific Ocean

Inforpress Centroamericana

Introduction

El Salvador is a country in civil war. Over the last decade two armies have battled to gain the upper hand in a war that has left over 70,000 dead and caused at least 750,000 to flee the country. It is a war that has deeply divided Salvadoran society and has become the focal point of the regional crisis.

Looking back over Salvadoran history, it could be said that this civil war was inevitable given the society's deep divisions between rich and poor and the long repression of the political and economic aspirations of the organized popular sectors. But others, including government leaders, say that the war can be better explained by looking outside Salvadoran borders to an international communist conspiracy involving the Soviet Union, Cuba, and Nicaragua. They charge that a dedicated minority of Marxist revolutionaries, supplied and trained by foreign communists, have incited peasants, workers, and students to seek change through political violence. This explanation of the war's origins is also advanced by the U.S. government whose dollars and weapons fortify the Salvadoran state.

There has also been considerable debate about the magnitude and nature of the conflict. Those forces gathered around the Salvadoran state—the U.S. embassy, the Salvadoran armed forces, the local business elite, and the centrist and rightwing political parties—have characterized the political violence as the product of isolated "terrorists," "communist subversives," and "delinquents." It is not a civil war at all, they say, but a terrorist assault that requires appropriate doses of counterterrorism and counterinsurgency.

In 1980 just such a campaign got underway. Its purpose was to isolate and then eliminate this subversive and violence-prone element in Salvadoran society. "Surgically removing a cancer" was the analogy used to describe the counterinsurgency effort. Superficially, the cancer analogy seemed an accurate description for most of the 1980s when the war was largely confined to certain rural areas and only barely touched San Salvador—the country's economic and political heart. Many among the society's middle and upper classes regarded the Farabundo Martí National Liberation Front (FMLN) as little more than a gang of bandits intent on disrupting the dominant civil order.

The $4 billion in U.S. aid to El Salvador during the 1980s was justified on this premise that a small group of terrorists was obstructing the country's economic and political progress. But Washington recognized that El Salvador had more than a strictly military problem and that political and economic changes were needed if the Salvadoran state was to be stabilized. Besides building up the army and police, the U.S. government put in place a "democratization" program designed to ensure civilian and constitutional rule. Acknowledging that the economically precarious conditions of most Salvadorans constituted a breeding ground for subversion, Washington spent three of every four aid dollars in economic assistance and stabilization programs.

But neither military nor economic aid succeeded in marginalizing and crushing the insurgency. Despite U.S. efforts, the country became more militarized, the government grew more unstable, and the divisions between the poor and the rich became yet more extreme. By the end of the decade the cancer of insurgency had been neither neutralized nor removed. No part of the country's economic, political, or military system was secure from the subversion. Even the country's most exclusive neighborhoods had at times become battlegrounds, and the enemy's military capacity was greater than ever.

* * *

In a guerrilla war, popular support is key—not just in logistical terms but also in political ones. As the strategists of low-intensity conflict and counterinsurgency war observe: "Over 90 percent of war is fought politically and only 10 percent militarily." The campaign to win the hearts and minds of the Salvadoran people began as soon as the armed conflict erupted. Salvadorans were offered an electoral democracy, a constitutional government, and a capitalist system softened by economic reforms and social services. The alternative, they were told, was terrorism, communist dictatorship, and economic ruin.

In 1980 the government announced political and economic reforms, which for the first time raised hopes that the country's economic and political systems would be modernized. A land-reform program was launched, and a centrist civilian government took office after elections, breaking the long tradition of direct military rule. For its part, the military offered civic-action programs to demonstrate the good will of the armed forces.

The guerrilla opposition has thus far been able to offer little more than promises. But its revolutionary program appeals to those Salvadorans, particularly the poor, who see the need for radical political and economic change. The FMLN guerrilla army has been able to count on the widespread belief in the country that nonviolent methods alone will not bring about significant progress for the large majority of poor Salvadorans. The FMLN's analysis of class struggle and critique of U.S. imperialism attracts other sympathizers and adherents. The *muchachos* have also won support as a result of their dedication and courage as guerrilla fighters and their support for ongoing struggles for higher wages, more land redistribution, and other popular demands.

After a period of unrelenting repression in the early 1980s, a popular movement reemerged in the middle of the decade. Speaking out were new union federations, student organizations, peasant associations, community groups, women's organizations, and human-rights groups. At first the Christian Democratic government of José Napoleón Duarte successfully incorporated new worker and peasant organizations into a progovernment alliance. But disenchantment with the Duarte administration grew as the war deepened and socioeconomic conditions worsened. By the end of his term and the beginning of the ARENA government of Alfredo Cristiani, most organized popular sectors were openly antigovernment.

Because the guerrilla's own political and economic demands so often parallel those of the popular organizations, the popular movement has proved fruitful ground for FMLN organizers. The FMLN's electoral and peace proposals, in particular, have found strong resonance among the country's popular organizations and churches. The government and the military have charged that the country's popular leaders, church activists, and intellectuals take their lead from the FMLN. It is undoubtedly the case that ties exist between the FMLN and some popular activists. But those organizations demanding peace and justice are not organizationally linked to the FMLN. They determine their own demands and political direction based on the needs and opinions of their members. In fact, the FMLN has often modified its demands to match those of the popular sector and churches rather than the other way around.

According to the FMLN, the faction that holds the support of the masses holds the key to victory.[1] Although the government acknowledges its own lack of support among the popular sectors, it disputes the FMLN's contention that the guerrilla forces have the sympathy of the "masses."

As evidence, the government points to the million or more citizens who go to the polls every several years to chose their mayors, Assembly deputies, and president. Furthermore, the FMLN's prediction of a popular insurrection is dismissed as largely a guerrilla illusion.

The popular support of the FMLN appears strongest among peasant communities and more tenuous among the urban poor. El Salvador is the most organized society in Central America, but there still exists a large unorganized and politically inactive population that is simply trying to survive the war and economic crisis. Also a challenge for the FMLN is the middle class whose support would be critical in any popular uprising against the government. As it is, however, the middle sectors have largely thrown their support to the government and have stood outside the popular coalitions.

*   *   *

The war in El Salvador broke out in 1980 but it is a conflict that has been building for at least a half a century. In the late 1920s a popular movement of students, workers, and peasants began coalescing around demands for basic political and economic rights. A U.S. Army officer visiting El Salvador in 1931 described the country this way:

> There appears to be nothing between these high-priced cars and the oxcart with its barefoot attendant. There is practically no middle class....Thirty or forty families own nearly everything in the country. They live in almost regal style. The rest of the population has almost nothing.[2]

After a civilian president, Arturo Araujo, proved unable to pacify this mounting internal dissension either with reforms or by repression, the country's vice president, Gen. Maximiliano Hernández Martínez, took over the presidency. In 1932 the general unleashed a scourge of repression that is still referred to simply as the *matanza* or massacre.

No one really knows how many died in that country-wide massacre. The most common figure is 30,000 but some say that the army did not have enough bullets to kill more than 10,000. One of those killed was the communist leader Augustín Farabundo Martí, whose name and cause was assumed in 1980 by a guerrilla coalition called the Farabundo Martí National Liberation Front (FMLN).

The repression of 1932 had the desired effect of smothering the dissident popular sectors in a blanket of blood. But neither General Hernández Martínez nor any of the generals or colonels that later ruled the country did anything to alter the desperate circumstances of the rural poor or to open up the country's military-controlled political system.

At first look, not much had changed in the five decades that followed the *matanza*. At the end of the 1970s an army general was still in the Casa Presidencial, terror was still used to repress popular organizing, hunger and poverty were the lot of the large majority, and the economic elite or oligarchy was, if anything, more ostentatious in its display of wealth and privilege.

While the country's narrow political and economic divisions remained largely intact, Salvadoran society had been changing in many important and, as it may turn out, decisive ways. In the 1950s the economy began to diversify. Sharecroppers who worked the traditional *latifundios* were pushed off the land as estates were converted into more modern agricultural enterprises relying on seasonal peasant labor. Other small farmers were pushed off their plots as the agroexport economy expanded beyond coffee to include cattle, cotton, and sugar. El Salvador also began to industrialize, which created new tendencies within the oligarchy and gave birth to larger working class. The changing economy also gave rise to an expanding middle class of professionals, technicians, small entrepreneurs, and bureaucrats.

New political and religious ideas began to circulate and challenge the traditions and structures of Salvadoran society. The alliance between the Catholic church and the elite began to break down after Vatican II and the Medellín Conference of 1968. The poor were empowered and dignified by new church teachings which equated morality and social justice. The revolution in Cuba reverberated throughout the continent, giving leftist organizers and intellectuals new hope that radical change was indeed possible. The economic reformism and attention to rural problems promoted by President Kennedy's Alliance for Progress, while not directly challenging the military and political elite, did stir the winds of change. So too did the emergence of new political parties like the Christian Democratic Party which created new hope for the country's political and economic future.

In the 1960s, and especially in the 1970s, the popular sectors began breaking the silence of fear that had settled over the country after the 1932 bloodbath. Peasants demanded land, and workers a decent wage. The booming economy and the expanding reach of the electronic media created rising expectations among the country's downtrodden majority. As if overnight, in the mid-1970s it suddenly seemed that Salvadorans were organized and demanding change.

But neither the oligarchy nor the military were ready to budge. During the 1970s the political opposition was kept out of government by fraudulent elections; and the peaceful protests of students, workers, and peasants were brutally repressed. Political and social tensions reached an apex in 1979-1980 — at which point the FMLN formed and the United States moved in to assist the Salvadoran state on its new path of political, military, and economic development.

Repression and uncompromising rule by the military and oligarchy had failed to keep the society pacified. In the 1980s a new combination of civilian rule, counterinsurgency, and halting economic reforms was tested. By the end of the decade, however, the Salvadoran state had not been stabilized. Class divisions had widened, and what had initially seemed merely a police problem had widened into a civil war.

*   *   *

The war, whose stated purpose was to eliminate the guerrillas, targeted mostly the civilian population. Particularly hard hit were those workers, students, squatters, peasants, and displaced who tried to organize themselves to protect their rights and improve their well-being. From 1979 through 1989, 40,000 to 50,000 civilians died in the conflict, mainly at the hands of the U.S.-trained and supplied military.[3] The combined death toll for civilians and combatants was over 70,000.

After a decade of U.S.-directed democratization and counterinsurgency, the military is more powerful and abusive than ever before — having quintupled in size and been fortified by more than a billion dollars in U.S. military aid. No longer is the magnitude of its human-rights abuses constrained by the number of bullets it possesses. The military now counts on unlimited firepower and a formidable air force, all of which it uses freely against nonmilitary targets. A civilian now wears the presidential sash but the military answers to no one — that is, no one except for the U.S. embassy.

By 1990 per capita income had fallen to one-quarter below the level of ten years before. Unemployment is over 50 percent, and 45 percent of Salvadorans cannot afford even a basic diet — let alone other necessities like health care and housing.[4] At least a third of the population is among the internally displaced or has been forced to flee the country because of the war. Around the major cities shantytowns of cardboard and other discarded materials have sprung up. Sixty percent of the urban population and 90 percent of those living in the countryside do not have the economic resources to live in decent housing.[5]

At the same time San Salvador saw a boom in the construction of luxury housing and commercial buildings. Services catering to the elite also prospered during the 1980s. A posh commercial center opened, and a new Pizza Hut and other fastfood places sprung up in wealthier neighborhoods. On Saturday nights the sons and daughters of the oligarchs—known as "garks"—check their guns at the door of nightclubs like Mario's.[6] Smartly polished BMWs, Mercedes, and Cherokees—many with tinted windows and some armor-plated—line up for the drive-thrus at such favorite spots as Pop's and McDonald's. Although the economy was stagnating, U.S. aid and credits have pumped billions of dollars into the highest reaches of Salvadoran society.

Meanwhile many peasants are still without shoes and only the more fortunate of them have oxcarts and a little patch of soil to call their own. Beggars abound, but private security guards are constantly clearing them away from the homes and entertainment spots of those who have *colones* and dollars to spare. The war kills the poor but so does poverty and lack of basic services. UNICEF has estimated that several hundred children die every week in El Salvador as a result of malnutrition, preventable diseases, and lack of medical care. Ten years ago three of every ten Salvadorans had easy access to safe drinking war, but only one in ten does now.[7]

Reverend Segundo Montes, former director of the Institute of Human Rights at the University of Central America, published a study in 1988 describing the economic makeup of Salvadoran society. He found that less than one percent of the population belonged to an upper echelon which owned most of the society's wealth; another 24 percent comprised the country's middle class, mostly professionals, bureaucrats, and small business owners; and at the bottom were 74 percent who were workers, peasants, and the unemployed—almost all of whom lived in poverty.[8] On November 16, 1989 Father Montes himself became a statistic, having been gunned down in the middle of the night by U.S.-trained troops.

The economic and social divisions in contemporary El Salvador are as shocking as they were to that U.S. officer who described them in 1931. The repression and killing by the Salvadoran army, "professionalized" by U.S. advisers, is as severe and mindless as anything experienced during the reign of the infamous Gen. Maximiliano Hernández Martínez.

But this time the popular rebellion has not been so easily repressed. The government troops face a sophisticated and dedicated guerrilla army—not simply peasants armed with machetes. Standing across the line from the government and the army is also a strong popular movement that refuses to be silenced. When one union leader or human-rights activist disappears or is tortured to death, another one takes her or his place. From the shantytowns and union halls to the universities and churches, the people and their leaders are demanding economic justice and a negotiated peace.

Despite escalating human rights abuses, not since the late 1970s has the popular movement been so unified, with the Christian Democratic-allied unions and peasant organizations joining a broad popular alliance demanding economic justice and a negotiated end to the conflict. What makes this civilian movement so threatening to the government is that its demands largely coincide with those raised by the armed FMLN.

The Cristiani administration took office with the confidence that it could reactivate the economy with neoliberal reforms and end the war with improved military/political collaboration. But nearly two years into his five-year term, the stability of the nation had become increasingly precarious. Facing the March 1991 elections, the ruling ARENA party found itself losing support on all sides. Its failure to spur economic growth and end the war alienated the private sector while its willingness to talk to the FMLN angered the ARENA's rightwing base. Government initiatives to privatize education, raise transportation prices, and impose new structural adjustment measures have angered the popular sectors.

In April 1990, when the FMLN and the government agreed to begin U.N.-mediated negotiations, there was widespread hope in the popular movement that a cease-fire would be signed by September 1990, but the negotiations proved fruitless. As the elections approached, the Christian Democratic Party and the Democratic Convergence threatened to sit out the elections if the government did not provide for international monitoring and a repression-free atmosphere for the vote. Opinion surveys in late 1990 showed widespread dissatisfaction with ARENA because of rising inflation and unemployment, and because of its failure to push the Jesuit case forward and to demonstrate the government's control of the military. Making matters worse was the control by the party's ultra-right over candidate selection and campaigning. The unity of the electoral left was also in doubt as pre-election politicking began, and it was doubtful that there would be much popular interest in the elections as long as the war still raged and the peace process was stalled.

Economic considerations have become increasingly weighty in the way the Salvadoran government and private sector view the civil war. During the 1980s the downpour of U.S. aid dollars washed aside concerns about budget deficits, falling demand, and decreased production. In the 1990s, however, the economy can no longer count on such large flows of aid. With the exception of the most ideologically committed, there is now widespread recognition among the private sector that terminating the war is essential to economic recovery. Neighboring countries are also pressuring El Salvador to end the war, which they regard as the main obstacle to efforts to expand regional economic integration.

After a long period of strong bipartisan consensus, U.S. policy in El Salvador began to break down by late 1990. The November 1989 offensive and army massacre of the Jesuits had irrevocably shattered the myths that the war was being won and that democracy was being constructed in El Salvador. Congress showed that the days of unlimited aid for the counterinsurgency were numbered, while the option of direct U.S. military intervention to defeat the FMLN seemed an ever more remote possibility. Still, Washington has not used its considerable leverage to push forward a negotiated solution.

Civil war has devastated this tiny country of 5.3 million people. It is a war that reflects the country's sharp class divisions and its tradition of militarization. It is also an ideological standoff between those who want to reinforce the private-enterprise system and those who demand radical structural reforms. At the extremes of this divide are rightwing ideologues who embrace fascism and leftist revolutionaries committed to socialist solutions. But more than a civil war, the bloodletting in El Salvador has been a product of U.S. determination to defeat the FMLN and maintain this U.S. client state in the region.

Since late 1988 the FMLN has followed a two-track strategy to bring about a negotiated end to the war. On the military side, the November 1989 offensive forced the government to recognize the FMLN's considerable strength and opened the doors to a U.N.-mediated negotiating process. On the political side, the FMLN declared its willingness to abide by the results of an electoral process, on the condition that an internationally monitored cease-fire is arranged and international monitors verify that the process is free and fair.

But before laying down its arms, the FMLN insisted that human rights violators be purged from the military and the size of the armed forces be reduced to pre-1980 levels. Echoing this "purge and reduce" demand have been the popular organizations, who are the main victims of continued repression. But the military has dismissed this demand, saying the Salvadoran people should "forgive and forget" the institution's bloody history.

Civil war remains the major issue in El Salvador. But when the war finally ends El Salvador will confront a host of development problems. As one of the most densely populated nations in the world, El Salvador will have a difficult time feeding itself while simultaneously increasing its agricultural exports. Infrastructure damage from the war will present a serious impediment to economic modernization and growth. On the positive side, however, Salvadorans are an admirably industrious and organized population with a strong will to survive and progress.

Chapter 1

Politics

Government Structure

Since 1979 the right and the power to govern have come under serious challenge in El Salvador. Although there exists a constitutionally established civilian government, the authority of that government has been severely limited by the following nongovernmental forces: the armed forces, the U.S. embassy, and the FMLN guerrillas.

The government of El Salvador is subject to the limits imposed by the military and the U.S. embassy. (See U.S. Military and Economic Aid) No policy decisions are made without first seeking the approval of these unofficial partners in government. Historically the military has administered government in El Salvador with the blessing of the dominant economic forces. Although the military relinquished formal power to civilians in 1982, it suffered little real loss of power. The authority of the army relative to the civilian government can be seen most clearly in rural areas, where zone commanders rule surrounding areas like personal fiefdoms. On a national scale, it is the military which makes the key decisions about how the war is fought and how (or if) its end will be negotiated.

Constitutional Government

The three major centers of governmental power in the country—as set forth in the 1983 constitution—are the presidency, the Legislative Assembly, and the Supreme Court. Another key focus of influence is the Central Election Council (CCE), whose objectivity in vote counting and regulation is often called into question by opposition parties. Like other Central American countries (except for Belize), El Salvador has a unicameral legislature whose 60 members are elected every three years. Members of the Assembly can be reelected consecutively, unlike the president, who has to leave office at the conclusion of a five-year term. A run-off is held for the presidency if no candidate receives an absolute majority in the first round.

The majority political faction in the Legislative Assembly exercises power over the judiciary in that it appoints the members of the Supreme Court. Local justices are then appointed by the Supreme Court.

The country is divided into 14 administrative departments, whose governors and deputy governors are appointed by the president. The local level of government, a typical Hispanic form of a town with its surrounding hinterland called the *municipio*, is governed, in principle, by an elected mayor and city council. During the late 1980s this system of local government was seriously disrupted as mayors became, quite literally, military targets. Out of fear, many mayors have not occupied their offices. New Assembly and mayoral elections are scheduled for March 1991 with the next presidential elections scheduled for 1994.

With the election of Alfredo Cristiani in March 1989 the Nationalist Republican Alliance (ARENA) assumed control over the three main branches of government — a level of power never matched by the Christian Democratic Party (PDC) whose control of government was undermined by a Supreme Court controlled by ARENA since 1984 and a Legislative Assembly that passed to ARENA's control after the 1988 elections. In addition, ARENA controls 70 percent of the municipal seats.

A Brief History:
Constitutions, Oligarchs, and Lieutenant-Colonels

Two powers — the oligarchy and the army — have historically stood behind the democratic facade that the constitutions of this country have traditionally erected. Political competition has occurred among elite groups, while the armed forces have assumed the mission of repressing any disaffection on the part of the masses.

Within these parameters a number of political variations were possible. Governments were sometimes one-man dictatorships, or at other times institutional regimes in which one military officer followed another with respect for constitutional formalities.The military governments served oligarchic interests, but also favored the military's own institutional interests when these occasionally deviated from those of the oligarchy. Repression of the masses was at times brutal and total; but it was often selective, used only when necessary and sometimes relieved by populist or progressive features of military rule.

Within this context, the Salvadoran oligarchy and military have long debated whether absolute repression is a more effective strategy than cooptation through concessions. Repression which is too absolute and brutal may alienate the more moderate members of the middle class and narrow a regime's base of support.

The popular uprisings of 1931-1932 grew out of frustrated hopes and deepening economic misery. A reformist civilian president, Arturo Araujo, was unable to deliver on his promised social benefits because of the depression-induced collapse of the world coffee market. Moving in to crush popular unrest and incipient revolutionary organizing were the armed forces under Gen. Maximiliano Hernández Martínez along with diverse vigilante bands formed by local oligarchs. The result was the infamous *matanza* of 1932 in which as many as 30,000 Salvadorans were massacred.

The repressive regime of General Hernández Martínez that followed the *matanza* endured 12 years. Finally, however, it could not withstand the epidemic of hope for a new world of democracy that broke out as World War II drew to a close. A national strike supported by military dissidents overthrew Hernández Martínez in May 1944. Three military coups between October 1944 and December 1948 kept the Casa Presidencial in constant upheaval. Major Carlos Osorio, who led December 1948 coup, ruled the country until September 1956, at which time the presidency was transferred to Lt. Col. José María Lemus, who was ousted in a military coup in October 1960. A six-man military junta ruled until January 1961 at which time a self-described "Civilian-Military Directorate" took over government for one year. A brief break in direct military rule came in January 1962 when Rodolfo Eusebio Cordón was appointed as provisional president.

Elections in July 1962 placed Lt. Col. Julio Rivera in office for five years until July 1967 when Gen. Fidel Sánchez Hernández won the next presidential election. After a blatantly fraudulent election in 1972, Col. Arturo Molina occupied the presidency until he was succeeded by Gen. Carlos Humberto Romero in another fraudulent election in 1977.

Each incoming set of military "progressives" would attempt some moderate social legislation – a minimum wage, a public-health program, even a land reform. But oligarchic resistance, frequently expressing itself through factional maneuvering within the military by pro-oligarchic elements, limited the effectiveness of any proposed changes while removing any threat to oligarchic predominance.

The current phase in Salvadoran politics dates from the military coup of October 1979. During the 1970s increasingly militant and radical popular organizations developed alongside an incipient revolutionary movement. The repression and corruption that characterized the regime of General Romero (1977-1979) closely resembled political life in Nicaragua under Anastasio Somoza—an analogy that made some army officers uneasy.

Rather than risking the revolutionary turn of events seen in neighboring Nicaragua, a reformist coup was organized by a group of young officers. It counted on at least passive support from the United States. The mixed military-civilian junta that was formed included two colonels (Adolfo Majano and Jaime Abdul Gutiérrez) and three civilians (Román Mayorga, Guillermo Manuel Ungo, and Mario Andino). Ungo, leader of the Social Democrats, had been the vice-presidential candidate on the ticket led by the Christian Democrat José Napoleón Duarte in 1972, a ticket that was which had been fraudulently denied victory in the elections.

In a sense, this "first junta" represented another chance at the reformist option blocked by the 1972 electoral fraud. Although a reformist military-civilian junta officially governed the country, real power remained in the hands of the hardline forces within the military under the control of Defense Minister José García. They countered the attempts of the junta to introduce social reforms, to restore respect for human rights, and to bring to justice those engaged in the repression of the Romero years. It became clear that the junta was ineffectual, and it began to be referred to as the junta of *chompipes*, or turkeys, who would be cooked and eaten by Christmas. In fact, the junta lasted till the first week of 1980. At that time the civilian members of the first junta resigned, having failed to receive assurances that the armed forces would recognize civilian control and would to stop the slaughter of the popular movement.

A second junta was formed in which the three civilians of the first junta were replaced by leading members of the Christian Democratic Party, which had held itself aloof from the first junta. These were Héctor Dada, José Antonio Morales Erlich, and José Ramón Avalos. Dada resigned in March 1980 and was replaced by José Napoleón Duarte. This coalition was favored by the United States, which had found the civilian members of the first junta too closely allied with left-leaning popular organizations. Despite the inclusion of the less progressive Christian Democratic leadership, the far rightwing elements in the military still felt that the second junta was still too reform-minded. A coup under the leadership of Major Roberto D'Aubuisson was planned for the end of February, but it was forestalled by the vigorous intervention of the U.S. charge d'affaires, James Cheek.

The repression of the popular movement and scourge of death-squad killings that caused the civilian members of the first junta resigned continued and deepened under the second junta (January 1980-April 1982). Political and economic reforms were introduced, but they were too little and too late. The reformist leadership that many Salvadorans had hoped for soon proved corrupt, inefficient, and subservient to the U.S. embassy and armed forces.

Constitutional government by elected civilian authorities became institutionalized in El Salvador during the 1980s. The transfer from military to civilian rule and the scheduling of regular elections began with the Constituent Assembly elections in 1982. In May 1982 the newly elected Assembly selected Alvaro Magaña as provisional president. A presidential election was held in 1984 followed in 1985 by mayoral and Assembly elections — with the Christian Democrats winning both times. ARENA came on top in the 1988 mayoral and Assembly elections and then went on to win handily the presidential election of March 1989.

Civilian government and the electoral system were consolidated through five major elections and the peaceful transfer of power from one elected civilian to another in 1989 — the first time in the country's history. But this U.S.-backed democratization has been weakened by a persistent decrease in the number of Salvadorans going to the polls and the failure of elected governments to resolve the country's two major crises: a widening civil war and worsening socioeconomic conditions.

Political Parties and Elections

The March 1989 election gave the presidency to Alfredo Cristiani and consolidated the control over government by the rightwing ARENA party. ARENA controlled the Supreme Court during all five years of the Duarte presidency and regained control over the Assembly in 1988 after having lost to the Christian Democratic Party (PDC) in the 1985 elections. The ARENA victory came as no surprise. It had trounced the PDC in mayoral and Assembly elections the year before — winning 48 percent of the vote to the 35 percent of the Christian Democrats. ARENA broadened its electoral victory in 1989 — gathering 54 percent of the vote to the 36 percent of the PDC.

On one hand, the successful transfer of the presidency represented the new strength of the electoral system in the 1980s. But on the other, the decreasing participation of voters in elections indicated an underlying weakness of this democratization process. Over 1,551,000 voters had gone to the polls in 1982 but only 1,003,000 cast ballots in 1989.[1] The million who voted in 1989 were among some 2.3 million eligible voters of whom 1.8 million had registered to vote with the election tribunal. For the

FMLN, this large abstention rate represented a popular rejection of the government and a large reserve of support for its own political project.

If the rate of abstention takes into account all 2.3 million potential voters, ARENA obtained only 22 effective votes out of 100 possible ones. If calculating only those registered to vote, ARENA won 28 of every 100 voters with an election identity card. But when considering only those who actually voted, ARENA won a clear majority — 54 votes of every 100 cast.[2]

The integrity of the 1989 elections was also undermined by the increasingly mud-slinging character and vituperative language of the campaigning. But the more serious problem with the democratization process was its failure to respond to popular demands for peace and economic justice. As the war dragged on and deepened, elections continued to be upheld as the only legitimate way of change and conflict resolution. Yet instead of contributing to resolving the civil war, honoring the elections and the constitution became an excuse for not negotiating an end to the conflict and for ignoring other pressing demands of the popular sectors.

After his inauguration on June 1, 1989 President Cristiani announced a program of "national rescue" and a "government of national unity." But neither the PDC nor the two parties that placed third (Party of National Conciliation-PCN) and fourth (Democratic Convergence-CD) in the 1989 election could be interested in joining the loyal opposition. Barring changes resulting from peace negotiations or a military victory by the FMLN, ARENA will have to defend its electoral mandate in the mayoral and Assembly elections scheduled for March 1991 and then again in the presidential election of 1994.

ARENA: The Party of the Right

The key figure in the creation of the Nationalist Republican Alliance (ARENA) in September 1981 and its maturation as a political party has been Roberto D'Aubuisson. In March 1980 D'Aubuisson, a former military intelligence officer, was arrested for planning a coup against the Duarte-led junta. As part of his political-military career, D'Aubuisson had worked under Gen. José Alberto Medrano, the founder of ORDEN (National Democratic Organization), a paramilitary network of informers and enforcers organized by the security forces to crush political discontent in rural areas. His coup attempt having failed, D'Aubuisson used the contacts he developed through ORDEN and his activities as an intelligence officer to lay the foundation of a new political party.[3]

D'Aubuisson first made a public splash in 1980 when he began appearing on television flashing documents and photographs of "suspected terrorists," warning them that they "still had time to change their ways."

Such broadcasts preceded death-squad killings such as the one that assassinated Attorney General Mario Zamora, brother of Rubén Zamora of the Democratic Revolutionary Front (FDR). Prior to his departure from the army, D'Aubuisson had removed the intelligence files accumulated by the security forces.

As a new party, ARENA brought together oligarchs, rightists, conservative professionals, and military hardliners around the themes of virulent anticommunism and nationalism. The party gained force in the 1980s as a defensive alliance of those who felt the nation was under attack by a conspiracy of terrorists, socialists, liberal academics, and soft-headed reformers. Dismissed at first as a marginal group of ultra-right extremists, ARENA soon became a serious political contender.

Although it initially had opposed the elections for Constituent Assembly scheduled for March 1982, ARENA later decided to enter the electoral contest and won 29 percent of the vote. A charismatic campaigner, D'Aubuisson electrified many voters with his macho image and fiery speeches. As the government party, the PDC was burdened by a sagging economy, capital flight, a drooping coffee industry, high unemployment, and its inability to control the armed forces.[4] Joining with the PCN, traditionally the party of the military, ARENA formed a rightwing coalition in the new Assembly, which elected D'Aubuisson Assembly president. Only pressure from the United States prevented the Assembly from naming him provisional president. In 1984 D'Aubuisson ran against Duarte for president but lost in the runoff election. The following year the PDC also won control over the Assembly.

A Face Lift for the Election

After its defeat in the 1985 Assembly elections, ARENA began a process of party strengthening in preparation for the 1988 and 1989 elections. The tasks at hand were to broaden the party's political base by reaching out beyond the oligarchy and extremists to members of the middle and lower classes who were frustrated and disgusted with the performance of the Christian Democrats. Essential to this broadening of ARENA was the shedding of the party's death-squad and extremist image. The resounding victory of ARENA in the 1988 elections demonstrated both the success of this new party-building effort and the degree to which the PDC had fallen out of favor with Salvadoran voters.[5]

D'Aubuisson began grooming Alfredo "Fredy" Cristiani as the new public image of ARENA in 1985 when he suggested that Cristiani be placed on the party's executive council. The next year Cristiani became party president although D'Aubuisson retained his position as "Maximum Leader." The position as the party's presidential candidate was D'Aubuisson's if he wanted it. But D'Aubuisson chose to step out of the electoral limelight in 1989, aware that his unsavory reputation as a death-squad organizer would undermine chances for international acceptance of an ARENA government. The collapse of the Christian Democrats had left the U.S. foreign policy of supporting the political center orphaned and discredited. Cristiani, with his moderate image and no known death-squad connections, proved the perfect candidate for the United States.

Despite his status as a leading member of the country's narrow oligarchy and a representative of the far-right ARENA party, Cristiani was hailed by White House and the U.S. Congress as El Salvador's new "moderate." Even before Cristiani's presidential campaign was launched, the "adjustment" of ARENA's image was underway in the United States. Writing in the *Washington Post* in 1988, Jeane Kirkpatrick called ARENA "a legitimate political party that espouses market approaches, private ownership, personal initiative, and deregulation." In a background report for the 1988 Republican Convention, Heritage Foundation also sought to legitimize ARENA as democratic political party.

Educated at the American School in San Salvador and later at Georgetown University, Cristiani speaks English flawlessly and projects himself as a political moderate. Brought into the party in 1984 by D'Aubuisson himself, Cristiani personifies ARENA's close connections with the agroexport oligarchy and the industrial bourgeoisie. Born into a a wealthy family, he came into more wealth with his marriage to Margarita Llach—a member of one of the country's mythic 14 oligarchic families. He is the epitome of the modern oligarch. Not only had he been president of the Salvadoran Coffee Exporters' Association (1977) and vice president of the National Private Enterprise Association (1977-1979) but Cristiani was also part of the industrial elite. Before becoming president, Cristiani would would fly each day between his pharmaceutical corporation in San Salvador and his coffee estates in San Vicente.

Aside from his several years as an ARENA member, Cristiani, 41, brought with him little national or international political experience. As a Christian Democratic leader quipped, "To make his resume fill a page, he had to list every sports team he's ever played with." The new president is in fact a nationally ranked sportsman (squash and motocross are his games) as noted in his biographical summaries. As far as political experience, his resume listed his having participated in "numerous roundtable discussions and forums about social and political problems."[6] During his first six months in office, however, Cristiani proved to be a capable politician and statesman.

Tendencies within ARENA

Nationalism, anticommunism, commitment to private enterprise, and deep distaste for the liberalism and opportunism of the Christian Democrats have been the unifying principles of ARENA. Like any other political party, ARENA is not monolithic but composed of various factions and tendencies, some being more extreme than others. But as much as Washington might like it, ARENA can in no way be characterized as a centrist political party with some ultra-right tendencies. It was founded as an extremist party which, though having broadened its political base and toned down its aggressive rhetoric, remains deeply anchored among the society's most extreme forces.

Politically, there is a strong extremist faction comprising early D'Aubuisson loyalists and military hardliners. These are the party's radical conservatives who will tolerate no compromise with the FMLN. They call for the pursuit of a quick military victory against the guerrillas no matter what the cost in human lives. Col. Sigifredo Ochoa Pérez (retired), an ARENA leader, has said that it would be better to quickly kill 100,000 FMLN guerrillas and their supporters than to kill the same number over the ten-year period that some U.S. military advisers say will be necessary to conclude the war.[7]

It is within this extremist faction that ARENA's nationalist tendency is also most strong. During the 1989 campaign ARENA loyalists professed patriotic indignation at Duarte's fawning before Washington and stirred party pride with chants of "Eat shit, gringo."[8] Within the ranks of these radical conservatives there also runs a strong neofascist current, manifested in the party's fist-to-heart salutes, the fanaticism of party youth, and its appeals to the defense of God and Fatherland. D'Aubuisson once said, "You Germans were very intelligent. You realized that the Jews were responsible for the spread of Communism and you began to kill them." And Colonel Ochoa, ARENA's former vice president of the Legislative Assembly, justified the party's extremism this way: "The methods of political solution are exhausted. Only violent means remain. Let us not kid ourselves....In 1945 the decision was taken to end a war by dropping atomic bombs on Hiroshima and Nagasaki."[9]

The ideological purity and fanaticism of the political extremists have been somewhat offset by the party's political pragmatists. Confronted with the difficulties of running a government, the pragmatist forces gained increased influence within ARENA. These realists recognize that any political, military, or economic solution promoted by the party must take into account the need to maintain international support. It was this faction that warned that a post-election outbreak of terrorism and massacres would destabilize the government by sparking wider popular opposition and cutting the country off from international sources of capital. The killing of six Jesuits in November 1989 and the harassment of other members of the religious community made it all the more difficult for ARENA government to claim that it was following a pragmatic, moderate course in El Salvador.

Economically, party unity is threatened by a similar split. Dominating the party rhetoric is a neoliberal economic-growth philosophy promoted by the U.S.-funded Salvadoran Foundation for Social and Economic Development (FUSADES) and its associated business organizations and think tanks. FUSADES represents a modernizing but extremely dependent sector of the business elite. Four of its members became part of the Cristiani cabinet while scores of others became undersecretaries or advisers in the new government.[10] FUSADES' economic-development philosophy calls for the liberalization of prices and trade, the promotion of nontraditional agricultural and industrial exports, the privatization of state corporations, and new government policies to facilitate private investment. Frequently cited economic models for ARENA are Taiwan (the prototype of an export-driven economy) and Chile (where General Pinochet reactivated the private sector following the neoliberal doctrine of the Chicago School).

All elements within ARENA salute the private sector as society's motor of economic growth and fountain of democratic principles. Yet among the country's private-sector elite, there is a traditionalist tendency that is less than enthusiastic about neoliberal solutions. The industrial sector would suffer from complete trade liberalization (lifting of protectionist tariffs and other import barriers) although the commercial sector stands to lose business as consumption patterns fall due to devaluation-induced inflation. This traditionalist tendency is supported by those who advocate a return to a pre-1979 golden age when the state protected industrialists and when there existed no debilitating reforms.

Within ARENA there are differing opinions about the extent to which the 1980 reforms should be rolled back. Generally, the political pragmatists and economic modernists argue against completely dismantling the agrarian reform for fear of narrowing ARENA's voter base. By contrast the political extremists and economic traditionalists want to erase all vestiges of Christian Democratic reformism no matter what the political and social cost.[11] (See Economy)

The choice of Francisco Merino as vice president and Minister of Interior was one indication of the continuing power of the party's hardliners. Merino, who was a member of a neofascist student group called the

Pyramid, selected as his vice-minister Carlos Humberto Figueroa, who is closely linked to death-squad operations.[12] Associates of D'Aubuisson control the Legislative Assembly. Two other ARENA extremists are Ricardo Alvarenga, president of the Assembly, and Col. Sigifredo Ochoa (retired), the Assembly's former vice president.

The demand that Cristiani appoint hardliner Juan Raphael Bustillo (then Air Force commander who was reassigned as military attache to Israel) as Minister of Defense was vetoed by the U.S. embassy. "Maximum Leader" D'Aubuisson continues to direct ARENA from his position of honorary chairman and his role as deputy in the Legislative Assembly. The party president is Armando Calderón Sol, who at the party's 1989 convention charged that the country's labor unions are "groups in service to Soviet expansionism."[13]

Shortly before his murder on November 16, 1989 Ignacio Ellacuria, rector of the University of Central America, described three tendencies with ARENA: the civilian tendency of Cristiani, the militarist tendency of D'Aubuisson, and the death-squad tendency. According to Ellacuria, "D'Aubuisson is not now responsible for the death squads because he understood the necessity of moderating his party to be able to win the elections."[14]

Differences in style between Cristiani and D'Aubuisson are easily observed and might signal a future of policy disputes between the two. It should be remembered, however, that D'Aubuisson himself groomed Cristiani as a political leader and selected him for the presidential nomination. The two contrasting images — the moderate, pragmatic image of Cristiani and the macho, extremist image of D'Aubuisson — have served ARENA well. Some observers like PDC leader José Antonio Morales Erlich have observed that differences within ARENA are mainly tactical and do not indicate variations from basic rightwing beliefs. ARENA, said Morales Erlich, has one line but two forms of action.[15]

The various tendencies within ARENA represent for the most part tactical not strategic differences. The party is unified, for example, around the need to eliminate the FMLN as a political force within the country but there are questions about whether the so-called "Guatemala Solution" is the appropriate path to follow. (See Military) There also exists essential unity over the need to preserve and increase the privileges of the private-sector elite but some debate about the best way to increase the wealth of this ruling class.

It is the challenge of ARENA to keep its various internal tendencies at peace. As the ruling party, it also needs to maintain the support of the military, oligarchy, and middle classes as well extend its political base among the rural and urban poor. To strengthen its support among the poor, ARENA announced a public-sector jobs program, the expansion of food-for-work programs, and a town-meeting program in which government officials talk to community gatherings. Although a natural constituency for ARENA, the middle sectors of entrepreneurs and professionals cannot be taken for granted.[16] ARENA has to be careful not to alienate them with economic policies that bring higher interest rates and higher prices. The continuation of the war might also drive these forces away from ARENA and to those political parties or organizations that support a negotiated settlement to the civil war. But more important still will be ARENA's ability to maintain support for the party among its main backers: the military, the oligarchy, and Washington.

To Arena's Right

To the right of ARENA are various business organizations, civic groups, newspapers, and think tanks of rightwing persuasion. These include the Chamber of Free Enterprise, Peace and Work Crusade, National Action Movement, and the Feminine Front. The opinions of the far right are published by *El Diario de Hoy*. The Rev. Ricardo Fuentes Castellanos, who represents the extreme right of the Catholic church, complained in one *El Diario de Hoy* article that ARENA was compromising its principles, while coffee oligarch and president of the Chamber of Free Enterprise Orlando de Sola charged in the same paper that the ARENA was serving as a vehicle for socialism.[17]

The Institute for International Relations (IRI), an ultra-right think tank and policy institute, forms the ideological spine of ARENA's right wing. The IRI sees the Jesuit-run University of Central America (UCA), liberation theology, peace negotiations, the State Department, and even the military doctrine of Low-Intensity Conflict as all part of an international Marxist conspiracy at work in El Salvador.[18] The institute, which regards itself as the national guardian of capitalism, has criticized the Cristiani wing of ARENA as betraying the principles of the party and tending toward socialism.

The high-profile murders of six Jesuit priests, their housekeeper, and her daughter placed new strains on the unity of ARENA and its alliance with the military and the extreme right. Many elements within ARENA as well as military hardliners and rightwing groups have long considered the Jesuits communists and FMLN sympathizers who should be silenced. In an effort to maintain high levels of unconditioned U.S. economic and military aid, the ARENA government was forced to take action against members of the army. In doing so, however, the government raised the ire of the party's ultra-right elements and factions of the military.

Rise and Fall of the Christian Democratic Party

In 1964 the Christian Democratic Party (PDC) became the first opposition party to win seats in the legislature since the repression of the 1931 uprising. The party, which was founded in 1964, went on to become the dominant power in the national capital, regularly winning the San Salvador mayor's seat. Its presidential candidates, José Napoleón Duarte in 1972, and Col. Ernesto Claramount in 1977, were deprived of victory only by fraud. These fraudulent elections led many moderate and progressive politicians and activists to believe that there was little hope for peaceful change in El Salvador.

The party's principles are the classic ones of Christian democracy: a denial of the necessity of class conflict, and populism and reformism that do not threaten established social and economic structures. The PDC has been a party preeminently of rising middle and working classes in urban areas, as well as people of all social levels of the countryside. Although progressive in tone, the party's position was never anti-imperialist, nor even clearly anti-military, but it always has stood for the principle of civilian control. Its reformist reputation, combined with its flexibility and the prestige of its leader, Duarte, made it an ideal civilian partner for the military in the 1980s. The party's right wing took the formal reins of government with the formation of the second military-civilian junta in early 1980.

Since 1980 the party has seen its political base shrink steadily. Its left wing split off in early 1980, disgusted with the party's willingness to join the military-civilian junta. In each election since 1982 the number of votes cast for the PDC has dropped — from 590,000 in 1982 to 340,000 in 1989. Thrust into national office in 1980, the party became the willing, although at times uncomfortable, instrument for the U.S. counterinsurgency project for most of the decade. Rather than taking advantage of its position as the ruling party to push through reforms and forge a base with the popular sectors, the PDC chose to maintain a close alliance with the military. Duarte was also careful never to stray out of favor with the U.S. embassy, even to the point of kissing the U.S. flag on one of his several trips to Washington.[19]

Once in office Duarte made little effort to maintain his support among the U.S.-backed unions and peasant associations that had thrust him into the presidential seat. Instead, the U.S. foreign-policy priority — defeat of the FMLN — became the government's top priority. Earlier promises to push forward economic reforms and pursue peace negotiations fell aside. His economic policy, like that of the United States, became increasingly oriented toward the private sector, leaving the poor majority to face deteriorating socioeconomic conditions. During the Duarte administration, government corruption soared to new heights, living standards kept falling, and human-rights abuses against labor leaders and popular activists continued unabated.

Disgusted with the subservience, corruption, and internal factionalism of the PDC, many voters joined with the right wing to push the Christian Democrats out of office. Much to the consternation of the U.S. embassy, ARENA in 1988 swept the local elections, gaining control over the Legislative Assembly and a clear majority of the municipalities. Only the presidential seat remained in the hands of the PDC, and that too became ARENA's in the March 1989 presidential elections. ARENA mounted an effective campaign against the PDC based on the widespread disenchantment with the PDC and preoccupation about the country's economic downslide. Cristiani campaigned on the slogan "Change to Improve" and benefited from compelling television ads, like the one showing a young couple lying in bed in the dark, agonizing over their lack of money and employment. A little girl whispers, "Mommy, I'm hungry."[20]

Running as the PDC's presidential candidate in 1989 was Fidel Chávez Mena, a founding member of the party and Duarte's former Planning Minister (1984-1987). A conservative technocrat, Chávez Mena was the favorite of the U.S. embassy. Although linked to the failures of the Duarte administration, Chávez Mena did not suffer from the reputation of opportunism and corruption that burdened his rival within the party, Julio Adolfo Rey Prendes. A longtime party hack with little personal appeal, Rey Prendes had served as the PDC government's Minister of Culture and Communications.

The fight for the party's nomination split the PDC in two, with the defeated Rey Prendes leaving the party ranks with other dissident Christian Democrats to form the Authentic Christian Movement (MAC). Ever the politician, Rey Prendes ran for president with Alfonso Salaverría as his vice-presidential running mate. Rey Prendes's MAC came in with just under 1 percent of the presidential vote. Following the election, MAC continued its trajectory to the right and moved closer to the ARENA voting bloc in the Legislative Assembly.

Having lost its base of popular support as a party that stood for reforms and negotiated peace, the Chávez Mena candidacy secured only 36 percent of the votes cast in the March 1989 contest. After the elections the PDC quickly adapted to its new role as the opposition party, seeing itself as the popular alternative in the 1991 Assembly elections.

Whereas the PDC government had refused to seriously negotiate with the FMLN "terrorists," the post-election party quickly found itself joining the FMLN's call for a negotiated settlement to the war while directing its epithets at the ARENA "fascists." The party sharply criticized the neoliberal economic policies of the Cristiani government, accusing it of "being against everyone" — inverting the new FMLN slogan of "everyone against ARENA."[21] Party officials began to talk publicly about a "confluence of interests" with the FMLN, and the PDC labor coalition UNOC joined the anti-government opposition alongside the leftist National Unity of Salvadoran Workers (UNTS) alliance. The PDC also publicly rejected Cristiani's offer to join as participants in a "government of national salvation."

Alliances on the Left

Foremost among the political forces of the left in El Salvador are those of the combatants of the FMLN. The popular organizations of peasants, workers, and students also are situated largely on the left. None of these organizations can be considered political parties, however, in the sense that they do not present candidates for office. (See Guerrilla Forces and Popular Organizing) The FMLN is at once both a political and military organization. Although it does not yet have its own political party, the FMLN has offered to enter into the electoral arena in the event of a negotiated settlement to the war.

The FMLN includes Communist Party of El Salvador (PCS), which founded the Armed Force of Liberation (FAL) in May 1980. Another component of the FMLN, the Popular Liberation Forces (FPL) was formed in 1970 by a break-away from the PCS, and was led by a former PCS secretary-general, Salvador Cayetano Carpio.[22] Another of the guerrilla organizations in the FMLN, the People's Revolutionary Army (ERP), also has a nominal identity as the Party of the Salvadoran Revolution (PRS); Joaquín Villalobos is the dominant figure in both organizations.

Since 1980 the main unarmed leftist organization has been the Democratic Revolutionary Front (FDR), formed in April 1980 immediately after the assassination of Archbishop Oscar Arnulfo Romero. In the months that followed virtually all the dissident groups in El Salvador — political parties, Christian base communities, mass popular organizations, unions, and peasant associations — joined the FDR, which went on to function in the 1980s as the diplomatic voice of the left opposition to the government. The FMLN-FDR alliance united the armed and unarmed left, although members of the FDR coalition sometimes have taken distinct positions from those of the FMLN. Despite continual rumors of its dissolution, circulated mostly by the U.S. embassy, the FMLN-FDR alliance has endured into the 1990s. The three political parties included in the FDR are the following:

National Revolutionary Movement (MNR): A party primarily of intellectuals, the MNR is affiliated with the Socialist International and is a member of the Permanent Conference of Political Parties of Latin America (COPPAL). Its political tendencies run from social democratic to revolutionary. Guillermo Ungo, a civilian member of the first junta formed in 1979 and the 1989 presidential candidate of the Democratic Convergence, serves as MNR's principal representative. In January 1990 a death squad in Guatemala killed Dr. Héctor Oquelí, a key MNR leader.

Popular Social Christian Movement (MPSC): This party was formed in March 1980 as a split from the Christian Democratic Party, which angered its progressive members by its continued association with *de facto* military rule. Rubén Zamora, appointed as a minister in the first junta, is the secretary-general of MPSC. Zamora served as the coordinator of the 1989 presidential campaign of the Democratic Convergence. Other important figures in the MPSC are Juan José Martell and Jorge Villacorta.

Nationalist Democratic Union (UDN): Formed in 1968 as a legal front for the outlawed Communist Party of El Salvador, UDN maintains a socialist ideology. Its leader is Mario Aguinalda Carranza, a founder of the Revolutionary Coordinator of Masses and the FDR. Carranza, a member of the FDR's political-diplomatic commission, returned from exile in 1988.

The Democratic Convergence

The unarmed political left had previously denounced elections as part of a counterinsurgency strategy to put a democratic front on a repressive state apparatus. It reversed this policy in 1988 and decided to participate in the 1989 election campaign. FDR leaders Guillermo Ungo and Rubén Zamora returned to the country for the first time since 1980 and helped forge the Democratic Convergence (CD). Three political parties composed this new electoral coalition: MNR, MPSC, and the Social Democratic Party (PSD), which was formed in 1987. Ungo was nominated as presidential candidate while the PSD's Mario Reni Roldán occupied the vice-presidential slot on the ticket.

Ungo, a former university professor, has been the key figure in the leftist political spectrum for 20 years. He ran as the vice-presidential candidate with Duarte in the fraudulent 1972 elections. The Democratic Convergence represented the latest stage of the process of cumulative coalition-building in which Ungo has been engaged since the resignation of the first junta in 1979.

Why the sudden change of the political left in its analysis of the strategic role of elections in El Salvador? Zamora, expressing a commonly shared opinion among left political observers, said: "The counterinsurgency project up until 1985 was on the ascent. But after 1985, instead of playing the role of stabilizing and legitimizing the project, elections started destabilizing the project."[23] This analysis parallels a similar conclusion by the FMLN leadership:

> Elections—conceived as a fundamental political component of low-intensity warfare strategy—are creating instability while working more against the counterinsurgency plan than for it. The elections cannot stop the social explosion nor realign the correlation of forces in favor of the counterinsurgency plan. They represent too little in the face of such a large-scale political and economic crisis and the current dimensions of the war.[24]

Given its lack of infrastructure, the ongoing repression, and the time constraint of its late entry in the race, the Democratic Convergence had no hope of winning the 1989 election. According to Zamora, "We don't have an electoralist position. Our participation seeks to improve the possibilities for reaching a politically negotiated solution to the crisis."[25] On announcing its participation, the CD stated:

> The upcoming electoral contest by itself will not solve the fundamental problems of our society—social injustice, lack of real democracy, subordination to the interests of the government of the United States, and the state of war imposed on our people—however, we are convinced that our participation will manage to bring together and mobilize the people in the broadest possible way around the goals of social justice, democracy, national independence, and peace.[26]

Even though the CD never harbored any illusion of winning the election, it did hope to do better both in the vote counting and in the realm of popular mobilization. It had projected winning 10-15 percent of the vote but collected only 3.8 percent, placing a sad fourth. The principal reason for this poor showing was the last minute call by the FMLN for an election boycott and a transportation stoppage on election day. Both measures particularly hurt the CD because its supporters were also largely FMLN sympathizers and because it did not have the ability to transport voters to the poll as did other parties. Army propaganda associating the CD candidates with the guerrilla forces also intimidated voters.

Yet another factor in the CD's failure to generate more popular support was the anti-electoral position taken by many popular organizations. Not only were the Salvadoran people tired of the war, but they were also in large part tired of elections. The CD did succeed in stretching the limits of political debate by participating, for example, in televised forums with the PDC and ARENA candidates. But it did not win the declared support of progressive organizations, such as those included in the UNTS popular coalition. While agreeing with CD's platform, which stressed the need for a negotiated settlement, the increasingly militant popular movement was not focused on the electoral arena. Instead, it stressed the need for building a strong anti-government opposition and establishing the basis for a "popular democracy."

It was the position of the FMLN that the CD made the wrong choice when it decided to stay in the election campaign even after the government had rejected its January 1989 peace proposal. Despite some bitter feelings after the elections, the FMLN contended that the FMLN-FDR alliance had in fact been strengthened owing to the mid-1989 FMLN offer to enter the electoral arena after a negotiated settlement.[27]

The unarmed left had been permitted to enter the 1989 elections, but by late 1989 its leaders were once against hostage to the extreme right and the military. In October 1989 the homes of MPSC leader Rubén Zamora and UDN leader Aronette Díaz were bombed by unknown attackers, presumably because of their strong support for a negotiated settlement. Three members of the MPSC were killed around the same time, and a MNR leader was assassinated in Guatemala.

Other Parties of the Right and Center-Right

The Party of National Conciliation (PCN) was the pro-regime party during the 1960s and 1970s. With the exception of an occasional reformist program, it represented the status quo of coexistence between military and landowners in the days before the country became dominated by the dynamics of revolution and counterrevolution. The PCN has survived the dramatic events of the 1980s, with ups and downs in its support, sometimes in alliance with ARENA, sometimes cooperating with the Christian Democrats. The party held 12 out of the 60 legislative seats in the 1985-1988 session, but dropped to 6 seats in the legislature elected in March 1988. It dropped to third place behind ARENA and the Christian Democrats in the presidential election of 1989, winning only slightly more than 4 percent of the vote for its candidate, Rafael Morán Castañeda. Following the election a shakeup in the party resulted in the positioning of Ciro Cruz Zepeda as the party's secretary-general. Hugo Carillo is another important figure in the party. Like the Christian Democrats, the PCN began positioning itself after the 1989 presidential election to become the centrist political alternative to ARENA in the legislative and municipal elections scheduled for 1991.

Popular Unity was a coalition of the three rightwing parties formed to participate in the 1989 presidential election. The Salvadoran Popular Party (PPS), a predecessor of ARENA founded by General Medrano, is the oldest of the three Popular Unity parties. The other two parties are PAISA, which is a rightist split from the PCN, and the Liberation Party (PL), the latest version of the tiny rightwing group Patria Libre. The Popular Unity ticket was headed by Hugo Barrera of the Liberation Party with María Julia Castillo running in the vice-presidential slot. The coalition came in with just under half of 1 percent of the vote in 1989, although its member parties had obtained between them 6 or 7 percent of the vote in the 1988 legislative elections. The presidential elections had a polarizing effect in the country's political arena as many Salvadorans apparently decided not to "waste their votes" on minor groupings but to vote primarily for the major contenders.[28]

Two minor parties of the center contested the 1989 presidential elections. The Democratic Action Party (AD) identifies with the Liberal International, whose leading members are the German Free Democratic Party and the center-right Italian Liberal Party. Its leader is Ricardo González Camacho, and it has experienced a steady decline in its vote from 3.68 percent in the 1985 elections to 1.7 percent in the elections of 1988 and 0.46 percent in the 1989 presidential race. The reformist-centrist Party of Renovating Action (PAR) similarly declined from 0.54 percent of the vote for the 1988 legislative elections to 0.34 percent of the vote in the 1989 presidential elections. In mid-1989 the CCE canceled the charters of the five political parties that did not win the required number of votes: PAR, PL, PPS, POP, and PAISA. The election council was also considering the revocation of the AD's charter, even though the PDC claims that this centrist party was part of a PDC-AD coalition in the 1989 electoral contest.[29]

Images Shaped by U.S. Consultants

During the 1989 elections, both the PDC and ARENA counted on U.S. firms to orchestrate their campaigns. ARENA hired the law firm of O'Connor & Hannan to lobby for Cristiani in the United States. Not new to El Salvador, the law firm had been lobbying for the private-sector association ANEP since the beginning of the decade. To handle its public advertising and media strategy inside the country, ARENA hired APEX Publicidad, a branch of the New York-based BBDO company.

To combat the aggressive media campaign of ARENA, the Christian Democrats opted for KRV International and the public-relations firm of Greer, Margolis, Mitchell and Associates. Commenting on the increasing role of U.S. companies in Salvadoran politics, Edward Herman, the author of *Demonstration Elections*, said, "The role of the PR firms violates the whole principle of indigenous elections. It's a reflection of the privatization of U.S. intervention in El Salvador."[30]

The Two Faces of Government

For the last decade El Salvador has been a country torn and divided by war. In this context the ability to govern has depended on military might and popular recognition. Using its own military force, the FMLN has limited the reach of governmental power, while the government's legitimacy has been increasingly questioned by the country's leftist popular organizations.

During the early part of the 1980s the areas of FMLN influence were limited to its "zones of popular control" in northern and northeastern El Salvador. After 1984 the significance of these popular zones diminished as the FMLN shifted its strategy away from maintaining liberated zones and toward exerting a broader political and military presence throughout the entire country.

The FMLN has disputed the state's power to extend its governing system into the villages and towns where guerrilla units operated. Not only has it attempted to drive back the advances of the Salvadoran military but it has also sought to destroy the infrastructure of civilian government in rural areas. When it became clear in the mid-1980s that the local systems of government and administration were being more closely integrated into overall counterinsurgency strategy, the FMLN launched a counteroffensive. Targeted were the local mayors who, in the opinion of the FMLN, were instruments of the strategy of low-intensity conflict. Not merely the political representatives of their communities, the mayors and their offices were "in effect a paramilitary structure of the army," according to FMLN Commander Villalobos.[31]

This attempt to use local governments as the political fronts for counterinsurgency efforts was first tested during the National Campaign Plan of 1983. (See Armed Forces) The concept later became integrated into the United to Reconstruct pacification campaign, which was kicked off by the army in mid-1986.[32]

The strategy of integrating local government more closely into counterinsurgency operations was also included in the Municipalities in Action Program initiated by the U.S. Agency for International Development (AID) in 1986. Under this program, AID sponsored economic-development and political-training projects for municipalities. Mayors were given political and managerial instruction by AID contractors and were encouraged to make government a more visible force in their communities through sponsoring small infrastructure projects. Besides fortifying the government in conflictive areas, the program also facilitated army plans to establish espionage and civil-defense networks through these local governments.[33]

The Municipalities in Action Program, according to an AID official in El Salvador, "has a political objective with the secondary objective being the development benefits." He noted that the army had selected the priority areas for the program and even the type of development projects to be carried out by the mayors.[34] In 1988 an AID-commissioned evaluation confirmed the FMLN's analysis of the role of municipal governments. The study concluded: "It is often overlooked that Municipalities in Action is a counterinsurgency strategy. Indeed, we will argue that in El Salvador it is the most effective counterinsurgency strategy."[35]

The FMLN successfully challenged the power of the army and government on the local level through a two-pronged offensive. One part of this assault was a campaign of intimidation against government officials, demanding that mayors in conflictive areas resign and issuing death threats to those who persisted in office. This practice, which was widely criticized by human-rights monitors, succeeded in undermining the political side of rural counterinsurgency. At least 75 of the 256 mayors resigned, and another five-dozen have fled to larger towns to administer their offices from the protection of military garrisons. In dozens of other towns controlled by the FMLN, no municipal elections were held in 1988. Eight mayors were assassinated by the FMLN, which claims that the murdered mayors were directly linked to the military or had themselves killed civilians.[36]

Another more constructive part of the FMLN's effort to weaken the hold of the state while increasing its own governing power was its *poder de doble cara* (two-faced power) strategy. Beginning in 1987 the FMLN began promoting the formation of local committees that would present a legitimate face to the military and a clandestine face to the guerrilla army. The *doble cara* strategy was in many ways a product of the FMLN's rising concern that it was unnecessarily endangering the welfare of its rural support by maintaining clearly identified zones of control. The FMLN's Mercedes del Carmen Letona ("Commander Luisa"), an architect of the *doble cara* strategy, explained this preoccupation: "The FMLN, by openly declaring its relationship with these people, made them illegal, placing them in confrontation with the enemy."[37]

Rather than creating organizations of local power directly linked to the guerrilla struggle, the FMLN favored the development of autonomous citizen committees among communities in conflictive zones. The successful creation of a network of these community organizations—which the FMLN regards as prototypes of a revolutionary "popular democracy"—substituted for community institutions linked to the central government. Villagers who came to identify with the *doble cara* organizations were not necessarily FMLN sympathizers but were attracted by the ability of these organizations to defend community interests before the government and the military.[38] (See Popular Organizations)

The FMLN has contended that the political and military situation in El Salvador is one of "dual power"—with the FMLN on one side and the U.S. embassy, the government, and the military on the other. Both the Christian Democratic Party and ARENA dismissed this description as an illusion of the beleaguered guerrilla forces. But the FMLN argued that Washington and the Salvadoran state refused to recognize the full extent of the guerrillas' political and military influence. By the end of decade the widespread popular sentiment for a negotiated settlement and the FMLN's military capability as demonstrated by the November 1989 offensive had given new weight to the FMLN's assertion that a state of dual power existed in the country.

But the FMLN had not yet succeeded in building a majority coalition for its revolutionary project. The strength of ARENA's showing in the March 1989 elections—in which over 1 million Salvadorans voted and gave the ARENA ticket a plurality of 54 percent in the first round—undercut FMLN's subsequent claim that the government was illegitimate. The FMLN's inability to spark the popular insurrection it had been predicting also weakened its claim that it had the firm support of majority of the Salvadoran masses. By the end of the decade the FMLN had neither the political or military might to overturn the constituted government. But it was nevertheless clear that the guerrilla army did count on a sizable and committed sector of the country's population and had the military capacity to make the country virtually ungovernable.

Foreign Policy

The Central American states, united during the colonial period, had originally become independent as a single federated republic. El Salvador was the last country to give up on the federation when it disintegrated in early 1800s. Centrally located on the isthmus, El Salvador has a tradition of promoting political and economic unity in the region. In 1951 the country took the initiative in the creation of the Organization of Central American States, which until then had only a paper existence. More significant and vital was the Central American Common Market, which became important in the 1960s. Along with Guatemala, El Salvador with its industrial base and cheap labor prospered mightily from the Common Market.

By contrast, neighboring Honduras had little to export and soon became flooded with Salvadoran industrial imports. Resentment against El Salvador began to build among the Honduran business community and soon was directed against the tens of thousands of Salvadoran peasants homesteading in sparsely populated Honduras. A long history of border disputes also contributed to building tension between the two nations. To generate nationalist support for the government, Honduran military officials began an anti-Salvadoran campaign that included the mass deportation of Salvadoran squatters in May 1969. The deportation of Salvadorans also was designed to reduce the pressure for agrarian reform within Honduras.

The Salvadoran military government, hoping to achieve a settlement of the border issues favorable to El Salvador, took the opportunity afforded by the heightened friction between the two countries to invade Honduras in July 1969. The conflict became known as the "Soccer War," so named because it followed disturbances at an international soccer match between the two countries. The United States and other Latin American countries organized a boycott of fuel supplies to the warring countries, thus effectively bringing the war to a halt within several days, with both sides claiming victory.[39] The war left a "no man's land" at the border from which the troops of both sides had withdrawn at the ceasefire. There was a concern that Salvadoran guerrillas were using these *bolsones* (pockets) of border territory as refuges and staging areas. The United States brought Honduras and El Salvador together in 1981 to resolve the border dispute. Washington was also interested in involving both nations in coordinated military actions against the FMLN forces. In the 1980s tensions between El Salvador and Honduras eased considerably, even to the extent that at one point Salvadoran troops were being trained at a U.S. base in Honduras. Nonetheless, an undercurrent of suspicion and hostility continues to characterize Honduras-El Salvador relations. The border remains undefined in six places, an issue that remains before the World Court at the Hague.

In most foreign-policy matters El Salvador follows the lead of the United States, voting loyally with the United States in the United Nations and other international bodies. Traditionally dependent on the United States for its international trade, the country is now also dependent on U.S. economic and military assistance. Despite the nationalism evident in ARENA rhetoric, there is a recognition by the Cristiani government that its very existence depends on good relations with the White House and the U.S. Congress.

While the Duarte government could count on an international network of powerful Christian Democratic parties from West Germany to Venezuela for support, the ARENA government is more isolated in international diplomatic circles. The failure of the ARENA government to join other Latin American governments in their condemnation of the 1989 Panama invasion and its early recognition of the Endara government underlined the strong alliance between the Cristiani and Bush administrations.

Peace Process

In 1984 the Christian Democrats and their candidate, José Napoleón Duarte, campaigned on a platform of peace. The faded slogan of that campaign – "Duarte/Paz" – remains stenciled in green paint on curbs and walls all over San Salvador – a sad reminder of how long this country has hoped, voted, fought, and prayed for peace. After the elections peace became a forgotten promise for the Duarte government.

The FMLN and many popular organizations were calling for a negotiated settlement, but the government, the army, and the U.S. embassy considered the war to be winnable militarily. The government dismissed guerrilla proposals for a cease-fire, dissolution of the army, and the formation of a transition government in which the FMLN would share power. Instead of entering into real negotiations, the Duarte government and the ARENA party asserted that the only road to peace was respect for the constitution, elections, and unilateral disarmament by the guerrillas.

The U.S. government and the Salvadoran army have blocked full-fledged negotiations with the FMLN. For them, the FMLN remains a delinquent, terrorist force not deserving of equal status at a negotiating table. The army, the PDC government, and ARENA based their objections to the peace and electoral proposals put forth by the FMLN on the grounds that they would violate the 1983 constitution. Since 1984 there has been an on-again, off-again series of dialogues between the warring parties. Both sides entered the talks to demonstrate their will for peace to national and international observers. But these talks never reached the level of serious negotiations between equal partners determined to end the civil war.

The sentiment for a negotiated settlement of the war grew steadily broader and stronger during the 1980s. The Archdiocese of San Salvador and the University of Central America have been the main institutions promoting negotiations, a position almost universally shared by popular organizations. The overwhelming support for a negotiated settlement by the Salvadoran people became clear at the National Debate for Peace. The National Debate, initiated by the Catholic church in late 1988, brought together a broad array of social forces to support a negotiated peace and national reconciliation.

Regional peace initiatives, which had from their beginning focused on Nicaragua, have done little to move El Salvador in the direction of peace. Following the withdrawal of the FMLN from talks with the government in October 1989 and the guerrilla offensive the following month, pressure again mounted for both parties to bring the war to a close. Although Washington announced its support for renewed dialogue, it stopped far short of pressuring the government and military to negotiate a settlement which would recognize the FMLN as legitimate political force. As long as high levels of U.S. aid continue to flow to El Salvador, it is unlikely that either the government or military will seriously negotiate with the FMLN. And given the demonstrated military capacity of the FMLN, it is unlikely that it will lay down its arms without having its basic demands met.

From La Palma to Tela

The first talks between the FMLN and the Salvadoran government were held in October 1984 in La Palma, Chalatenango several months after Duarte was inaugurated as president. A second meeting was held in November in La Libertad at which the FMLN presented a broad peace proposal calling for the formation of a transition government, official recognition of guerrilla-held territory, and the fusion of the FMLN and army troops. The proposal was dismissed the Duarte government which insisted that the FMLN lay down its arms and incorporate into the constitutionally regulated democratic process. Three years later in June 1987 the FMLN presented the government with a new proposal calling for the humanization of the war and the renewal of talks. This was also rejected by Duarte and the military.

Running parallel to the bilateral talks between the FMLN and the government have been the regional peace talks. The Central American peace process was set in motion in February 1987 at the Guatemala border town of Esquipulas. Presidents from four Central American countries — El Salvador, Honduras, Costa Rica, and Guatemala — met in Esquipulas to discuss regional peace initiatives put forth by President Arias of Costa Rica and President Cerezo of Guatemala. Initially, the U.S. government encouraged this regional effort because it diverted attention from the Contadora peace initiative sponsored by several Latin American nations.[40] But when Nicaragua was invited to the second Esquipulas meeting, the peace process assumed a regional dynamic that at times deviated from U.S. foreign-policy goals.

Just as it had in the earlier Contadora peace process, Nicaragua confounded U.S. diplomats by accepting the general outlines of the new Central American peace initiatives (variously called the Arias Plan and the Esquipulas II Peace Accords) and supporting the resulting accords in its own search for an end to the contra war. The agreement signed by the five heads of state in August 1987 specified symmetrical measures to be implemented among all five signatory nations. These included: a cease-fire and dialogue between the government and the armed opposition, an amnesty for political offenses, resettlement of refugees, elections, open political competition, and monitoring of the agreement by nationally constituted "commissions of reconciliation."

Although the Duarte government signed the Esquipulas accords, it implemented them in a superficial and self-serving way. A dialogue of several days, mediated by Archbishop Rivera y Damas, did take place in San Salvador in October between the FMLN, the government, and the army. But little was achieved other than an agreement to study the formation of a cease-fire commission, a proposal that was soon discarded as both sides began to escalate military operations.

The first set regional peace accords signed in 1987 resulted in no serious efforts to end the civil war or to achieve internal peace. The Duarte government persisted in its demand that the guerrillas lay down their arms and join the ongoing political process. There were, however, a few tangible steps forward including an amnesty declaration. Under the amnesty decree several hundred political prisoners were released from Salvadoran jails. Members of the security forces and death squads were also given amnesty for any human-rights violations they may have previously committed. For the guerrillas to benefit, they were required to surrender themselves and their weapons within two weeks. Herbert Anaya, president of the nongovernmental Human Rights Commission of El Salvador (CDHES), announced his group's opposition to the amnesty of members of death squads, and was himself promptly assassinated. The killing of Anaya caused the breakdown of the cease-fire talks.

As required by the Esquipulas accords, there was some resettlement of refugees in late 1987 and in 1988, but this occurred at the initiative of the refugees themselves and in spite of the objections and threats of the Salvadoran armed forces. The regional peace process also had the effect of broadening the political space in El Salvador enough to permit FDR leaders Guillermo Ungo and Rubén Zamora to return to El Salvador to found the Democratic Convergence.

The Esquipulas accords, while not bringing peace to El Salvador, did bolster popular and guerrilla pressure for a negotiated settlement. By 1988 calls for a settlement of the civil war echoed throughout the region — from the increasingly unified popular movement within the country to regional meetings of presidents and foreign ministers. With the winding down of the contra war against Nicaragua, the civil war in El Salvador became the main impediment to regional peace. The government still characterized the FMLN forces as "delinquents" and "terrorists;" and the army continued to insist that the guerrillas were on the run. But the effectiveness of the transportation stoppages, the FMLN's new ability to mount well-coordinated attacks throughout the country and even within the capital, and an aggressive diplomatic campaign indicated that the guerrillas were hardly a spent force. To the contrary, they seemed to be making a political and military comeback.

The FMLN had been calling for peace negotiations since the early 1980s but its insistence on the formation of a transition government and the dissolution of the army seemed insurmountable obstacles. In January 1989 the FMLN announced an innovative electoral proposal that even the U.S. State Department said deserved serious consideration. Dropping their long-held demand for a transition government, power-sharing, and the dismantling of the armed forces, the FMLN said that it was willing to cease hostilities and abide by the results of a presidential election. But rather than participating in the upcoming March election, it proposed postponing the election until September, thereby gaining time to prepare an election campaign together with the FDR and the Democratic Convergence. The proposal apparently represented an attempt by the FMLN to align itself more closely with the demands for peace by the National

Debate and other social forces as well being the result of an increasing realization that there was little international support for a sustained guerrilla war.

The January 1989 proposal was rejected by the Christian Democratic government, ARENA, and the military on the grounds that it would violate the Salvadoran constitution. The government and the U.S. embassy charged that the proposal was little more than a ploy to advance the political and military projects of the FMLN. Although rejected, the FMLN peace proposal did serve to increase the credibility of the guerrilla army. In fact, the proposal reordered the entire political and diplomatic landscape — bringing the FMLN closer in line with the peace demands of the country's popular sectors while at the same time placing it well within the scope of the regional peace initiatives.[41]

Having had its political project rebuffed, the FMLN expanded and intensified its military project — attempting to undermine official claims that the guerrilla forces were simply isolated terrorist bands. Pushed on the political defensive by the bold electoral proposal of January 1989, the Salvadoran state also found itself increasingly on the defensive militarily. The FMLN, considering the March 1989 election "a fundamental political component of the low-intensity war strategy," called for a voter boycott, while pursuing its political goals through increased diplomatic initiatives.

The Tela Accords, signed by the Central American presidents in August 1989, were a product of the forward momentum for peace created by the Esquipulas accords and new Sandinista initiatives. The Salvadoran government, which had argued for the demobilization of the FMLN similar to that stipulated for the contras, was forced to back down from its insistence on symmetry between the contras and the FMLN and to sign the accords which called for direct talks between the government and the FMLN. The Tela Accords, however, also called for the FMLN to lay down its arms, recognize the ARENA government, and incorporate itself in the country's political process.

FMLN and ARENA Maneuver to End War

Local, regional, and international pressure pushed both the FMLN and the new ARENA government to enter into talks following the ARENA victory and the Tela summit. Although the FMLN's proposals basically followed the outlines of its electoral proposal of January 1989, they did also represent a hardening of its position. In its April 1989 proposal, for example, the FMLN insisted that ARENA declare itself to be a government of transition.

During later talks in Mexico and Costa Rica, the FMLN offered new compromises and initiatives that kept the new government on the defensive and off guard. Again dropping its previous demand for power sharing, the FMLN stated its willingness to cease hostilities and convert, together with other dissident forces, into a political party that would campaign in Legislative Assembly and municipal elections. "We don't seek a quota of power, but space and guarantees to compete for power," explained the FMLN's Joaquín Villalobos. Besides its political offer, the FMLN also agreed in September 1989 to end its sabotage campaign, to terminate its use of anti-personnel mines, and to call a unilateral cease-fire during negotiations.

The FMLN peace proposal demanded the following in return: an end to all repression of the popular movement, reorganization of the judicial system, punishment of those responsible for the assassination of Archbishop Romero, advancement of the 1991 elections including an election for the now-appointed department governors, a purge of the abusive and criminal elements from the army, a reduction in the size of the army, an end to government economic programs that impact most severely on the poor, and respect for the 1980 reforms. In addition, the FMLN suggested that further U.S. aid be used for the reconstruction of the war-devastated country.

The government presented no overall peace proposals of its own, and appealed to the inviolability of the constitution as its main argument for rejecting the FMLN's new offers. Cristiani hoped that by entering into negotiations the government would gain more political space and stability. Any offhanded dismissal of the FMLN peace proposals or the regional accords would have faced widespread reproval within El Salvador and would have the effect of further destabilizing the government. The government also risked angering the rightwing base of ARENA if it responded seriously to the guerrilla initiatives.

When talks between the FMLN and the new government began in September 1989, it seemed to many that El Salvador was closer to peace than at any other time since the civil war broke out. But it remained difficult to visualize a negotiated end to the conflict. The army, which would necessarily have to approve any such settlement, declined to participate in peace talks and persisted in its illusion that the FMLN was at its "politically and militarily weakest point." Defense Minister Humberto Larios said that the military supported the government's efforts to talk with the FMLN, but he noted that "a dialogue is a conversation between two parties, but to negotiate is another thing. The government has nothing to negotiate."[42] Rather than responding in kind to the FMLN's deescalation of the war (by halting the use of sabotage and car-bombs) and its unilateral cease-fire, the army took advantage of the lull in guerrilla strikes to mount its own offensive, trying to regain an upper hand in the war.

Many government and military strategists apparently saw the FMLN's new electoral proposals as evidence of its growing international isolation in a world moving dramatically away from communist parties and socialist agendas. They asserted that the FMLN was victim of *perestroika* and the global move toward capitalism and Western democracy. In other words, the FMLN had come to the talks not from a position of strength but out of its increasing weakness. Privately, however, military leaders acknowledged the FMLN's growing military capabilities and worried about a possible insurrection.

Following the October 31, 1989 bombing of the FENASTRAS union headquarters, the FMLN unilaterally broke off the talks, charging that neither the government nor the army was seriously interested in putting an end to political violence. On the contrary, the military had unleashed a campaign of repression against popular organizations and those leaders suspected of FMLN links. Less than two weeks later the FMLN launched its most daring offensive of the war. The army responded with aerial bombings of San Salvador *barrios* where the guerrillas were entrenched, causing many hundreds of civilian deaths and forcing the evacuation of some 50,000 frightened residents.

At their December 1989 summit the five Central American presidents again called for peace in the region. President Ortega had presented the FMLN's proposal: internationally supervised cease-fire, end to human-rights violations also with international verification, removal of major military figures, and a "definitive" dialogue with the ARENA government. The proposal was rejected by Cristiani; and in a diplomatic setback for the FMLN, the five presidents hammered out a compromise statement that condemned the FMLN offensive, likened the FMLN to the contras, and supported peaceful resolutions to regional conflicts.[43]

The FMLN condemned the summit declaration as one-sided and rejected the implication that a symmetry existed between it and the contras. By early 1990 plans were being made for a new round of talks between the FMLN and the government. This time the FMLN insisted that the talks be mediated by UN Secretary-General Javier Pérez de Cuellar. In addition, the FMLN expressed willingness to initiate negotiations to end the war "with the participation of the country's political parties and social groups with the objective of obtaining solutions reflecting the multifaceted and pluralist interests of the nation." It also proposed an immediate cease-fire if the United States would suspend its military aid.

Following the 1989 offensive the government responded to increased domestic and international pressure to maintain ongoing talks with the FMLN. But fearful of further alienating the rightwing leadership of the ARENA party and unable to control the army, the Cristiani administration repeatedly dismissed the FMLN's demands for political and military reforms.

By late 1990 the peace negotiations had become another facet of civil war as the series of talks failed to bring the country any closer to a peaceful resolution of the conflict. As the government and the FMLN continued to present mutually exclusive positions at the bargaining table, human rights abuses and military repression intensified. There was hope that a cut in U.S. military aid would force the military and government to negotiate more seriously. But there also existed the possibility that the peace talks would be discontinued as the FMLN saw improved chances for military victory and as the military and the ARENA right wing became increasingly unresponsive to solve the Jesuit case and to negotiate with the guerrillas.

During the 1989 government-FMLN talks, the FMLN's Villalobos said that "at present there is not much international space to maintain a war." The dramatic reduction in East-West tensions and the momentum established by the Esquipulas accords certainly narrowed the space for war-making. Within El Salvador there also exists a growing sentiment that the civil war must come to a peaceful end. But this will for peace is counterbalanced by three other factors: the determination of the FMLN to show tangible gains from its decade-long insurgency; the extremist and entrenched positions of ARENA and the army; and, perhaps most important, the reduced but still substantial U.S. aid package to El Salvador.

Human Rights: War and Repression

Despite continuing denunciations of human-rights abuses by local and international monitoring organizations, gross violations of human rights have become virtually an institutionalized way of politics and war in El Salvador. Aside from the large numbers and the persistence of violations, the human-rights situation is characterized by:

* Military disregard of international conventions regarding humanitarian treatment of civilians and injured combatants in war-time conditions.
* Increased use of arbitrary detentions, beatings, and torture to stem dissident activity

* Government failure to prosecute and sentence officials of the security forces involved in human-rights violations.

* Labeling of popular organizations as guerrilla fronts by Salvadoran army, government, and U.S. embassy.

* Existence of governmental and nongovernmental human-rights groups that give widely varying reports on the quantity and sources of abuses.

/* The return to the totalitarian and repressive environment of the late 1970s and early 1980s, making public dissent and popular organizing increasingly risky. |

Since 1980 human-rights monitoring groups have denounced El Salvador for the estimated 40,000 to 50,000 civilians that have been killed or disappeared by the country's security forces. Organizations like Amnesty International and Americas Watch have also charged the guerrilla forces with abuses but on a considerably smaller scale. /Amnesty International describes El Salvador as a country where the "ordinary citizen has no protection when threatened with anonymous violence...as the police or the military themselves carry out death-squad killings."[44] In its 1988 report *Nightmare Revisited*, Americas Watch warned that the situation in El Salvador was on the verge of returning to the massive killings of the early 1980s.[45]|

The denunciations by human-rights monitors contrasted greatly with the generally positive picture of the security forces painted over the decade by the U.S. government. In an October 1988 letter to the House Foreign Affairs Committee, the Reagan administration listed the following achievements of the Salvadoran government: "complete freedom of expression, restoration of full political and civil rights, massive resurgence of free labor-union activity, and a dramatic decline in human-rights abuses by government forces and the radical right."[46] The State Department's *Report on the Human Rights Situation in El Salvador* said the armed forces' military operations are "characterized by general commitment to respect of El Salvador citizens." A later State Department report acknowledged that an increased number of death-squad killings "were probably committed for ultra-right political motives," but goes on to say, without giving any evidentiary support, that "some of the killings are quite possibly the work of common criminals. Others may have been committed by the FMLN in an effort to portray a deteriorating human-rights situation."[47]

In its monitoring and reporting of the human-rights situation, the U.S. embassy typically does not gather information itself, but uses press reports—which are based usually on army press releases.[48] The establishment press in the United States does little better, with the *New York Times* particularly falling down egregiously on its responsibilities.[49] James LeMoyne of the *New York Times* even gave credence to a claim by the military that the FMLN had assassinated Human Rights Commission director Herbert Anaya. It was later shown that a confession to that effect, made by a man held captive by the army, was obtained fraudulently.

There are obvious problems in trying to hold a country to a decent standard of human-rights performance while a civil war is going on. Nevertheless, El Salvador is a party to Protocol II of the Geneva Convention, which requires certain standards of performance in the protection of victims in domestic armed conflict. The Salvadoran government has acknowledged its responsibility under the protocol. Human-rights violations are committed by troops, who take no care to spare civilian casualties; who kill noncombatant medical personnel; and who rape, torture, and assassinate prisoners. Security forces have targeted FMLN clinics and field hospitals, while the government has obstructed the evacuation of wounded FMLN combatants.

A characteristic feature of human-rights violations in El Salvador are the cover-ups and obstructions of justice that take place when any serious attempt is made to use the legal system to punish the perpetrators of abuses. Amnesties are declared, witnesses are intimidated, and judges are coopted. Uncooperative judges are killed, as are human-rights workers. Four of the founders of the nongovernmental Human Rights Commission of El Salvador (CDHES) were killed within ten years of the founding of the organization.[50] On the other hand, no military or police officers have been tried and convicted of human-rights abuses against civilians.[51] Some enlisted soldiers have been convicted, principally where the victims were U.S. citizens.[52] The arrest in January 1990 of a Salvadoran colonel, two junior officers, and five soldiers for the murder of the Jesuits, their housekeeper, and her daughter may lead to the first exception to this pattern.

The routine procedure used by security forces to incriminate detainees is to have them sign a blank sheet of paper on which the confession is later typed. Prisoners often say, "Why not confess? If I refuse, they will make up something anyway." Nevertheless, the security forces set great store by the extraction of confessions, for which they use different techniques. The National Police is said to favor smothering prisoners with hoods and using beatings, electric shocks, and drug injections. The Treasury Police has been reported to string up prisoners by their wrists and submerge them in vats of filthy water. Army counterinsurgency units run to beatings, mock executions, and tying the prisoners to anthills.[53]

In October of 1987 an amnesty was extended to any military officers against whom charges of human-rights violations were pending. Meanwhile, 92 percent of the people being held in prison as of July 1987 had not been tried and legally condemned.[54] In effect, El Salvador has no system of justice worthy of the name.

The pattern and intensity of human-rights violations have varied over the years. The rate of killings during the years of the juntas, from 1980 to 1983, was high. Major political figures were assassinated: Mario Zamora, the attorney general; Enrique Alvarez Córdoba, president of the FDR; Juan Chacón, secretary-general of the Popular Revolutionary Bloc; and, most dramatically, the Archbishop of San Salvador, Oscar Arnulfo Romero, in March of 1980—while he was saying mass.

With the "normalization" of the situation after the election of Duarte as president, the number of death-squad killings dropped. This clearly occurred as a result of pressure from the United States for the country to clean up its image so that Congress would continue to finance the war. It would, however, be a mistake to see the reduction in the number of assassinations as a significant or fundamental change. Killing could be more rational and selective since so many major figures had already been removed from the scene, and so much of the population was intimidated. In 1988 the rate of killings and disappearances began to increase again as an apparent response to increased popular organizing.

Numerous human-rights organizations have emerged as part of the popular movement. These include the Human Rights Commission (CDHES), Committee of Mothers and Relatives of Political Prisoners (COMADRES), Federation of Committees of Mothers and Families (FECMAFAM), and the Christian Committee of the Displaced (CRIP-DES). The State Department labels such groups "FMLN fronts" and dismisses their human-rights reports as "highly distorted" and "fabrications." CDHES, which has been nominated for the Nobel Peace prize three times, is, according to the State Department, "the FMLN human-rights organization."[55]

Two organizations associated with the Catholic church that document human-rights abuses and provide legal assistance to victims are Socorro Jurídico Cristiano and Tutela Legal. The Institute of Human Rights of the University of Central America (IDHUCA) also monitors human-rights violations and publishes reports. The government has its own Human Rights Commission (CDH) that focuses almost exclusively on charging the FMLN with human-rights abuses.

Although CDH is more a propaganda arm of the military than a bona fide monitoring group, it is certainly the case that the FMLN is responsible for some human-rights abuses. These have included executing suspected government informants, causing civilian deaths through the placing of land mines, assassinating municipal mayors, shooting at people who violate transport stoppages, and occasionally kidnapping people for ransom. According to Tutela Legal, 48 civilians were killed by the FMLN in 1988. Some of these victims were bystanders of car-bombs used in the FMLN's escalating urban war. Responding to criticism, the FMLN announced that it was suspending the use of car-bombs, although it still makes wide use of land mines, which also result in accidental civilian deaths.

The human-rights situation worsened dramatically in late 1989. The United Nations General Assembly denounced the aerial bombing of civilian neighborhoods in San Salvador by the Salvadoran Air Force. Americas Watch observed that "the hundreds of civilian casualties resulting from army attacks in slum neighborhoods strongly suggests a double standard. The army's ability to avoid significant casualties in a rich neighborhood demonstrates that it may have been feasible to have used greater care to protect slum residents and their fragile dwellings."

The imposition of martial law, increased media censorship, the enactment of a new penal code, and the widespread arrest of union leaders, church activists, and representatives of popular organizations also resulted in international condemnation of the ARENA government. The penal code, which has been characterized as "fascist" by the Christian Democratic Party, authorizes the arrest and imprisonment for up to four years of those found distributing or printing literature that subverts the public order. Finally, the massacre of the Jesuits on November 16, 1989 focused world attention on the deteriorating human-rights climate in El Salvador.

The massacre of the six priests and a mother and her daughter raised questions about the degree to which the military high command and elements within the ARENA party were involved in that and other attacks against those labeled as guerrilla sympathizers. President Cristiani pledged to prosecute all responsible for the November 16 killings. But most foreign observers felt that there would be an attempt to pin the blame on only the actual perpetrators, overlooking the intellectual authors of the crime. "We believe that such a grave act cannot be carried out just like that," said the Auxiliary Bishop of San Salvador, Gregorio Rosa Chávez. "I think it is not enough to punish a few."[56]

Chapter 2

Military

Salvadoran Military and Police Forces

A coup by Gen. Maximiliano Hernández Martínez in 1931 commenced a half-century era of almost uninterrupted direct rule by the military. In October 1979 this period was brought to a close by a reformist faction of young officers which forced Gen. Carlos Humberto Romero out of the Casa Presidencial. For two and a half years, until May 1982, the country was ruled by a military-civilian junta. Between March 1980 to May 1982 this junta was headed by José Napoleón Duarte.

With the selection of Alvaro Magaña as provisional president in mid-1982 the transition from military to civilian rule was complete.[1] Two years later, the election of Duarte as president further institutionalized civilian government and installed the president as the commander-in-chief of the armed forces. But the switch to a civilian government did not weaken the military. Instead, its power deepened as its budget and ranks expanded with the injection of U.S. aid.

Despite over $1 billion in U.S. military aid and substantial clandestine support by U.S. intelligence agencies, the Salvadoran military has never become the professional army its U.S. sponsors were hoping for. It remained a highly corrupt institution with little respect for human rights and without the capacity to defeat an underequipped guerrilla army less than one-sixth its size.

The November 1989 offensive by the Farabundo Martí National Liberation Front (FMLN) highlighted the shortcomings of the military. Despite many signs that the FMLN was preparing a general offensive, the army was taken unawares by the breadth and intensity of the FMLN's campaign. The offensive demonstrated the army's inability to wage counterinsurgency war in the cities. Only by relying on aerial bombings of poor neighborhoods was the military able to drive the guerrillas from their urban strongholds. The offensive shattered the belief that the military had the upper hand in the war and that the FMLN was a guerrilla force in the process of disintegration. The military's difficulty in turning back daring advances by the FMLN seriously damaged its prestige while aggravating tensions within its ranks.

As it entered its second decade of war, the Salvadoran armed forces also faced serious political problems. In the United States, public opposition to U.S. military aid to El Salvador was growing stronger and there was new talk in Congress of imposing human-rights conditions on further aid. Within El Salvador, the military's efforts to isolate the FMLN politically looked more difficult than ever. Billboards and other army propaganda proclaiming "The People and Army Together" still seen around the country are faded remnants of a time when the military believed that it could indeed unite the people around its counterinsurgency war. But strong support among the Salvadoran people for the war had become difficult to find except among the wealthy and ideologically committed. Instead there was widespread popular support for a negotiated settlement of the war — an eventuality seen by most military leaders as tantamount to defeat.

Also weakening the position of the military in the counterinsurgency war was the inability of the government to sustain a project of national reconstruction and rescue. For a couple of years it seemed that the Duarte administration was successfully building a government that enjoyed local and international credibility and support. The Cristiani administration too has attempted to shape a government which would present a strong foundation on which to base a counterinsurgency war. But like its predecessor, it is burdened by an economy in which the conditions for the poor seem only to worsen. The government's association with extremist military and political elements, its lack of success in building coalitions with popular sectors, and its difficulty in attracting international support all undermine its value and effectiveness as a partner with the military in counterinsurgency.

Despite these handicaps, the armed forces remain a formidable institution that has proved capable of preventing a military victory by the FMLN. Its superior firepower, greater numbers, and billion-dollar backing by Washington keep the Salvadoran military strong, giving it the resources it needs to continue but not to win the war.

Structure and Organization

The two main figures within the military are the Minister of Defense and the Chief of Staff of the Salvadoran Armed Forces, the former selected by the president and the latter chosen by the military hierarchy itself. There are three armed forces: Army, Air Force, and Navy. Together they number some 55,000 officers and soldiers — having more than quintupled in size since 1980.[2] The army (comprising eight brigades, seven regional detachments, and 33 battalions) forms the bulk of the armed forces. Military reserves and a civil-defense force constitute auxiliary components of the armed forces.[3]

Also operating under military authority are the country's three main security forces: National Guard, National Police, and Treasury Police. Founded in 1912, the National Guard is a rural gendarme which has traditionally functioned as a security force for plantation owners. The National Police, established in the mid-19th century, maintains security on roads and highways. The newest service, the Treasury Police, was created in 1937 to enforce treasury regulations against smuggling and moonshining but has developed into a political and intelligence police force with associated death-squad and terrorist operations. During the war, the three police units have provided the main protection for San Salvador.

About 30 percent of the government's budget is reserved for defense and public security but these functions actually absorb closer to 45 percent of total operational expenses of the government.[4] Even so this percentage does not represent the full extent of funding for the armed forces since it does include the U.S. military, police, and intelligence aid that flows directly from the United States to the country's army and security forces. (See U.S. Military Aid)

Two major weaknesses of the military are its reliance on forced recruitment and its system of automatic upgrading of officers (the *tanda* system). The constitution mandates universal military service, but the legislation needed to structure a military draft has never been passed. To fill its ranks, the military forcibly recruits from 12,0000 to 20,000 poor youth into service annually. At movie theaters, soccer fields, and even schools, youths as young as 14 are forcibly conscripted. Unless a family has money or connections to win their release, the young men are required to serve for two years, receiving about $80 a month. Commenting on the class bias of the current recruitment system, Auxiliary Bishop Gregorio Rosa Chávez said, "I am sure that well-off people who vehemently defend the military solution would think differently if their own sons, who now study, work, or simply idle away their youth in frivolous or superficial life, had to go fight on the battlefields."[5]

Although this conscription method is simple and cheap, it contributes to the lack of commitment and low morale of the young recruits. As one U.S. military adviser observed, instead of having search and destroy units, the Salvadoran army has "search and avoid" patrols. Many desert, and only 25 percent reenlist for a second two-year term, leaving the military with an inexperienced fighting force.

The weaknesses of the recruiting system are paralleled by deficiencies in the officer corps. Officers are largely the product of the Gerardo Barrios Military School, which graduates classes of junior lieutenants.[6] Each class, or *tanda*, then jointly rises in grade until reaching the rank of colonel. Bound by loyalty to their *tanda*, the officers mutually assist one another in what is, according to a U.S. military report, "a West Point Protection System gone berserk."[7] This system of advancement and solidarity means that officers rise to high positions regardless of merit or competence. Despite U.S. attempts to "professionalize" the Salvadoran armed forces, the *tanda* system dominates the hierarchical structure.

In October 1988 the 35th class, which graduated in 1966, rose to top positions within the armed forces. Known as the *tandona*, or big class, it had 45 members, approximately double the normal, and is known for its hardline officers and extreme solidarity. Members of the *tandona* include ARENA's Roberto D'Aubuisson; another ARENA leader, Col. Sigifredo Ochoa Pérez (retired), named by President Cristiani to be head of the public corporation that generates electricity for the country; Col. Juan Orlando Zepeda, appointed Under-Secretary of Defense by Cristiani; Col. René Emilio Ponce, appointed Armed Forces Chief of Staff in November of 1988; Mauricio Staben, a battalion commander against whom charges of running a kidnapping racket for ransom were dropped "for lack of evidence" after members of the *tandona* had rallied in his defense; and Col. Mauricio Vargas, the army's foremost counterinsurgency theorist and one of the few Latin American officers to have taught at the U.S. School of the Americas in Panama.

By 1989 the *tandona* had assumed control over ten of the 14 military zones, five of seven military detachments, five of six prestigious brigades, the three police forces, and three of the military commands (intelligence, operations, and personnel). Several generals were replaced by lower-ranked colonels belonging to the *tandona*. For years, the *tandona* had been complaining about the inability of the military command to end the war. With the control of the military, and to a large extent the government, in the hands of the *tandona*, it was, according to one Western diplomat, "time for the young bucks to put up or shut up."[8]

The implication of one of its members, Col. Guillermo Alfredo Benavides, in the November 1989 murder of the Jesuits indicates cracks in the unity of the *tandona* and is a sign that the military high command might be willing to forsake one of its high officers in the interest of continued high levels of unrestricted U.S. aid.

Divisions within the Military

Large and cohesive, the *tandona* has spread itself through the top positions of the armed forces, but not without creating resentment and suspicion among junior and older officers. They are concerned that the *tandona* will force their way into all positions of authority and that their mutually reenforcing power will allow the *tandona* set to overstay its rotation.

The unity of the military was also weakened by the relative independence of the Air Force. Over the last ten years, the Salvadoran Air Force evolved from being little more than a small transport division to becoming one of the most well-equipped and powerful air commands in Latin America. But rather than responding to the authority of the Defense Minister and central military command, the Air Force has established its own priorities and politics.[9] "In theory part of a unified defense establishment, the Salvadoran Air Force is in reality," according to one U.S. military evaluation, "an autonomous fiefdom, deploying its infantry without prior coordination, as likely to support on the basis of amicable relations with a brigade commander as on the basis of actual need."[10]

Another source of fractioning within the military is debate over the thrust of military strategy. Widespread discontent has been rising from within the ranks for several years. Discouraged at the slow pace of the war and the largely defensive position of the armed forces, there was much criticism of the Duarte-era leadership of Chief of Staff Adolfo Blandón and Defense Minister Vides Casanova, both of whom were considered moderates and sycophantic adherents to the U.S. doctrine of Low-Intensity Conflict. Rejecting the concept of low intensity, other elements — especially Col. Sigifredo Ochoa, Col. Juan Orlando Zepeda, and Gen. Juan Rafael Bustillo — called for the armed forces to take off its gloves and increase the intensity of war. They contended that, if unconstrained by the concerns of international disapproval of human-rights violations, the military could quickly end the war, albeit with widespread bloodshed. In contrast to low-intensity war, they call for "total war." This type of unconstrained counterinsurgency campaign is also known as the "Guatemala solution" within El Salvador.

Calls for a "total war" were quickly vetoed by new ARENA government and the new military chief Col. René Emilio Ponce. It was commonly agreed that any escalation of counterinsurgency would have to be preceded by successful government efforts to reactivate the economy and establish a secure political base. Only from this foundation could a more intensified counterinsurgency campaign be effective in breaking the FMLN's links with the popular sectors. Both the ARENA government and the military command were also well aware than any clean break with U.S.-approved war conduct would be unthinkable, given the degree of their dependence on U.S. aid.[11] In fact, the military conditioned its support of the ARENA government on its promise to modify its practices so as to not jeopardize U.S. support.[12] Generally, only the most extreme elements in ARENA saw the "total war" strategy as a viable option.

As demonstrated in the 1979 coup, the solid front of the military is sometimes broken by reformist or patriotic dissident factions. The Hernández Martínez dictatorship was dragged down in part by a military revolt in 1944; and other internal rebellions occurred in 1960 and 1972 after the electoral fraud. Although there have been no recent indications of similar discontent, the FMLN does not rule out another such "patriotic" revolt connected with popular insurrectional fervor. Nationalism and anti-oligarchic sentiment, as well as growing unwillingness to risk their lives fighting an unwinnable war, are factors that might instigate such a split in the military.[13] One small indication of a growing split was an anonymous statement on October 25, 1989 by a group of young officers which condemned human-rights violations by the military. The officers said they were "responsive to the people's struggle, which our fellow officers, especially those of the security forces, have tried so many times to suffocate."[14]

Yet another source of tension within the armed forces is the investigation into the November 16, 1989 murder of the Jesuit priests. The naming of one *tandona* officer and three junior officers upset many officers and other *tandona* members who either supported the massacre or contend that the military should not have to answer to civilian authorities or to foreign governments.

Corruption and Wealth within the Officer Corps

Besides the *tanda* system, corruption within the officer corps is also part of the Salvadoran military tradition. The first taste of the economic privileges that accompany an officer rank comes upon graduation from the Military School. Graduating officers have the right to import a car duty-free, a payoff that most young officers sell to wealthier members of the society. According to one retired officer, "Their goals are largely materialistic." The military represents a path to the middle class for poor young men.[15]

Once officers rise to command positions they control a lucrative system of patronage and graft. One source of extra funds is the common practice of renting out troops as security guards to plantation and factory owners, charging $200 to $300 per man per month. Colonels also grow rich siphoning off money from their base's payroll and food budgets. One of the most inventive ways of making the army a business is to fill your command with ghost soldiers or *plazas ficticias*. One major told the *New York Times*, "Just about every brigade lists at least one 50-man company that isn't there. Each of those 50 pay slots brings 500 *colones* [equivalent to $100] a month."[16] Rather than filling all the re-enlistment positions — over 10,000 a year — commanders fill them with the names of nonexistent soldiers. The pay and the food money for those soldiers is then channeled into the unit's slush fund. As Joel Millman, writing in the *New York Times*, pointed out: "Every time a soldier deserts, or dies in action, the commander can add to his list of ghost soldiers, earning himself yet another salary."

Another wellspring of graft is the practice of mandatory deductions or *descuentos obligatorios*. Soldiers are charged for food, boot polish, toothpaste, and uniform accessories, and lower officers collect the profits as a type of commission. Soldiers of the Third Brigade even paid to build a wall around their own base.

Following the Guatemala model, the Salvadoran army in the 1980s became an economic power in its own right. Its major cash reserve is the Social Provision Institute of the Armed Forces (IPSFA), a social-security fund into which each recruit pays $150 upon leaving the army. Since 1989 the fund has grown from $2 million to more than $100 million. IPSFA has become a major investor and the largest source of liquid capital in the country. It recently bought a $2 million oceanside resort and is also backing a 500-lot housing development. The *New Times Times* reported that IPSFA is also invading the country's financial markets, making mortgages and car loans and co-signing small business loans. It is negotiating with the government for permission to enter into joint ventures with multinational corporations. There are also plans for an army insurance company and a land bank, and the new Bank of the Armed Forces is set to open in 1990.

High-level officers are also getting rich from this booming military-business complex. Salvadoran firms commonly place colonels on their boards of directors, and many officers run their own agribusiness operations — with the luxury of never paying any taxes.

Limits and Contradictions of Low-Intensity Conflict

The course of the war in El Salvador has demonstrated the truth of the counterinsurgency maxim that politics and popular support are at least as important as military tactics in winning small wars. This basic principle of counterinsurgency strategy was given new prominence in the U.S.

military's upgraded counterinsurgency doctrine called Low-Intensity Conflict. By the mid-1980s the importance of the nonmilitary aspects of counterinsurgency also became recognized by the Salvadoran military. When announcing the army's United to Reconstruct rural pacification program in 1986, Chief of Staff Adolfo Blandón warned that the "subversive war to take power is 90 percent political, economic, social, and ideological, and only 10 percent military." It was necessary, he said, to unite all the country's resources and energies to confront this sophisticated challenge. "Obtaining a military victory is not enough. It is also necessary to win in the economic, political, ideological, social, and international fields."[17]

The Salvadoran armed forces and their U.S. trainers showed at least a cursory understanding of the nonmilitary dynamic of counterinsurgency. Civic-action programs were established, a new military psychological operations division of the central command was created, national security and development plans were formulated, and government job projects and resettlement programs were closely integrated with military strategy. Nonetheless, the course of the war has demonstrated their inability to take the political and economic steps necessary to win public support for a counterinsurgency campaign. Given the severity of socioeconomic conditions, nothing less than radical economic and social reforms were necessary to preempt the revolutionary movement and quiet social unrest. More than just token development projects and slogans about the "Army and People Together" were needed to create an effective popular base for counterinsurgency—but neither the armed forces nor their U.S. benefactors have been willing to take the campaign to win hearts and minds that far.

The furthest that the counterinsurgency project in El Salvador was ever taken in this direction of preemptive reforms came during the first year of the war. To stave off the growing leftist rebellion, Washington pushed through a limited land-distribution program and the nationalization of the banks and foreign-export trade. But the agrarian-reform program was never fully implemented, and it left the oligarchy largely intact while doing little to improve the lot of the poor. (See Agriculture)

In early 1983, even before talk of low-intensity conflict became common, the counterinsurgency war incorporated some developmental programs advocated by U.S. military advisers. The National Campaign Plan of 1983-1984, which concentrated on the San Vicente department, was the first feeble step in this direction. Trying to sweep the guerrillas out of the region, the army only succeeded in terrorizing the inhabitants. The follow-up pacification program of building and road repair projects was only half-heartedly instituted and quickly fell victim to government corruption and inefficiency. Few hearts and minds were won in San Vicente.

The civic-action programs and the United to Reconstruct campaign that followed similarly failed. Passing out food and giving free haircuts proved insufficient to refurbish the image of the army. Initially, civic-action programs were enthusiastically supported by those within the military who regarded them as an important part of a strategy to create a reserve of good will for the army among rural villagers. Today these programs are have become little more than patronage projects administered at the whim of local commanders.[18]

Having succeeded in silencing the popular movement and terrorizing rural communities, there were fewer massacres and murders after 1983. But as the military capability of the FMLN improved, the armed forces struck back in the mid-1980s with a devastating air war and scorched-earth tactics. For the FMLN, the massive bombings of rural communities and poor urban neighborhoods and the forced resettlement of the displaced demonstrated the impotence of the armed forces and their U.S. advisers. It said, for example, that the 1985-1986 Operation Phoenix campaign against the communities of the Guazapa volcano was further evidence of "a military strategy that has no other choice but to run counter to political logic, feeding its own defeat."[19]

Despite the failure of the military's various pacification strategies, its high command has not abandoned the principles of low-intensity conflict. Indeed, Chief of Staff Ponce asserted in 1989 that under his command there would be more emphasis placed on the "hearts and minds" campaign. Echoing the words of his predecessor Blandón, Ponce said, "The victor in this war will be the one with popular support. The war will not be won with guns and bullets but with all sectors of society working together."[20] But the armed forces have never taken these proclamations to heart and instead view all popular dissidence as part of the revolutionary threat.

As a logical extension of its own belief that the popular organizations are nothing but front organizations for the guerrillas, the military has lashed out against unions, leftist political parties, and human-rights groups. But this has only increased anti-government sentiment and further skewed the political balance in favor of the FMLN. Massive terror did succeed once in eliminating the popular movement from the political balance. But if it resorted again to terror on the scale of the early 1980s, the military knows it would risk losing the U.S. aid on which it now so thoroughly depends. The late 1989 killing of the Jesuit priests and the ensuing international outrage brought this lesson home.

The FMLN offensive of late 1989 raised new questions about the ability of the military to keep the guerrilla forces from gaining the upper hand in the war. For the first time, the FMLN proved capable of successfully operating within San Salvador, what had been until then the near inviolable rearguard of the armed forces. The offensive also highlighted the inability of the army to fight an urban war, without resorting to politically damaging aerial bombings. The FMLN offensive exploded the myth propagated by the military that the guerrillas were simply bothersome terrorists and not a serious military threat.

Furthermore, the offensive showed that the military, despite its superior numbers and firepower, was operating at near capacity and would be hard put to expand the war. Prior to the offensive the army was already largely on the defensive, pinned down to defending fixed positions like bridges, barracks, and coffee plantations. The opening of a serious urban front further strained the military's resources, limiting its ability to maintain the kind of strong offensive posture needed to keep the FMLN on the run.

Paramilitary Groups

With names like the Secret Anticommunist Army, White Warriors Union, and the Revolutionary Anticommunist Extermination Action, death squads have terrorized the popular movement since the 1970s. These bands of heavily armed, uniformed men have kidnapped, tortured, and killed tens of thousands of Salvadoran labor leaders, church activists, students, suspected guerrillas, and community organizers. It would be a mistake, however, to categorize death-squad members simply as rightwing extremists, something the U.S. embassy regularly does. In its 1988 report, *El Salvador: Death Squads—A Government Strategy*, Amnesty International concluded that the so-called death squads "are simply used to shield the government from accountability for torture, disappearances, and extrajudicial disappearances committed in their name....Squads are made up of regular army and police agents under orders of superiors."

Just as the death squads should not be considered apart from the armed forces, neither should they be regarded simply as a national occurrence. There is good reason to believe that the emergence of death squads in El Salvador and throughout Latin America was directly related to U.S. counterinsurgency, intelligence, and police training programs. One important source of supplies and training for anticommunist terrorism was the Agency for International Development's Office of Public Safety which trained Salvadoran police and the National Guard between 1962 and 1975. The police training program was established by President Kennedy to "counter communist inspired or exploited violence and insurgency" and for the purposes of "detecting and identifying individuals and organizations engaged in subversive insurgency in its incipient state." The program instructed the Salvadoran police in such areas as intelligence systems, interrogation systems, and even bomb-making. A National Police detective and D'Aubuisson associate, Lt. Edgard Pérez Linares, was the longtime chief of the Secret Anticommunist Army.

The CIA was another major influence on the formation of military-linked death squads. Together with U.S. Green Beret instructors, the CIA conceived and organized ORDEN (National Democratic Organization), the rural paramilitary and intelligence network described by Amnesty International as a movement designed "to use clandestine terror against government opponents." Out of ORDEN grew the White Hand, one of the first Salvadoran death squads.[21] The CIA also established AN-SESAL, the elite presidential intelligence service that was, in the words of one U.S. official, "the operative arm of intelligence gathering." Gen. José Alberto Medrano (director of ORDEN and ANSESAL) served as a CIA agent, along with Col. Nicolás Carranza (former chief of the Treasury Police). In addition, the CIA and the U.S. embassy have regularly shared intelligence information on leftists and popular leaders with military and police intelligence units.[22]

The military-civilian junta of October 1979 abolished ORDEN and ANSESAL but death-squad violence, now fully integrated into the armed forces, did not stop. Rather it rose to new heights in the 1980-1983 period in conjunction with the U.S. sponsored counterinsurgency project. Together with the political and economic reforms instituted by the March 1980 junta came a wave of terror in which some 800 civilians were killed a month. Roberto D'Aubuisson, a protege of General Medrano, protested the closure of ORDEN in 1979 and, to continue the work of ORDEN, immediately formed the Democratic Nationalist Front, which later became ARENA. With ARENA in control of the Constituent Assembly, the center of death-squad operations switched to the special police unit run by Assembly president D'Aubuisson.

By late 1983, with the popular movement having been decimated by disappearances and murders, death-squad violence was on the decline. The Reagan administration sent Vice President Bush and Oliver North to San Salvador in December 1983 to warn the Salvadoran military that gross human-rights violations would no longer be tolerated and to stress the importance of cleaning up death-squad activity prior to the presidential elections scheduled for the following year.

With the reconstitution of the popular movement in the late 1980s, death-squad violence again became common. The main target of the death squads are activists of popular organizations that the U.S. embassy terms "FMLN fronts." Among the newly named death squads are the National Movement for the Salvation of El Salvador, Revolutionary Anticommunist Extermination Action, Eastern Solidarity Action, and the Central American Anticommunist Hand. In May 1989 the most extreme elements within ARENA working with First Brigade Commander Colonel Zepeda (later assigned to the Ministry of Defense), formed the Patriotic Defense Committee—a new open paramilitary organization—as an "integral front" against the FMLN. But local pressure, especially from the Catholic church, forced the the government to disband the paramilitary group.

It is commonly believed in El Salvador that the rash of bombings of popular organizations such as UNTS, COMADRES, and FENASTRAS are the work of special operations teams associated with military intelligence. The old ANSESAL apparatus has been replaced, with CIA and Pentagon support, with a sophisticated intelligence network directed by the National Directorate of Intelligence (DNI), which falls under the authority of the Defense Ministry.[23] Other intelligence organizations are the C-2 of the Combined General Staff of the Armed Forces which works directly with the D-2 or S-2 intelligence units of the three security forces: National Police, Treasury Police, and National Guard. The D-2 of the Air Force is also widely suspected of coordinating the increased death squad-type activity in the eastern part of San Salvador.[24]

In late 1989 a deserter from the D-2 intelligence division of the First Brigade, César Vielman Joya Martínez, acknowledged that he had participated in death-squad murders organized by the intelligence division. Joya Martínez, who was in charge of executions while others handled the "heavy interrogation" or torture, charged that U.S. advisers were aware of the activities of his "special corps." In fact, one U.S. military adviser shared an office with him. He said U.S. advisers gave his clandestine unit instruction in "special planning" for urban counterinsurgency war and that they received special compensations from the U.S. military. Col. Elena Fuentes, commander of the First Brigade, admitted that Joya Martínez was a former member of the Brigade but dismissed him as a thief and liar.

The myth that most bombings of popular organizations and the murders and disappearances of activists were the signature of the ultra-right vigilantes was finally laid to rest in early 1990, when the government itself acknowledged that elements within the army were responsible for the murders of the six Jesuits.

Guerrilla Opposition

The Farabundo Martí National Liberation Front (FMLN) takes its name after Augustín Farabundo Martí, the leader of the 1932 insurrection who was executed by the military. Now widely recognized as the strongest guerrilla army in Latin American history, the FMLN is the unified front of five guerrilla armies. The FMLN is, however, much more than an army with a political agenda. As the country's leading nongovernmental political force, the FMLN has demonstrated that political considerations generally guide its military strategy, not the other way around.

FMLN: Origins and Components

In the aftermath of the 1969 war with Honduras and frustrated by continued electoral fraud, several leftist groups decided that armed struggle was fundamental to changing the country's repressive and unjust economic and political structures. The five guerrilla organizations that constitute the FMLN are the following:

Popular Liberation Forces (FPL): Founded in 1970 by Salvador Cayetano Carpio and other dissidents of the Communist Party of El Salvador, the FPL had strong links with the Popular Revolutionary Bloc, a large popular coalition formed in the mid-1970s. Internal political and personal disputes led to the murder of Melinda Anaya Montes ("Commander Ana María") in 1983 and the subsequent suicide of Carpio. The FPL advocated the revolutionary strategy of "prolonged people's war." Its commander is Salvador Sánchez Cerén (nom de guerre "Leonel González").

People's Revolutionary Army (ERP): Founded in 1971 by leftist student leaders, ERP was associated with the People's League of February 28 (LP-28). Long considered to be the most militaristic of the FMLN armies, the ERP was responsible for assassination of mayors who refused to leave their posts. Ana María Guadalupe Martínez and Joaquín Villalobos have been ERP's main *comandantes*.

Armed Forces of National Resistance (FARN): Founded in 1975 as a split from the ERP, FARN has stressed building mass political support and was linked to the country's second largest mass organization, People's

Action Front (FAPU). Eduardo Sancho ("Fermán Cienfuegos") is the FARN commander.

Central American Revolutionary Workers Party (PRTC): Founded in 1976 as the Salvadoran component of a proposed regional guerrilla army, PRTC was the smallest of the FMLN armies. Its commander is Francisco Jovel ("Roberto Roca").

Armed Forces of Liberation (FAL): Founded in May 1980, FAL was established as the military arm of the Communist Party of El Salvador, which had previously rejected armed struggle. FAL's commander is Jorge Shafik Hándal, who had succeeded Carpio as chief of the Communist Party.

Until 1980 the four existing guerrilla groups were not armies but clandestine political organizations whose operations were largely limited to kidnapping oligarchs and political organizing among the mass popular organizations. But with the resignation of the progressive civilians from the first junta and intensifying repression, the role of the armed resistance increased dramatically. In March 1980 the four armies (FPL, ERP, FARN, and PRTC) formed the Unified Revolutionary Directorate (DRU), which together with the FAL became the FMLN in October 1980.

During the 1980s, and especially after 1983, the distinctions between the five organizations eroded. Although the different armies are still not completely integrated, they function under one five-member general command, which is the FMLN directorate. As the FMLN itself admits, the differences between the five organization, particularly ideological squabbling, was one reason why the revolutionary forces were unable to seize power in late 1981 in the "Final Offensive."[25] Now divisions between the armies and the various commanders seem a matter of history, discussed more by the State Department and U.S. academics than a cause of real tension within the FMLN.

The FMLN does not release information about its internal structure and numbers. It is, however, generally accepted that the number of organized full-time combatants has declined from its peak of some 12,000 in the early 1980s — a time when its ranks were swelled by thousands of refugees from the popular movement. At the end of the decade, the FMLN's forces numbered about 7,000. These troops were divided into guerrilla units which fight in areas where they live; regular units that move throughout the country; and special forces which have long political and combat experience.[26] After the November 1989 offensive, the FMLN claimed that its ranks swelled with new recruits.

These full-time troops are supplemented by militias, including part-time combatants and auxiliaries. Colonel Zepeda, former head of military intelligence, described militia members this way: "They are fighters. But their main role is to carry messages, gather intelligence, carry out propaganda and sabotage, provide logistical support, and stage hit-and-run attacks." Militias are active FMLN supporters who, because of family and work commitments, cannot or do not wish to join the guerrilla forces but who significantly augment the FMLN's military capacity. In addition, these "weekend warriors" serve as important links between the FMLN and the popular organizations and are a key element in its insurrectional strategy.[27] Although not institutionally linked to the FMLN, the militant popular organizations, the *doble cara* structures of power in rural areas, and large number of guerrilla sympathizers amplify the power of the FMLN.

FMLN Political and Economic Philosophy

The U.S. embassy characterizes the FMLN leadership as Marxist-Leninist ideologues, and it is clearly the case that the ideological formation of the FMLN is deeply Marxist-Leninist. As the civil war evolved, however, the FMLN leadership has gradually backed away from earlier revolutionary dogmatism. No longer do they promise to install a socialist government after the military defeat of the Salvadoran armed forces.[28] Today the FMLN's rhetoric carries a more moderate tone, overflowing with assurances of its commitment to democracy, negotiations, pluralism, and broad class alliances. FMLN theoretician Joaquín Villalobos claims that reality, not ideology, is the FMLN's main guide for action. Political and economic democracy are its declared goals.[29]

Although adopting a new and "more mature" pluralist rhetoric, the FMLN does not deny its Marxist-Leninist convictions:

> The FMLN understands Marxism-Leninism as a scientific discipline for analyzing reality and as an organizational theory for struggle. But we do not convert the tenets of Marxism-Leninism into dogma that might isolate us from reality.[30]

An unmistakable feature of reality in El Salvador is that most Salvadorans are desperately poor — and it is this poor population that is the main social base of the guerrilla army. Its ranks are filled with young peasant women and men who regard the FMLN as a poor people's army. FMLN actions to protect and improve the life of the poor, not simply its promises of a better life after victory, underlie this allegiance. Its encouragement of rural communities to empower themselves through *doble cara* committees and its pressure on coffee growers to raise wages explain the depth of FMLN support in the countryside. The class dynamic of the war becomes all that much clearer when peasants see the FMLN defending the coffee workers while the army protects the property of coffee oligarchs.

The class nature of the revolutionary struggle dates back to the organizing by communist Farabundo Martí. The FMLN represents, however, more than a peasant war against the oligarchy. For most of the 1980s the thrust of guerrilla political organizing was in rural areas where its forces were based. The peasantry—downtrodden, repressed, and deeply cynical about reformist claims of the military and government—proved the natural allies of the revolutionary army. But the FMLN commanders also brought to the mountains strong their strong roots in the unions, universities, political struggles, and popular movements of the cities. In the last few years, as the war extended into urban areas, the FMLN has gone a long way toward renewing its links with the newly energized popular movement. It has also sought to broaden its appeal among the critically important middle class.

Although Marxism-Leninism remains the principal analytical tool of the FMLN, there is also a strong foundation in progressive Christianity. For many revolutionaries, the martyred Archbishop Oscar Arnulfo Romero is their main hero and inspiration. Significantly, the Christian Base Communities in Morazán were among the first recruits of the ERP guerrilla army.[31] The FMLN's commitment to sexual equality and its success in integrating women into the military and political leadership are other prominent components of the guerrilla struggle.

When held in the context of the civil war, elections have always been dismissed by the FMLN as part of a counterinsurgency strategy. Beginning in January 1989, however, the FMLN substantially altered its demands for a negotiated settlement. It announced that it was abandoning its call for power-sharing in a transition government and was ready to compete for power in the electoral arena once hostilities ended. According to Villalobos, the FMLN "pursues an El Salvador that is open, flexible, pluralistic, and democratic in both the economic and political spheres."[32]

In stating its revised position on the role of elections in the revolutionary process, the FMLN noted that since its founding the armed struggle has maintained an unbroken alliance with social-democratic elements through the Democratic Revolutionary Front (FDR). The three political parties of the FMLN-FDR alliance—National Revolutionary Movement, Popular Social Christian Movement, and National Democratic Union—have kept the FMLN linked to social-democratic and socialist political currents and philosophy throughout the world. Rumors of the imminent dissolution of the FMLN-FDR alliance, promoted mostly by the U.S. embassy, have frequently floated through diplomatic and media circles. Much to the dismay of Washington, the unity has endured. It continues to exist as evidence of the FMLN's commitment to political alliances and political solutions.

It is the conviction of the FMLN that, under fair conditions, the majority of Salvadorans would vote for revolutionary change. Through a negotiated settlement to the civil war, the FMLN hopes to establish the conditions in which it could incorporate as a political party and seek power in an open election campaign. According to Villalobos, "Electoral democracy confers legitimacy on the revolution, reaffirms its mass support, and allows the balanced participation of all sectors in exercising power." But democracy, according to the FMLN, is about more than political parties competing for power. It also must be participatory, meaning that political parties act as a catalyst for the increased political participation and self-management of the citizenry.[33]

Despite these offers to transfer its revolutionary struggle to the election arena, fears persist that the FMLN remains committed to a narrow political future administered by a dictatorship of the proletariat and peasantry. In other words, there is concern that the FMLN's new political program is little more than another communist trick. The FMLN replies that it has been calling for a government of broad participation since 1983 and that domestic and geopolitical realities would make a socialist regime in El Salvador impossible, even if the FMLN was still committed to such a project. It is not forsaking socialism but sees it as a long process. The first necessity, according FMLN Commander Cienfuegos, is an economic modernization that "is nothing more than [a program for] the development of capitalism in El Salvador." First, the FMLN intends to develop a minimal program and "later we look for bases to construct socialism."[34]

The minimal program includes an agrarian reform "since land is the fundamental factor in the economy and the fundamental source of social conflict." Villalobos calls the land-tenure system "the heart of the oligarchy's power" and "it must change." Modifications in the country's economic structure and reforms to guarantee the welfare of all Salvadorans are what the FMLN labels "economic democracy." It asserts that for political democracy to be meaningful, "people must eat, become educated, and have access to health care."[35] Concerning the role of the private sector, the FMLN offers this vision:

> The private sector should operate in a new structural context: In today's world, a combination of the private and public sectors can

lead to more rapid development of Salvadoran society than a supposedly more radical and closed model....Our objective is development. An ideological approach is of no use if it does not resolve the problems of poverty.[36]

Guerrilla Strategy of War and Peace

The FMLN began its "strategic counteroffensive" in January 1989 — a new phase of war incorporating an expanded political project and a wider military offensive. The new strategy, in preparation since 1986, reflected wide agreement within the FMLN that a purely military victory would be impossible because of the logistical superiority of the armed forces and continued U.S. military aid. Instead, the war will be brought to a close either by negotiations or by a popular insurrection in conjunction with a military offensive.

Insurrection has long been part of the FMLN strategy. In the first phase of the revolutionary struggle (1979-1981), hope was placed on a Nicaraguan-style popular insurrection that would be spearheaded by the inchoate FMLN army. But that hope was crushed by unprecedented repression aimed at eliminating the revolution's social base. The Final Offensive of December 1981 fell far short of FMLN expectations, and resulted in a new resolve by the FMLN to establish itself as a formidable armed force, capable of conventional and unconventional warfare. At the same time the FMLN set about to develop its military capabilities, it also established "zones of control" in the isolated northern and eastern regions of the country.

Meanwhile, the scourge of repression continued unabated until 1983. During that time, tens of thousands of civilians lost their lives in death-squad killings and military terrorism. The terror was accompanied by a parallel counterinsurgency strategy of pacification and democratization.

The next stage of the war began in late 1983 when the FMLN battalions began posing a serious military challenge to the armed forces. Recognizing the new military threat represented by the FMLN, the United States responded with increased military aid and training. With its strategy of economic and political reforms showing success in building a popular base for a civilian government, Washington was convinced that with adequate assistance a decisive military victory was possible in the short term. The plan was for the Salvadoran military to isolate the FMLN army from its narrow geographical base of support and then, with superior firepower and logistical capacity, wipe out the remaining guerrillas.

But rather than leading to victory, the strategy led to a military stalemate. Quickly adjusting to the new air war and ground offensives, the

FMLN switched its emphasis from large units and zones of control to smaller irregular units and a countrywide network of support and military action. Unable to respond in kind to military firepower, the FMLN developed a homespun weapons industry and seriously inhibited army mobility with extensive use of landmines. The switch to small mobile units that could strike throughout the country also reflected an awareness on part of the FMLN that political organizing among rural communities was more difficult when operating in large guerrilla units. Smaller groupings facilitate more direct political contact with rural communities.

Another new element in the guerrilla's strategy was sabotage aimed at the country's economic and transportation infrastructure. The objective was not only to debilitate the country's "economy of war," but also to keep army troops pinned down to guarding fixed positions, like bridges, dams, and the electrical system. Causing $2 billion in infrastructure damage, the FMLN's campaign of economic destabilization effectively counterbalanced Washington's aid for economic stabilization. The sabotage campaign also stretched the army's personnel and logistical limits, while keeping it largely on a defensive footing. For the Salvadoran military and the U.S. embassy, the sabotage campaign demonstrated the guerrilla's weakness and essentially terroristic nature. Defending the sabotage campaign, Commander Villalobos stated:

> What is at issue here is not the FMLN's military abilities, but rather the army's inability to defend its political-economic power base, its reason for being. The war is not a jousting match between medieval knights.[37]

During the early years of the Duarte government, Washington came to accept that the FMLN could not easily be defeated militarily. But it felt that its political and economic stabilization project, combined with the eventual exhaustion of the FMLN, would succeed in marginalizing the guerrilla army, making it more of an irritant than a real threat to state power. What it did not count on was the continued determination and tactical flexibility of the guerrillas. Nor did U.S. planners figure in the exhaustion of the political side of counterinsurgency. Salvadorans grew disillusioned with elections that did not solve the country's main crisis and a reformist government that seemed only interested in pursuing the war. The stagnating economy and worsening socioeconomic conditions also undermined support for the government and the war.

In formulating its strategic counteroffensive, the FMLN rejected the thesis of stalemate. Instead, it insisted that it held the strategic advantage because of its successful political initiatives. The state of the war, it said, could not be measured by numbers of combatants or battle victories but also had to be evaluated in political terms. It was the FMLN's contention in mid-1989 that the popular movement was quickly accumulating force and would soon reach the levels seen in 1979 and 1980. If a negotiated settlement was not accepted, the FMLN predicted that an insurrection, in conjunction with an expanded FMLN offensive, would bring the government down.

Essential to any insurrectional strategy is urban support—probably the FMLN's weakest point. But during the late 1980s, the FMLN made great strides in building an urban network of support. It dramatically increased its urban military actions, even to the extent of launching attacks against military bases within San Salvador. The FMLN also encouraged the formation of an infrastructure of clandestine urban cells made up of the most radicalized members of the popular movement which could spark wider insurrectional response. Rather than integrating all new militants into the guerrilla army, the FMLN has advocated locally initiated insurrectional activity.

The FMLN calls itself "the political actor most in touch with the people." As such, the FMLN "has a decisive piece in its hands—the masses—and it is going to use them for the checkmate." When this will happen, the guerrillas say is impossible to predict—but they are confident that it will be in the short term. There is no more talk of prolonged people's war. Why the confidence? The FMLN points to a history of powerful mass action, from the 1932 rebellion to the union and teachers' struggles of the 1960s and the explosion of the popular movement in the late 1970s. It also cites the willingness and courage of the popular sectors to regroup despite the recent memories of massive disappearances and assassinations of the early 1980s.

The military side of the war is necessary to keep the government and army unstable and on the defensive. In the FMLN's strategic counteroffensive, the nonmilitary factors are the decisive elements working in its favor. "From now on, the people will determine the pacing, the timing, and the intensity of the battles" of the conflict, asserted Villalobos in 1989.[38]

Father Ignacio Ellacuria, in an interview shortly before his murder, observed: "The FMLN has never been so strong politically, militarily, and in relation to the masses. And it can grow even stronger in a very short time. The FMLN has clearly not abandoned its preparation for a general offensive accompanied by a popular insurrection, mainly in the countryside, but also in the city. It has used reason to pressure [the government] to change its position, but has not abandoned the pressure of force."[39]

Escalating the War

Following the October 31, 1989 bombing of the FENASTRAS head-quarters, which left ten union leaders dead, the FMLN broke off talks with the ARENA government. On November 11 it launched its largest offensive of the war, attacking military positions throughout the country and sending 3,500 troops to San Salvador. As a minimal goal, the FMLN hoped the offensive would significantly alter the balance of political and military forces. It was also thought that the offensive might spur a widespread public insurrection against the ARENA government. Early on in the offensive guerrilla leaders predicted that this would be the final offensive and that they would never leave their newly established positions in the cities.

The offensive would not have been possible without broad and committed public support, but it did not ignite the long-predicted popular insurrection. Many students and other young Salvadorans picked up arms during the offensive, but for the most part these were members of the FMLN clandestine urban networks rather than streams of new recruits. The aerial bombing of the poor neighborhoods where the FMLN units were entrenched brought to a tragic end guerrilla predictions for an immediate urban uprising.

The FMLN, however, counted the offensive as a political and miltary victory. It had demonstrated its military capacity while at the same time increasing domestic and international pressure for the government to enter into serious negotiations. Assessing the post-offensive atmosphere, the FMLN observed: "For the first time the army couldn't say that the FMLN is a scattered force with no combat capabilities."[40] With the November 1989 offensive, the FMLN demonstrated it was a military force to be reckoned with. Nonetheless, the war remained stalemated with both military forces capable of denying victory to the other but neither able to defeat the other militarily.[41]

By late 1990, the intransigence of the government during the U.N.-mediated peace talks, the weakening state of ARENA and the Cristiani administration, and the prospects of a substantially reduced U.S. commitment to the war encouraged some elements within the FMLN to adopt a harder negotiating line and to re-commit themselves to a military solution. A negotiated end to the war and FMLN's insertion into the electoral process with the guarantee of international verification remained, however, the preferred option of the guerrilla directorate.

Chapter 3

Economy

The State of the Economy

The Salvadoran economy enters the 1990s in a precarious state. Its principal characteristics are the following:[1]

Costs of War: Since 1975 current expenditures for defense have increased 8 times, while the overall government budget has trebled. In 1988 nearly 45 percent of current government spending was for defense and security.[2] This prioritization of war spending has contributed to the budget deficit and inflationary problems while causing budget cuts in the agriculture, education, and other government ministries. The war has also created serious obstacles to industrial and agricultural production because of the overall conditions of insecurity and the damage to the nation's economic infrastructure.

War-related damage to the economy as result of guerrilla sabotage is estimated to be over $2 billion — about the same amount that the U.S. Agency for International Development (AID) has pumped into the country for economic stabilization. Preliminary estimates by the Ministry of Planning showed that the guerrilla offensive of late 1989 and the military's response caused $30 million in infrastructure damage and as much as $90 million in direct and indirect losses in economic production.[3]

Dependence on External Aid: Economic aid in El Salvador is not just a booster, but a central part of the economy. Without U.S. aid, the economy and the government would stop functioning as if an electric cord were disconnected. The foreign aid that enters El Salvador, mostly from the United States, is much larger than the revenues the government itself generates. Economic aid from AID increased in amount and significance throughout the 1980s. In 1983 AID funds were equivalent to almost a third of the country's export revenues but by the late 1980s represented two-thirds of export income. The foreign aid from the U.S. government in 1987 represented 105 percent of the government's own revenues — a proportion of dependency that is much higher than any other country receiving U.S. aid. Most of the U.S. economic aid is designated as the country's "extraordinary budget" and is administered by the Ministry of Planning under guidelines imposed by AID.

During the 1980s the U.S. government pumped almost $3 billion of U.S. economic aid into the country. Congressional sources have reported that 75 percent of the U.S. aid program is for war-related expenditures.[4] The $300 million in average annual economic assistance in recent years has been complemented by generous funding (over $600 million between 1980 and 1988) from the Interamerican Development Bank (IDB), a multilateral bank largely controlled by the United States. As crucial as this wealth of economic aid is to the economy, it has not proved an adequate substitute for an energetic local economy, especially since much of the aid is lost to corruption, consultants, and military-related programs.

So dependent is El Salvador on U.S. economic aid that even slight decreases could cause a crisis in government. The ARENA government faces just such a prospect, as it is highly unlikely that U.S. aid commitments will increase and very probable that the annual U.S. assistance will steadily decline for a variety of reasons: decreased U.S. interest in maintaining El Salvador as a client state, reduced congressional enthusiasm for the ARENA government, U.S. budget constraints, demands for U.S. aid by other countries like Panama and those of Eastern Europe, and the inevitable momentum of the regional peace process. Nonetheless, as long as Washington is committed to waging war in El Salvador, the country will probably continue to be favored by large, although not increasing, allocations of U.S. economic aid.

Dependence on Remittances: Remittances from Salvadorans living abroad inject more dollars into the Salvadoran economy than either the coffee industry or the U.S. economic-aid program. A 1987 study by the University of Central America estimated that over one-third of the Salvadorans living in the country have family members in the United States. Those family members were sending an average of $188 dollars a month to relatives in El Salvador.[5] Estimates of total remittances range from $500 million to over $1.3 billion annually. Only some $225 million of this is directed through official channels, the balance being exchanged on the thriving black market. During the 1980s, remittances — which have been called a form of "people's aid" — became a major factor in holding up the economy and sustaining consumption levels.[6] Although remittances will continue, it is unlikely that they will increase due to tighter immigration controls in the United States.

Falling Exports and Widening Trade Imbalance: The balance of trade has dropped precipitously, from a positive $112 million in 1980 to a projected negative $515 million in 1989. A sharp drop in coffee exports and an accompanying fall in coffee prices in 1989 meant that the country was importing a half billion dollars more than it was exporting at the end of the decade. Some planners, like those at AID and the U.S.-funded Salvadoran Foundation for Social and Economic Development (FUSADES), have pinned their hopes on the growth of nontraditional exports both in the industrial and agricultural sectors. Despite tens of millions of dollars to promote such growth, nontraditional exports outside the region increased only about $15 million since 1979, while nontraditional exports to other countries in the region have been cut in half over the last decade.

Attempts to adjust the economy through increased trade liberalization and currency devaluation are likely to adversely affect this commercial imbalance, given the extreme import dependence of El Salvador. An average of 70 percent of the country's import bill is for intermediate goods (raw material, semi-processed goods, agricultural inputs — about 50 percent) and capital goods (machinery — about 20 percent) needed by Salvadoran producers. The currency-devaluation process initiated by the ARENA government is making it increasingly costly to purchase these necessary imports and will likely further inhibit economic growth.

If the economy is to grow, there needs to be a substantial increase in imports of intermediate and capital goods. During the several pre-1979 periods of economic expansion, the pace of economic growth was paralleled by a significantly faster rate of import growth. In other words, the possibilities of economic recovery depend a great deal on the capacity the country has to import. Declining export income, increasing debt service, and foreign aid dedicated to stabilization not investment are all factors that contribute to the economy's increasing inability to afford imported intermediate and capital goods.[7]

Absence of Investment: Despite some early success at economic stabilization, the Salvadoran economy is once again sliding backwards. During the 1979-1983 period, the economy experienced negative growth, but this was followed by a few years of cumulative economic growth that resulted from a sharp increase in U.S. economic aid. By end of the decade, however, the economy was stagnating again. In per capita terms, the Salvadoran economy steadily fell in the 1980s (except for 1984) at the rate of one to 2 percent a year, and Salvadorans found themselves living with an economy one-fourth smaller than in 1978 and lower than it was a quarter of a century ago.[8]

Decreased public-sector investment and an all but dormant private sector explain this retrogression. Agriculture is experiencing continuing reverses; the construction industry, which boomed because of cheap credit and post-earthquake building, has lost its momentum; and manufacturing has barely kept up with per capita growth.[9] The private sector has been the focus of AID efforts to energize the economy but its promotional efforts have largely fallen flat — understandable when one considers the insecurity and disruption resulting from the ten-year civil war.

Although the public sector also benefits from substantial injections of foreign aid, this aid is not oriented toward productive ends but is used largely to balance the budget, cover imbalances in external accounts, and for war-related purposes (pacification programs, infrastructure repair, etc.). Little is left over for public-sector investment projects which could increase employment and bolster economic growth.

Persistent Budget Deficits: When measured against many other third world countries, the country's budget deficit is not extremely serious.[10] But when taking into account the tremendous influx of budget-balancing AID monies, the deficit is serious indeed. Despite constant U.S. efforts to plug the budget deficit with local currency generated from its balance-of-payments assistance (ESF and Title I aid), the gap only seems to grow wider.

Since over 90 percent of the government's budget covers routine operating expenses (the public-sector investment budget is handled almost exclusively by the foreign donor-generated extraordinary budget), it makes it difficult to cut. Already public services have been cut bare. Education's portion of the budget dropped from 35 percent to less than 20 percent during the 1980s, and public-health expenditures were halved.[11] This means that it would be impossible to close the budget deficit without laying off thousands of public employees — which is exactly what the ARENA government started to do in late 1989.

Higher taxes and more efficient tax collection can also play a role in closing the deficit. The government is already heavily dependent on indirect or consumption taxes, which fall most heavily on the poor. There is little room to increase taxes in this area, although the Cristiani administration has attempted to push the limits of what the poor can bear by increasing utility rates and public-transportation costs. Although the ARENA government has committed itself to more efficient tax collection, it is unlikely that it will risk angering its middle-class and wealthy supporters by raising property and income taxes or even strictly enforcing current tax laws.

When ARENA won control of San Salvador's city hall in 1988, one of the first acts of the new mayor, Armando Calderón Sol, was to write the city's wealthiest residents begging them to pay their property tax bills, which are traditionally discarded. One Salvadoran observer told the *New York Times*, "To say that his request was ignored is putting it politely."[12] In El Salvador, the poor shoulder the tax burden while many businesses avoid their full tax obligations.

During the Duarte government, there was a joint government/army effort to increase direct taxation to cover the costs of the war. Rejecting this "war tax," the private sector, led by the National Association of Private Enterprise (ANEP) and Chamber of Commerce and Industry, organized a highly successful business slowdown, forcing the government to modify its tax measures. The ARENA-controlled Supreme Court ruled that the war tax was unconstitutional on the grounds that national sovereignty was not at stake in the war, which was a conflict among Salvadorans.

Instead of increasing taxes on those who can best pay—the agroexport sector—the ARENA government's economic package included tax breaks for sugar and shrimp exporters and other tax breaks for producers of nontraditional exports. At the time ARENA took hold of the government, the shortfall between budget revenues and expenses was approaching 30 percent. Things were made worse by the fact that the outgoing government had already spent most of the first-quarter government revenues. Weak coffee production—the worst in 30 years—further aggravated the government's revenue problems. It is the stated intention of ARENA to reduce the budget to manageable levels through further austerity measures, increased government efficiency, and privatization. Given the continued drain caused by war-related expenses and the dismal state of the export economy, even small reductions in the deficit will prove extremely difficult.

External Debt: El Salvador's external debt is approximately $2 billion, 70 percent held by the public sector, 24 percent by the nationalized banking system, and 6 percent by the private sector. By the standards of other Latin American countries, this is not a serious burden. The continued flow of U.S. economic aid—at least half of it directly targeted for balance-of-payments assistance—lightens the load of annual debt servicing, which represents about 40 percent of export income.

Devalued Currency: Devaluation has been on the economic agenda of El Salvador for the last ten years. At the start of the 1980s, the *colón* was valued at two *colones* to the dollar. Pressure from the multilateral banks and a growing black market resulted in the creation of a legal parallel market by the Duarte government followed by an official devaluation in 1986, reducing the *colón*'s value to five to the dollar.

Devaluation pressure began building again in 1987 and a promise of devaluation became part of ARENA's economic platform. But once elected the new government decided to postpone indefinitely the promised devaluation. It was thought that a devaluation might provoke widespread popular disapproval and ignite a popular insurrection. Instead the Cristiani administration opted for what amounts to a gradual devaluation process or a "sliding" currency exchange in which the importers are permitted to buy dollars on the black market for the going rate. A similar process was unleashed when President Duarte authorized a parallel exchange rate prior to the official devaluation in 1986. By the end of 1989 the dollar was valued at 6.5 *colones* on the black market. Observers expect an eventual devaluation on the order of 50 to 100 percent.[13] Recognizing the sensitive nature of devaluation, the term was dropped from the government lexicon. Instead of devaluation, the Cristiani administration in 1989 began to talk of instituting "an exchange policy that would permit the creation and maintenance of a realistic currency exchange."

Devaluation is an adjustment measure advocated by AID, the World Bank, and the International Monetary Fund (IMF) and heartily supported locally by the agroexport sector. Devaluation would broaden the impact of foreign aid and remittances by increasing the sum of local currency generated by that assistance. It would also increase the profits of the agroexport sector since the dollars earned by exports would be converted into a larger number of *colones*.

It is argued that devaluation is an appropriate structural-adjustment measure because it spurs increased investment and production in the export sector — the engine of the economies in third world countries like El Salvador. The idea is that a devalued currency makes a country's exports more attractive and competitive on the international market. In some cases such as the production of some nontraditional exports, this might be true, but for the most part Salvadoran exports face an inelastic world market which will not make room for increased Salvadoran coffee, cotton, and sugar exports.[14]

Although its benefits are for the most part doubtful, there are many direct negative consequences of currency devaluation. It negatively impacts the economy and society by raising prices, increasing the cost of debt service, and discouraging the import of intermediate and capital goods. The initial hesitation of the ARENA government to impose the promised devaluation was not the result of any change of economic philosophy but of a close reading of social history. The 1986 devaluation by the Christian Democratic government was one of the factors that sparked the creation of the UNTS coalition and popular rejection of the Duarte administration. Army and government officials are concerned that devaluation and increased austerity in the context of the ten-year civil war might prove to be the detonator of a "social explosion" predicted by the FMLN.

Given the widening dependency on remittances, the effect of a devaluating currency is not as severe in El Salvador as in other countries where there is little dollar-based income. Just as agroexporters benefit from a devalued currency, so do the families that receive remittances from relatives in the United States. Each dollar that comes into the country has a higher value in local currency. Those families that do not receive checks and money orders from family members in the United States are, of course, hard hit each time the *colón* loses more of its value.

Deepening Poverty: The most recent estimates (Ministry of Planning, 1988) place unemployment in urban areas at 50 percent and in rural areas at 71 percent. But even those with jobs generally cannot afford basic necessities. Since 1980 per capita national income has dropped by 25 percent, while inflation had raised the cost of living by 360 percent. Real wages have dropped by at least a third since the war began.

As a result of unemployment, depressed wages, and inflation, at least 45 percent of Salvadoran families in 1985 were considered living at or below absolute poverty levels — meaning they do not have enough income to cover basic food needs. Ninety percent of the population were living in relative poverty in the mid-1980s — meaning that they did not have the economic capacity to provide a dignified life for themselves and their family (housing, education, health care, etc.).[15] It is expected that those measures of poverty have significantly worsened in the last five years because of inflation, a weaker currency, and static wage levels.

When President Duarte was inaugurated in June 1984, he promised to institute a Social Economic Policy that would change the oligarchic model of the economy and place new emphasis on meeting the needs of the poor. Instead he froze wages and cut the social-service budget while allowing continued the repression against unions and popular organizations demanding higher wages and better living conditions.[16] Priority attention was given to the war and to the private sector with new policies to promote investment and increase exports. These priorities have been renewed and expanded by the ARENA government, offering little hope for the country's poor.

Rescuing the Economy

Given the magnitude and length of the civil war, the economic crisis in El Salvador cannot be addressed without also seeking an end to the war. Yet throughout the 1980s that is exactly what foreign donor and lending organizations (principally AID) and the country's private-sector elite have tried to do. The widely expressed belief has been that with proper stabilization, austerity, and investment-promotion measures, the economy could be rescued from stagnation. According to AID:

> Without realistic economic policies to enhance production, investment, and employment, substantial economic and social progress will not be possible in El Salvador. AID continues to press the Government of El Salvador to enact policies that promote a productive economy, based on better dialogue between the public and private sectors. To stimulate the economy, the government must move quickly...to increase production of traditional exports, develop new exports, and improve agricultural productivity.[17]

To address falling exports, the focus of the prevailing economic development strategy has been to promote nontraditional exports. To spur private investment, there have been efforts to increase credit and provide subsidies to new investors. To ease the fiscal deficit, the tendency has been to hold public-sector wages down, cut budgets of essential social services, and finally lay off government employees. Devaluation, decreased government intervention, and removal of protectionist trade barriers are among the other favored economic-stabilization and growth strategies.

Initially at least, ARENA breathed new life into the myth that the country's economic problems have economic solutions. It is ARENA's contention that the private sector has been stifled by reforms, bureaucracy, and excessive interventionism of Christian Democratic governments. In its campaign the party promised a "national rescue" of the depressed and dependent economy. Being a party largely of businessmen, it promised that an ARENA-run government would know how to promote private-sector growth. The private capital that had fled the country during the 1980s would come rushing back to the country.

ARENA's formula for success is based on the tenets of neoliberalism, including the freeing up of prices, trade, and market forces. Its emphasis on free enterprise and the primacy of the international market paralleled the growth strategies proposed by FUSADES, an economic think tank and promotional organization funded almost entirely by AID.

The rhetoric of neoliberalism may be new in El Salvador but the interests that live behind this economic "solution" are not. It is an economic philosophy that eminently suits the narrow and short-term economic interests of the agroexport oligarchy. It is a philosophy of self-interest, and those who will benefit are dominant sectors of the private elite. Neoliberalism opposes state intervention in the economy, which translates into privatization, price liberalization, deregulation, the priority of capital, and the dissolution of state-sponsored reforms.

Joining in ARENA's call for private-sector solutions, the Chamber of Free Commerce charged that the origin of the economic crisis of the 1980s is the "socialist misspending of former regimes." The National Association of Private Business Owners (ANEP), the country's most important business association, said that the "so-called structural reforms are what distorted the institutional order of the country, provoking the backward movement."[18] As the undisputed representative of the oligarchy, ARENA has promised that its government would "stimulate and rationalize the free movement of economic forces." True to its campaign platform, the ARENA began to impose its neoliberal agenda on the country soon after taking control of the government. But it immediately was confronted by the limits and weaknesses of neoliberalism and economic policies that relied on private-sector investment.

Privatization of state enterprises, for example, is limited by the relatively low degree (about 18 percent) of state economic involvement. Contrary to the impression created by ARENA, there was no increase in government intervention in the economy under the Christian Democratic government. There is important state investment in such areas as the ports, airport, telecommunications, and electricity services, but these are the very sectors controlled by the military — and are obviously off limits. (The military also has privileged access to lines of credit, which might be threatened by privatization of the financial system.) Ironically, ARENA has targeted for privatization the corporations held by CORSAIN, which are in fact generally private firms that went bankrupt. Although not exactly privatization, the government promises to eliminate all subsidies to government agencies and semi-autonomous state institutions that provide water, electricity, phone, and educational services — a policy that will have its most grave impact on the poor.

Where privatization will have its greatest impact is in the rollback of the 1980 reforms: agrarian reform, nationalization of banking, and nationalization of trade. Five banks and nine other financial institutions are scheduled to be reprivatized. If this occurs, it will affect the distribution of credit since the nationalized financial sector had been managing about 80 percent of the country's local credit. The main obstacle to this reprivatization of financial institutions is that they are heavily burdened with bad debt, making them unattractive to private investors.

No wholesale return of redistributed lands is on the agenda but ARENA has given its approval to judicial rulings returning some cooperatively held land to former owners and to a process of parceliza- tion. (See Agriculture) The fate of the state institutions established to regulate agroexport trade (mainly INCAFE and INAZUCAR) is uncer- tain. It is likely that INCAFE and INAZUCAR will be left standing to compete in the market with other private coffee-trading houses. New government agencies may be created to define and manage government tax, credit, and foreign-exchange policies related to coffee and sugar production. The 1980 nationalization of export trade did not result in any redistribution of the country's wealth but only increased control by the government and the Christian Democratic functionaries over the sugar and coffee industry. Privatization will likely spur increased concentration and may cause capital flight and decreased tax collections.

Although it did not immediately announce a currency devaluation, the ARENA government took measures that allowed the *colón* to slip inex- orably toward an official devaluation. Recognizing that a devaluation could ignite widespread popular opposition, the government decided not to devaluate the currency as ARENA had promised. But to prepare the way for an eventual official devaluation the government legalized black- market currency exchange—thereby putting in motion an unofficial devaluation process.

Liberalization of prices, dismissal of public-sector employees, and in- crease of interest rates were other economic measures announced by President Cristiani. In proceeding with its economic program, the new government's neoliberal principles are being tested by the reality of run- ning a government in the middle of the civil war. The Cristiani administra- tion is aware that uncompromising neoliberalism might drive the middle class toward a leftist popular alliance while pushing the poor and workers, particularly in the cities, toward rebellion.

The Cristiani government is also aware that his government's stability also depends on its image among the poor. To polish that image, Cristiani announced a series of social-assistance measures including expanded food-for-work projects, the creation of temporary public-works jobs for 20,000 unemployed workers, and a school-lunch program. In the August 1989 speech announcing these programs, Cristiani described ARENA's economic model as a "social market economy" and referred to Pope John

Paul II's notion of the economy as a "virtuous circle" which generates employment allowing workers to satisfy their needs.[19]

Grim Economic Prospects

There is, of course, little doubt that El Salvador needs to adjust its precarious economy. Policies are needed to diversify its exports, increase private investment, narrow the gap in the fiscal deficit, and adjust its external financial and trade imbalances. But there are many questions about the appropriateness of many of the remedies proposed by the Cristiani program of "national rescue." It is possible that the neoliberal policies will lead only to increased capital flight, higher inflation, deeper misery for the poor, and stagnant economic growth.

The main economic problem for El Salvador is not government economic policy but the war — a basic fact that was made clearer than ever for the ARENA government by the FMLN offensive of November 1989. The prospects of any plan for economic recovery or improved conditions for the poor are dismal in the context of war. Although ending the civil war is the necessary first step toward recovery, a post-war El Salvador would also face a bleak economic landscape. The problems of uncertain export revenues and deep structural inequities in the distribution of land and resources would remain.

A post-war economy would likely be confronted with a sharp drop in U.S. aid as well diminishing remittances from Salvadorans living in the United States as they return home. The loss of U.S. food aid, for example, would cause severe food shortages within the country while further aggravating its balance-of-payments crisis. Aside from problems caused by traditional structural injustices and weaknesses in the export sector, the prospects for future economic and social stability are also limited by the country's devastated environment. Even with better land and resource distribution, this small environmentally ravaged country will not easily be able to meet the basic needs of its large population.

Agriculture: Foundation of the Economy

Agriculture is the heart of the Salvadoran economy, accounting for nearly a quarter of the national product and two-thirds of its export income and directly employing a third of the workforce.[20] Actually, agriculture is a dual economy, sharply divided between the export and local food production. Traditional agroexports are down over 50 percent since 1979 and grain production is not able to meet local demand. Prospects are not good for the 1990s. The end of the war would immediately result in increased agricultural production but the country's producers would probably still be faced with low coffee prices, increasing international prices for fertilizer and pesticides, lack of credit and technical assistance for grain production and for small farmers, and the concentration of the best land in a relatively few hands.

Agroexports: Province of the Oligarchy

Coffee, shrimp, sugar, and cotton are, in that order, the leading agroexports. Coffee has been the undisputed king of the export sector for more than a hundred years. By the 1920s coffee accounted for 95 percent of the country's exports.[21] The plummeting coffee prices of the Great Depression era sparked a rural rebellion among Salvadoran peasants, which was suppressed by the infamous *matanza* of 1932 when the army and vigilante bands killed as many as 30,000 suspected rebels and sympathizers. The terror of 1932 quieted widespread rural unrest for a half a century.

Historically, El Salvador has been the largest coffee producer in Central America, and the fourth largest in Latin America following Brazil, Colombia, and Mexico. But the disruption caused by the war has halved coffee production since the late 1970s. Nonetheless, coffee dominates the agroexport sector, producing 60 percent of total export income, 90 percent of agricultural-export income, and some 25 percent of the government's tax revenues.[22]

While the country's oligarchy spreads over all economic sectors, it is firmly based in the coffee estates that cover the rich volcanic uplands. The coffee oligarchy fought successfully against the enactment of Phase II of the 1980 agrarian-reform program, thereby excluding most coffee estates from the land-redistribution program. Thus, the economic base of the most reactionary elements of the oligarchy remained intact.

The coffee industry has been battered by low international prices, coffee rust, and bad weather. Another major problem has been the economic destabilization campaign mounted by the FMLN, which has targeted the warehouses and processing plants (*beneficios*) of the coffee elite. The 1988-1989 harvest was particular disappointing—amounting to only a third of what the country had exported a decade before. Improved weather contributed to a 50 percent increase in the 1989-1990 harvest but a precipitous drop in international coffee prices made it impossible for exporters to cash in on the increased production. The chief reason for the low coffee prices—down to 70 cents a pound from a former high of

$1.45—was the dissolution of the International Coffee Organization which has historically set country quotas and floor prices for coffee.[23]

More than coffee oligarchs are hurt by the debilitated state of coffee production. The many small coffee farmers are also hard hit, as are the tens of thousands of peasants who depend on seasonal work on the coffee plantations. The stability of the government itself is affected by the projected drop of $100 million in export earnings and $25 million in export tax revenues. A sensitive issue confronting the ARENA government is the degree to which it will privatize coffee marketing.

In 1980 the government nationalized coffee trade and established IN-CAFE as the government institute which would control all international marketing. In mid-1989 the Supreme Court declared INCAFE unconstitutional because it monopolized coffee exports. Subsequently the Legislative Assembly approved legislation opening up coffee marketing to private firms. It is likely, however, that the government will attempt to maintain its control over foreign revenues generated by the coffee trade. Any complete relinquishment of government and Central Bank controls over the coffee trade would result in reduced tax revenues and increased capital flight—the very reasons why coffee trade was nationalized in the first place.

Another sad story in the agroexport sector is that of the disappearing cotton industry. Cotton is grown mainly in areas disrupted by the war, but the feeble state of the cotton industry is also the result of the industry's heavy reliance on expensive inputs and the weak world market. Not only is El Salvador no longer exporting much cotton, the country has had to resort to importing vegetable oil formerly produced locally by the country's cotton gins. A large part of the country's effective demand for vegetable oil is now covered by the U.S. food-aid program.[24]

Sugar and shrimp production are the only export crops that have maintained or increased former production levels, although together they still account for less than 10 percent of agricultural exports. Sugar production is important for its role in the domestic economy, meeting the large internal demand and providing a major source of rural seasonal employment. There is a tobacco industry in El Salvador, but the British-owned Salvadoran Tobacco Company sends raw Salvadoran tobacco to Guatemala for processing, explaining why almost 50 percent of the tobacco used in cigarette manufacturing is imported from Guatemala.

Much is being made over the need to diversify agricultural production in El Salvador. There is, however, little to show for the nontraditional agroexport projects administered by FUSADES and backed by AID and the Interamerican Development Bank (IDB). Besides shrimp, melons are the only significant new nontraditional agroexport. Cantaloupe and cucumber production is also being promoted but with discouraging results. Most of the small local demand for fruits and vegetables is met by imports from Guatemala. El Salvador is, as a result, a net importer of fruits and vegetables.

Less Food and More Import Dependence

The crisis in food production has not yet become a major issue in El Salvador because of the immense U.S. food-aid program that fills the gap in local production with imported wheat, corn, vegetable oil, soybean meal, and rice. Domestic production of corn, sorghum, beans, and rice is unable to keep up with the demand for those grains even though per capita consumption is declining.[25]

The U.S. food-aid and commodity-credit programs cover virtually the entire value of the country's food-import bill. Increased dependency on food imports is one result of this food aid. Another is changing consumption patterns as wheat (which cannot be produced locally) becomes increasingly integrated into the national diet.

Aside from its increasing inability to meet local food demand, the booming poultry industry is the other major change in the local food sector. During the 1980s the poultry industry rapidly expanded to meet the demands of the middle and upper classes. It also exports large quantities of eggs and broiler chickens to other Central American countries. During the 1980s corn consumption by humans actually declined while corn consumption by animals doubled.[26] Not only does the poultry industry benefit from yellow corn imports under the U.S. food-aid and credit programs, it is also bolstered by imports of wheat and breeder chicks.

Death of the Agrarian Reform

The 1980 Land Reform Law was a key element of the "hearts and minds" strategy for defeating the guerrillas. It was thought that the land-redistribution program would simultaneously create a popular base for a centrist government, undermine the power of a reactionary oligarchy, and open the way for increased agricultural production. Ten years later the agrarian-reform program is being largely dismantled by the rightwing government.

On many counts, the program failed. Over the decade the oligarchy maintained its dominant economic position while increasing its political power. In economic terms, the program has been a disaster. Between 1980 and 1986 grain production dropped 56 percent in the reform sector, while falling just 6 percent in the non-reform sector. In export production, the reform sector showed an 11 percent drop in production against a negative 17 percent in the non-reform sector.[27] The reform sector proved an important source of support for the Christian Democrats and gave credibility to reformist image of the government, particularly through the critical 1981-1986 period of the U.S. counterinsurgency project.

In its electoral campaign, ARENA promised to substitute the agrarian-reform program with an agricultural development program that stressed privatization and support for commercially viable farms. Although it is unlikely that the ARENA government will seek to reverse completely the results of the land redistribution for fear of peasant reaction, it has begun to cut off public-sector support for the Phase I cooperatives and push for the dissolution of these cooperatives in favor of individually owned parcels.

The new director of FINATA (one of the AID-funded sources of credit for the reform sector) declared his intention "to break with the communist system of agricultural land distribution." He also announced the dissolution of the Committee of Campesino Organizations (CCC), which the Duarte government established to adjudicate peasant cooperative claims. CCC was replaced and renamed the Campesino Consultative Committee, which will move to distribute cooperative property to "individual and independent" peasants. At the same time, ARENA's Roberto D'Aubuisson and the new director of the Salvadoran Land Transformation Institute (ISTA) began maneuvering to replace the leadership of agrarian-reform cooperatives with ARENA partisans.[28]

There is mixed reaction among the cooperative sector to ARENA's parcelization proposals, but most oppose the measures. At the Los Pinos cooperative, Eugenio Rivas observed, "Five fingers can hold back the force that breaks one. If I go as an individual to a bank for credit, they won't bother with me. If we all go together, we're more likely to get a loan." Jorge Villacorta, an author the original reform law, doubts that the cooperatives will survive if the government "uses competition and profitability as the only yardsticks for agrarian credit." He added, "I have no doubt that in a few years most peasants would sell or have their lands put up for sale by banks holding their property as collateral. Then we're back to the days when a few families owned most of the land—the same agrarian inequities that brought us to war in the first place."[29]

The agrarian reform did give the peasantry increased access to land, credit, and technical assistance. But it fell far short of providing the reform sector with the support it needed. While the AID project did fulfill its guarantees to compensate expropriated landowners, it left the beneficiaries burdened in debt and without adequate government support. Only one-quarter of the reform sector benefited from government credit during the 1980s, and most agree that beneficiaries will never be able to pay off the accumulated debt.[30]

Underutilization and stagnant or declining levels of production characterize the reform sector. One factor has been the war. At least 28 cooperatives on Phase I lands have ceased to function primarily because of their location in conflictive zones. Another factor has been the withdrawal of 34,000 acres by the original landowners as a legislatively approved expanded Right of Reserve. Throughout the 1980s the uncultivated portion of the reform sector has steadily risen.[31] According to a 1987 survey by the government agency PERA, the main reasons for this underutilization and consequent weak production were lack of credit, technical assistance, training, machinery, and investment funds to make underutilized lands productive.[32]

Three Phases of the Agrarian Reform

In 1980 the Duarte-led junta instituted a land reform in three distinct redistribution programs (Phases I, II, and III). Phase I provided for the transformation of estates of more than 1200 acres into cooperatives. Compensation for land expropriated under Phase I has been provided to a majority of the former owners in the form of interest-bearing government bonds.

Phase II, which has been seriously undercut by legislative amendments and was never implemented, was to have affected holdings between 220 and 1200 acres—which would have included the richest and most productive estates.[33] Phase III included all rental lands under 17 acres and allowed peasants who worked those lands to apply for title.[34] Altogether, 40-45 percent of the country's agricultural lands were to be redistributed.

The reform has fallen far short of its original redistribution goals. Only 15 percent (about 904,000 acres) of the country's agricultural lands have been affected. Within this reform sector, Phase I cooperatives control about 62 percent and Phase III parcel owners control 22 percent, with the balance in the hands of ISTA. Total beneficiaries of the reform as of 1987 were 77,296 peasants, of whom 30,268 were cooperative members—falling far short of the 300,000 beneficiaries initially promised by AID.[35]

Some cooperatives have become efficient and profitable producers, but these constitute fewer than a third of all cooperatives.[36] The individualization of ownership within the cooperatives would follow a tendency that had already been developing to allow members to farm individually rather than cooperatively. By 1987 about 28 percent of the land of the collectives was farmed on an individual basis, 72 percent collectively.[37]

Industry

Import Substitution to Export Processing

El Salvador, historically an industrial leader in Central America, has seen its industrial sector shrink as a result of falling internal consumption and sharp decrease in regional trade in the 1980s. Beginning in the 1950s Salvadoran industrialists aggressively pursued the dual strategy of import substitution and regional marketing, developing important local industries in the areas of textile manufacturing and food processing. The country became an export platform for assembled electronic products by such U.S. firms as Texas Instruments. (See U.S. Trade and Investment)

The rapid growth of the 1960s and 1970s was arrested by a decline during the years of political uncertainty from 1979 to 1982. Since then there has been steady, though modest growth, although the industrial sector has still not regained its previous strength and momentum. The manufacturing sector currently contributes about 18 percent to GDP and employs about 22 percent of the labor force.[38]

Industry has not been adversely affected by the war nearly as much as agriculture and transport, although it has been affected somewhat by infrastructure sabotage and transportation disruptions. Industry is concentrated in the San Salvador area, although there are other centers in La Libertad, Santa Ana, San Miguel, Usulután and San Vicente.

While large enterprises controlled by the leading families employ a majority of the industrial workforce, microenterprises with fewer than five employees account for 95 percent of the country's businesses. These small businesses produce 16 percent of the industrial product and employ 45 percent of sector's workers.[39] So small are 75 percent of all "industrial" enterprises that they provide only a subsistence income for the proprietor. The construction industry has been very active following the 1986 earthquake, helped by foreign assistance and low local interest rates. There is virtually no mining industry in El Salvador.

Government industrial policy historically stressed both production for export and import substitution. Although there is a significant import-substitution sector, this sector is dependent on the import of raw materials and of intermediate and capital goods for the manufacturing process. As in other Central American countries, AID and the multilateral banks are encouraging a shift away from import-substitution industry in favor of export-oriented production. Locally, this growth strategy is being directed by the AID-funded FUSADES.

The ARENA government has promised to place increased emphasis on the promotion of labor-intensive export manufacturing, particularly textiles. The plan, pushed forward by the Trade and Investment Promotion Program (PRIDEX) of FUSADES, is to model the country's industrial sector after those of the so-called Four Tigers of Asia (Hong Kong, Singapore, Taiwan, and South Korea). A key part of this strategy is to keep wages low to maintain the country's "comparative advantage" in relation both to other third world countries and to industrial countries. The AID-supported initiative to promote nontraditional agroexport production rests on the proposition that wages remain low and that the government adopts programs to facilitate and encourage such investment.

Economic strategists at FUSADES see no reason why El Salvador, with its cheap and skilled labor force, cannot become the Caribbean Basin's number one exporter of textiles.[40] Backing this economic development strategy, AID has funded the PRIDEX program since 1985 and is financing the expansion of the San Bartolo free trade zone and the construction of a new export processing zone. This development strategy is based on the dubious assumption that the private sector is capable of taking the bold steps and necessary risks that such a plan would need for success.

FUSADES does represent a forward-looking element within the private sector, but it is not a source of new private investment. Rather FUSADES is more like a government agency that studies economic policy and offers technical assistance, marketing help, and credit for investors. The problem is that the investors are not coming forth; and when they do, they demand what amounts to a risk-free investment environment. As a whole, the country's private sector, dominated by a conservative landowning oligarchy, is very traditional and reluctant to take risks. For its part, the existence of FUSADES depends solely on AID funding, not on its ability to modernize and restructure the economy. Despite all the subsidies and promotion, there was virtually no growth in export-oriented assembly manufacturing in the 1980s, and the prospects for increased foreign investment in war-torn El Salvador appear dim despite all the enthusiasm being generated by FUSADES.

Although the private sector has largely united behind the neoliberalism and free-market rhetoric of FUSADES and ARENA, the country's industrialists are resisting government economic policies that put this rhetoric into practice. For over three decades the industrial sector has benefited from protectionist tariffs and tax exemptions on imports. Industry owners now fear that the elimination of protectionist measures will seriously reduce their profit margins, while opening up the country's market to foreign products. The Association of Salvadoran Industrialists (ASI) has therefore demanded that the government back off from its plan for the immediate imposition of neoliberal measures. ASI also wants the government to help local industries restructure their production capabilities to make industry more competitive on the international market. The ARENA government, in desperate need for new tax revenues and with no extra funds to invest, will be hard put to meet the demands of the country's important but inefficient industrial sector.[41]

Society and Environment

The Popular Movement

The pace of the war in El Salvador and the fortunes of the political parties have dominated the news about this troubled country. But the guerrillas, the political parties, and the army are not the only sectors that are organized and active in Salvadoran society. During the 1980s most of the popular sectors—from squatters and refugees to workers and women—formed strong organizations to defend their political and economic rights. In the shadow of war, El Salvador has become the most organized society in Central America.

The country's backward and exploitative structures were challenged for the first time by peasant communities, labor activists, and communist organizers in the late 1920s. This popular threat to feudal rule of the famous "14 Families" (*Los Catorce*) and their military protectors was crushed by the *matanza* of 1932. That bloodshed silenced the popular sectors for several decades.

It was not until the 1960s that a new popular challenge began to coalesce. Cooperatives were formed, workers began to organize, and the expanding numbers of the middle class called for political change. A strong popular movement had formed by the late 1970s. In the process of struggle for basic rights, the leadership of this movement was radicalized, demanding not only reforms but a revolution to overhaul the society. The leading popular coalitions were the Popular Revolutionary Bloc (BPR), the Unified Popular Action Front (FAPU), and the People's League of February 28 (LP-28). These three, together with the Nationalist Democratic Union (UDN) united in 1980 to form the Revolutionary Coordinator of Masses (CRM).

The proverbial combination of carrot and stick was then employed to crush the popular movement, which by 1980 was threatening to bring down the government. Political modernization and an agrarian reform were the carrots; widespread repression that left thousands of activists dead was the stick. This two-pronged counterinsurgency strategy seriously weakened the militant popular movement and facilitated the creation of pro-government worker and peasant organizations supported by U.S. economic-aid programs.

Popular Organizing in the 1980s

The repression of the early 1980s wiped out the strong popular coalitions that formed in the previous decade. In the midst of the repression, only organizations linked to the government and the U.S. embassy could operate openly. Activists from the older popular organizations had either fallen victim to death-squad terror or had joined the ranks of the FMLN guerrillas.

Labor organizations were among the first reemerge.[1] Several labor federations and peasant associations had formed Democratic Popular Unity (UPD) but this organization was closely linked to the Christian Democratic Party and the American Institute for Free Labor Development (AIFLD). It was not until 1983 that a strongly anti-government labor movement started to organize. The first to form was the leftist MUSYGES labor federation, founded in 1983 but quickly cut down by repression. But within two years, a powerful new confederation of labor unions and peasant associations rose up to challenge the economic policies and war-making of the Duarte government. This was the National Unity of Salvadoran Workers (UNTS). Shortly after the formation of UNTS, a pro-government, U.S.-financed coalition called UNOC (National Union of Workers and Campesinos) was formed. UNOC was largely made up of rural associations and unions funded by AIFLD.

By the late 1980s an extraordinary variety of new popular organizations had surfaced. The student, worker, and peasant movements that had been crushed in the early 1980s reemerged with different names and often with different leaders. They were joined by new organizations from every popular sector. These included organizations of the displaced, squatters, earthquake victims, the unemployed, women, political prisoners, and families of the dead and disappeared.

From Squatters' Associations to Insurrectional Organizing

As the counterinsurgency war extended throughout rural areas, Salvadorans were forced to abandon their villages, some fleeing to other countries and others seeking safety in larger towns and cities. The repopulation movement began with the 1984 founding of the Christian Committee for the Displaced (CRIPDES), which insisted that the internally displaced had the right to return to their former villages. Defying the military, CRIPDES helped displaced families to return home. CRIPDES gave birth in 1986 to the National Repopulation Coordinator (CNR), which not only helped the internally displaced resettle their communities but also worked closely with returning refugees from Honduras.

During the 1970s the country had seen its first popular organizing among urban squatters. The Union of Residents of Tugurios (UPT) brought most of these groups into a national coalition that in 1975 joined the BPR. It was not the mid-1980s that marginal communities began to pick up the momentum lost because of the repression of the late 1970s and early 1980s. Fifteen communities formed the Committee of Marginal Communities (CCM) in 1984.

In the wake of the 1986 earthquake, which had left 56,000 poor Salvadorans homeless, there was a new surge of urban organizing. Two groups, the Coordinating Committee of Communities (CCC) and the National Union of Disaster Victims (UNADES), formed to represent and respond to the needs of the increasing number of urban Salvadorans who found themselves without homes and jobs. UNADES protested that the Duarte government was squandering the earthquake relief it had received, charging that the government "was more interested in fighting the war that in the living conditions of Salvadorans."[2]

CCC, CCM, and UNADES in 1987 formed a broad umbrella group called the Unity of Salvadoran Communities (UCES). Then in mid-1989 an even broader coalition of community organizations called the Salvadoran Communal Movement (MCS) came together to protect the interests of the marginal communities. One CCM director summarized the convictions of the coalition: "We are human beings and we have rights, we have dignity. We want to get out of the ravines and river banks where we are exposed to death, and the only solution is the organizing of all communities, because in organization there is strength."[3]

The 1980s also brought an explosion of women's organizing, and International Women's Day was publicly celebrated for the first time. In addition to the growing presence and militance of labor unions, unemployed and fired workers formed their own organization called CODYDES, which became part of the UNTS coalition in 1986. Street vendors and other members of the expanding informal sector formed CONAVIDES, and an organization of poor children called CIPOTES was also established.

The popular movement also gave birth to various human-rights groups, including COMADRES (Committee of Mothers of Prisoners, the Disappeared, and Murdered Political Activists), CDHES (Human

Rights Commission), and FECMAFAM (Federation of Committees of Mothers and Relatives of Political Prisoners, the Disappeared, and the Assassinated). There has been organizing even within the prisons by groups like the COPPES (Committee of Political Prisoners).

The cooperative movement also showed signs of new life and strength in the 1980s. Supported at first by the Catholic church, the cooperative movement expanded in the 1960s with the support of Alliance for Progress funding to develop savings and credit cooperatives. Today COACES, a member of UNTS, is the coordinating alliance of most of the country's cooperatives including the FEDECACES (savings and credit), FENACOA and FEDECOOPADES (agriculture), FENACITES (transport workers), and consumer cooperatives. Another group of cooperatives, most of them associated with the agrarian reform, is linked to AIFLD and UNOC.

In 1987 a new dimension of the popular movement took hold in conflictive rural areas where government services and representative were almost nonexistent. Local and regional groups formed to take the place of absent or unresponsive government institutions. Communities began forming their own committees to represent their interests and to carry out development and service projects. These committees took their complaints to the military and even sent delegations to foreign-aid agencies proposing new development projects. Over 400 of committees from the departments of Morazán, San Miguel, La Unión, Usulután, San Salvador, Santa Ana, and Ahuachapán came together in January 1989 to form PADECOES (Patronato for Communal Development in El Salvador).

These rural community organizations began calling for a "popular democracy," a concept popularized by the FMLN. Leaders of these new village committees say they are working to create a communal model of development, more in line with that of their Indian ancestors than with the capitalist model, which they say does not care for the marginalized, poor, widowed, and orphaned. In its statement of principles, PADECOES observed that the development projects of the 1960s and 1970s had failed and those of the 1980s were directly linked to counterinsurgency. Furthermore:

> Today the manipulation of politics and population is more evident. Both rural and urban communities now have an accumulated experience that allows them to more quickly identify and determine the real objectives of government programs and plans....In contrast, our communal organization channels this popular participation within the context of popular democracy and self-sufficiency—working principles that generate true human

development — development that arises from popular participation in decision-making and in the solution of their most serious problems as they work to change their reality.

By the end of the decade a clandestine and extremely militant sector of the popular movement formed the Bread, Land, Work, and Liberty Movement (MPTL). Closely associated with the student political front called FERS, MPTL in 1988 began organizing for a violent popular insurrection in the cities. It aimed to radicalize the urban population and prepare them for increased repression and stepped-up resistance. Rather than organizing by popular sector, MPTL organized by streets and neighborhoods, "reaching into peoples' homes." Santiago Flores, a MPTL militant, said, "We've demanded, side by side with the people, credit, land, freedom to organize, wage increases, and the right to strike, decent housing, and better living conditions."[4] Characteristic of MPTL militance, during a 1988 protest one activist raised the banner: "MPTL — with our blood, we write history." Reacting to increased attacks against the popular movement, the MPTL popularized the slogan, "Against more repression, more struggle."

The broad base of the popular movement in the 1980s was best seen in the wide participation in the National Debate for Peace in El Salvador. Archbishop Rivera y Damas in June 1988 called for a national dialogue about peace. The National Debate for Peace that resulted brought together some 60 popular organizations, ranging from the Association of Salvadoran Medium and Small Businessmen to UCES and CDHES. Only the private-sector elite boycotted the session. The combined membership of the participating organizations totaled over one million, one-fifth the country's population. A Permanent Committee of these organizations was formed to search for solutions to the Salvadoran civil war, and its recommendations were largely in line with the FMLN's call for a negotiated settlement and structural change. After the 1989 elections, the unity of the popular movement was considerably strengthened. Formerly pro-government union federations like UNOC, Confederation of Salvadoran Workers (CTS), and General Association of Municipal Employees (AGEPYM) which had previously distanced themselves from the more left-leaning unions joined with the UNTS in its demand for an negotiated end to the war.

In response to the escalating repression in mid-1989, a new popular coalition formed called the Popular Democratic Coordinator (CDP), which included peasant, student, human rights, and union organizations. Also evidence of the increasing strength and unity of the popular movement was the formation in October 1989 of a new peasant coalition called the Democratic Campesino Alliance (AD). The coalition brought together more than a dozen *campesino* associations and cooperative organizations with the objective of defending the agrarian reform. Marco Tulio, the director of the COACES federation, said that "we are prepared to suffer bloodshed" to block further evictions.[5]

The rising repression in 1989 hit the popular movement hard. The offices of many popular organizations, including COMADRES, UNTS, and FENASTRAS, were bombed. Other groups had their offices ransacked and leaders arrested and tortured. The repression that followed the FMLN offensive of November 1989 forced hundreds of activists into hiding. For many, the offensive and the military's aerial bombing of poor neighborhood was the moment of definition. Some leaders and members of popular organizations decided to take up arms. "For many it was stay open and be killed [by the army], or incorporate," explained the UNTS leader Humberto Centeno.[6] But most popular movement leaders like Centeno remained determined to build the country's unarmed popular movement despite the increased risks and the closing of political space in El Salvador.

El Salvador is a society that has been waiting for a radical social change for a half a century. But the oligarchy and the military have always stood in the way of social, economic, and political modernization. The expanded popular movement that developed in the late 1980s was a political movement in that its demands for a negotiated settlement and economic reforms largely paralleled those of the FMLN. But it was also a grassroots movement that arose primarily to protect the interests of women, workers, peasants, squatters, and the displaced.

Labor and Unions

Workers in El Salvador are known throughout the region for their industriousness and proclivity for organizing. At least half of the workforce, however, is unemployed, and the real wages of those who still have employment have fallen by a third since 1980. The minimum wage is about 40 cents an hour in the city and 20 cents in the countryside — meaning that the average monthly earnings of a two-income family can only provide for only half the minimum cost for a basic nutritious diet.[7]

The labor codes that govern the legal situation of Salvadoran workers date back to 1971 (for the public sector) and 1972 (for the private sector). These antiquated codes obstruct legal labor organizing. Public employees are not permitted by law to organize unions or strikes, while employees of autonomous institutions in the public sector like the Social Security Institute may form unions but may not strike. In practice, however, most public employees have formed unions and many have gone out on strike, some successfully. The 1983 constitution provides agricultural workers with the rights to organize and strike. Most farmworker unions, however, have not yet been legally recognized, since the appropriate implementing legislation has not been passed.

Despite the legal provisions, labor-union activity goes on. Where unions are not authorized, "associations" are created; and where unions are authorized but strikes are not legal, they occur illegally anyway. One estimate is that only 5 percent of all strikes in the nation's history have taken place according to the legally prescribed rules.[8]

By the same token, employers frequently ignore their obligations under the law. The law does stipulate minimum wage levels, for both industrial and agricultural workers. Minimum wages were raised in 1986 but the simultaneous imposition of Duarte's austerity measures and a currency devaluation meant that workers saw no increase in their real wages.

According to the law, workers have an eight-hour day and a work week of between 39 and 48 hours, depending on the type of work performed and the region. Beyond those hours workers should be paid overtime. They are also guaranteed paid vacations and a Christmas bonus. Enterprises employing more than five people must participate in the Social Security Program, which provides medical treatment, sick pay, and survivors' pensions. Many employers, however, do not contribute to the social security fund and consequently the Social Security Institute is bankrupt. Government corruption and the prioritization of the war effort have also caused a steady decline in the quality and extent of government health services. Some unions have even opened their own health clinics to care for their members.

A revised Labor Code, higher minimum wages, and increased respect of the right to organize are among the demands of the country's strong but heavily repressed labor movement. Concerns of the labor movement in El Salvador extend far beyond economic issues. Unions are highly politicized and, especially since 1984, have assumed a leading role in the anti-government popular movement. For most of the 1980s, however, often bitter divisions existed between that part of the labor movement that stood behind the Christian Democratic Party and that part which shared a leftist critique of the Christian Democrats and the U.S. counterinsurgency project. The advent of an ARENA-controlled government, however, pushed virtually the entire labor movement into the anti-government opposition.

Brief History of Worker and Peasant Organizing

Although union organization goes back to the founding of the Central American Congress of Workers in El Salvador in 1911, unions were outlawed from 1932 to 1944 during the dictatorship of Gen. Maximiliano Hernández Martínez.[9] This reflected the fact that agricultural unions such as the Regional Federation of Salvadoran Workers had provided much of the organizational base for the insurrection of 1932. After the overthrow of the dictatorship in 1944, union organization resumed but received a setback with the failure of a general strike in October 1946 and the resulting exile of the strike leaders. The constitution of 1950 was the first in El Salvador's history to concede the right of urban workers to organize, bargain collectively, and strike.

The military government headed by Col. Oscar Osorio (1949-1956) and those that followed attempted to control the incipient labor movement and peasant organizations through the Ministry of Labor and the government's own rural organizations like the National Democratic Organization (ORDEN). In the 1950-1977 period, military governments consorted with the international operations department of the AFL-CIO and the American Institute for Free Labor Development (AIFLD) (created in 1962) to maintain moderate, pro-government unions and peasants groups. These included the Salvadoran General Confederation (CGS) for trade unions and the Salvadoran Communal Union (UCS) for peasant associations.

Neither repression nor pacification succeeded in containing the independent and often leftist oriented organizing of urban and rural workers. The 1970s were an especially fruitful period for labor organizing. Advances in the cities were paralleled by the growing militancy of peasant groups — all forming part of an increasingly dynamic popular movement. A case in point was the Federation of Christian Campesinos (FECCAS), which moved increasingly away from its roots in the Catholic church to become an important element in the growing progressive movement of peasants. Within the trade-union sector, this radicalization was reflected in the dissipation of the AIFLD-linked CGS federation as its base split off to form the National Federation of Salvadoran Workers (FENASTRAS), which is currently one of the strongest and most militant federations.

Repression in the late 1970s and the early 1980s all but wiped out the overt functioning of trade unions and peasant associations associated with the anti-government popular movement. Between 1980 and 1984 hundreds of labor leaders were openly murdered or disappeared. Although independent organizing was silenced, this was a period of rapid growth for AIFLD-sponsored groups, not generally subject to the same level of repression. AIFLD guided the formation of a new labor coalition called the Popular Democratic Unity (UPD). The UPD, which brought together several rural and urban organizations, served to build support for the Christian Democratic Party while acting as an effective counterweight to the repressed organizations clustered on the left.

The UPD included the UCS, Construction and Transport Workers Federation (FESINCONSTRANS), and a coalition of agrarian-reform associations including the the Confederation of Cooperatives Association (ACOPAI) and the Salvadoran National Indigenous Association (ANIS) – all of which were funded by AIFLD. The only UPD member not directly associated with AIFLD was the Salvadoran Workers Central (CTS), a federation of public-sector employees affiliated with the Latin American Federation of Workers (CLAT), a Christian-democratic regional organization.

In 1984 labor organizing markedly increased and the independent labor movement began to reemerge with the "democratic opening" that resulted with the move toward elected civilian government and increased international press coverage of El Salvador. Two new important federations formed: the Coordinator of Worker Solidarity (CST) and the State and Municipal Coordinating Council (CCTEM). It was, however, the formation in February 1986 of the National Unity of Salvadoran Workers (UNTS) that marked the beginning of a strong progressive labor movement.

In response to the creation of UNTS, the Duarte government, the U.S. embassy, and AIFLD quickly collaborated to form a pro-government confederation called the National Union of Workers and Campesinos (UNOC). From 1986 through 1988 UNTS and UNOC remained sharply at odds. UNTS assumed a leading role in an expanding popular movement, demanding an end to U.S. intervention and a negotiated settlement to the war, while UNOC passively supported the government and charged that UNTS was a guerrilla front.[10] Despite continuing claims of AIFLD to the contrary, UNTS by early 1988 assumed the leading role in the labor movement. Even the Salvadoran Ambassador to the United States admitted as much, saying that "fully 77 percent of collective bargaining agreements were between employers and UNTS affiliates."[11] To combat the growing strength of the UNTS unions, the government and AIFLD worked to create parallel unions in the public and private sectors with the objective of delegitimizing and isolating the UNTS-affiliated organizations.

By late 1988 UNOC began inching away from the politics of its AIFLD sponsors, joining the UNTS in the national dialogue and cautiously applauding FMLN proposals for a negotiated settlement to the war. UNOC, however, stood solidly behind the Christian Democratic Party in the 1989 presidential election while the UNTS encouraged voter abstention. Following the ARENA victory UNOC quickly moved closer to the antigovernment stance of the UNTS, joining a coalition with the leftist confederation in opposing ARENA's economic policies. The backtracking of the U.S. Agency for International Development (AID) and the U.S. embassy as well as a common hatred of ARENA and the military have brought most sectors of the union movement together, although the various federations have retained their separate identities and UNOC remains associated with AIFLD. Bereft of its link with state power, UNOC has nonetheless insisted on its centrist position, careful to blame both the FMLN and the army for human-rights violations.

Main Labor Confederations[12]

The National Unity of Salvadoran Workers (UNTS), founded in February 1986, is the country's largest and most militant labor confederation and includes the following trade union federations: CCTEM (which includes such public-sector unions as ANDES, ASTTEL, and STISSS), CST (a broad confederation which includes such unions as the CGS, FENASTRAS, FESIAVICES, FEASIES, FESTRAS, and FUSS federations). Most cooperative associations belonging to UNTS are grouped together in the Confederation of Cooperative Associations (COACES). These include leagues of cooperatives in transport, savings, and agriculture such as FENACOA, FEDECACES, FEDECOOPADES, FENACITES, and FECORAPCEN. Rural workers and peasants of the eastern part of the country are grouped together in the UNTS-affiliated CCTO (which includes FENACOA, FECORAO, and ANTA). Another rural federation associated with UNTS is the UNC.

Although principally a labor confederation, UNTS also includes under its umbrella a wide range of popular organizations, including CRIPDES; the Committee of Laid Off and Unemployed (CODYDES), University Unity, which represents two student federations and organizations of university faculty and staff; FECMAFAM, a human-rights organization; and the Pro-Unity Committee of Women. Since its formation in 1986 the U.S. embassy and AIFLD have tried to dismiss UNTS and its affiliated organizations as "guerrilla fronts" and marginalized elements within Salvadoran society. A report prepared by the U.S. embassy in 1988 asserted that UNTS is "composed almost entirely of unions headed by members or sympathizers of the FMLN/FDR." The same report charged that FENASTRAS has "close links with the FAPU/FARN guerrilla groups."[13] Such assertions opened the way for military attacks on UNTS unions such as the October 1989 bombing of the FENASTRAS headquarters that left ten dead including the federation's secretary-general Febe Elizabeth Velásquez. The UNTS headquarters was also destroyed by the military and its leaders forced into hiding in late 1989, but by early 1990 the UNTS was already making plans to open a new office and renew its organizing work.

The National Union of Workers and Campesinos (UNOC), founded in March 1986, is the labor confederation which is sponsored by AIFLD and closely identified with the Christian Democratic Party. One of the founding principles of UNOC, formed immediately after the formation of UNTS, was to "defend the social-economic reforms of the government" and to "counterbalance the UNTS' opposition to the government."[14] It includes the CTD confederation whose strongest federations are FESINCONSTRANS and FECORACEN; the CGT confederation which has strong conservative social-Christian roots;[15] and the FESACORA association of rural cooperatives in the central and western party of the country. UNOC also includes UCS and ACOPAI, which are rural associations closely connected with AID and AIFLD's agrarian-reform projects. Following the 1989 elections tensions between UNOC and its U.S. government sponsors (AID and AIFLD) developed as a result of UNOC's joint declaration with UNTS and the U.S. government's failure to support the agrarian-reform program.

The Popular Democratic Union (UPD), founded in September 1980, has been associated with AIFLD. For a brief time (1984-1986), UPD, guided by AIFLD, played a key role in organizing worker and peasant support for the Duarte government. Since the formation of UNOC, UPD has played only a marginal role in the labor movement. It is a ghost of a labor federation, including such small or phantom unions as STISTA, CUTS, ANC, and UTIC. The faction of UPD directed by Arístides Mendoza threw its support behind ARENA in the 1989 elections.

The United Workers Front (FUT), founded in October 1987, is Social Christian in political orientation and includes the important public-sector federation AGEPYM and the CTS.

Repression and Trade Status Controversy

Two divergent positions have existed within the U.S. labor movement regarding the situation of labor rights within El Salvador. The dominant position has been that of the AFL-CIO and its international branch

AIFLD, which has persistently claimed that labor-rights conditions are "improving" in El Salvador and that the main threat to the rights of worker is the leftist insurgency and its alleged popular facades, namely the UNTS.

Another more critical position is maintained by labor activists associated with National Labor Committee in Support of Democracy and Human Rights in for El Salvador, an organization founded by the presidents of many of U.S. major labor unions. Although it has not yet succeeded in reversing the foreign-policy direction of the AFL-CIO hierarchy, the National Labor Committee has offered a strong counterbalance to the official AFL-CIO positions concerning Nicaragua and El Salvador. Owing to the initiative of the National Labor Committee, the AFL-CIO's foreign-policy positions and operations were openly questioned for the first time on the floor of the federation's 1985 annual convention.

In its call for an end to U.S. military aid to El Salvador, the National Labor Committee cites reports by such groups as Americas Watch, Amnesty International, and the International Confederation of Free Trade Unions (ICFTU) about the increased repression of the Salvadoran labor movement. In March 1988 Americas Watch concluded that: "Government repression against organized workers in El Salvador in all labor sectors—industrial workers, agricultural workers, public employees, and employees of autonomous institutions—is extensive, systematic, and often brutal." The government has "employed a variety of tactics—from assassination to arrest—to maintain quiescence and to suppress legitimate union activity."[16]

In contrast to the AFL-CIO's practice of blaming most human-rights violations on the FMLN and publicly denouncing large sectors of the country's labor movement as being FMLN fronts, the ICFTU, with which the AFL-CIO is associated, condemned in 1988 "the continuation of uncontrolled criminal actions while the army protects the extreme right-wing groups, the thousands of cases of 'disappearances' that have occurred in recent years which have not been investigated, [and] the countless examples of anti-labor practices and laws."[17]

Besides calling for an end to U.S. military aid and AIFLD intervention, critics of U.S. and AFL-CIO policy in El Salvador demanded that the U.S. trade status with the country be revised. They insisted that trade sanctions, mandated by U.S. law for labor-rights violators, be invoked against the El Salvador government. The 1984 Trade Act denies countries preferential trade status, like El Salvador currently enjoys, if "such country has not taken or is not taking steps to afford internationally recognized workers' rights." Similarly, the Caribbean Basin Initiative (CBI) requires that the president assess the degree to which a country's workers "enjoy the right to organize and bargain collectively" when determining its eligibility for duty-free access to the United States. If these trade privileges were revoked, it would prove a serious blow to the economic-recovery strategy promoted by AID and the ARENA government, which focuses on the use of cheap labor to assemble manufactured goods and to produce nontraditional crops for export to the United States.

In mid-1989, as repression against the labor movement worsened, some one hundred members of Congress petitioned the U.S. Trade Representative to undertake a formal review of labor-rights problems in El Salvador. In March 1989 Americas Watch submitted its third such petition.[18] These requests for a review or change of El Salvador's trade status have been consistently denied by the U.S. Trade Representative, citing the AFL-CIO's hostility to such requests.[19] In September 1989 UNOC recommended that El Salvador's trade privileges with the United States be rescinded because of the extreme human-rights violations against labor unions. AIFLD declined to push forward the UNOC demand in Washington, but said that it would ask for a review in June 1990.

Schools and Students

Salvadoran students and teachers have been in the forefront of political protest movements dating back to 1944 when a general strike initiated by students and faculty of the University of El Salvador (UES), known as the National University, helped bring down the Hernández Martínez dictatorship. The ANDES teachers' union was at the center of the popular movement in the late 1970s and was decimated by the 1979-1982 wave of repression. The National University was closed down in 1980 after the army invaded the campus killing and wounding scores of students.[20] In late 1989 the FMLN used the university as one of its bases to launch its urban offensive, and the National University was subsequently bombarded and invaded by the military.

Throughout the 1980s the Jesuit-run University of Central America (UCA) served as an important center for research and analysis about the civil war. In the late 1980s, tensions between the educational community and the government and army began heating up again after a period of relative calm, resulting in disappearances, shootings, and mass arrests of students and professors. The November 16, 1989 massacre of six Jesuit priests, including the rector of the UCA, brought international attention to what was increasingly described as the country's "death-squad democracy."

Demands of student and faculty organizations in El Salvador range from increased government spending for education to the initiation of serious negotiations with the FMLN. The state of siege and the escalation of the war in November 1989 further narrowed the political space available to the the student movement.

The Educational System

Official statistics show a 65 percent literacy rate in El Salvador with only 40 percent literacy in most rural areas.[21] As mandated by the constitution and a series of legislative acts, primary education is free and compulsory; this involves nine years of education divided into three cycles of three years each. According to Ministry of Education statistics, only two-thirds of the relevant age group is actually enrolled. Moreover, although there are no tuition payments, there are expenses for supplies which serve as a deterrent to some families. Primary education is compulsory, but many areas have no schools or teachers.

Half the workforce has, at best, a third-grade education. The sad state of primary education has been aggravated by decreases in per capita government expenditures for education, which dropped 66 percent in relative terms between 1978 and 1987.[22]

At the secondary level, nine separate tracks exist leading to the *bachiller* certificate. While only one of these is academic and the others vocational, all of the tracks include a common core of general education in Spanish language and literature, English, mathematics, sciences, social studies, and art.

Post-secondary education offers several options. The government administers nine technological institutes throughout the country which train teachers and technical specialists, as well as a national school of agriculture and a higher school of physical education and sports. The military operates its own school (Escuela Militar), as well as a school of nursing. These are both two-year programs leading respectively to commissioning at the rank of second lieutenant, and a credential as nursing aide. There is also a nursing program at the medical school of the National University.

Striking changes have occurred in higher education. Until 1970 El Salvador had only one public university, the National University, and one private university, the UCA. However, in 1965 a system for accrediting private institutions was established, and four new private universities were recognized by the Ministry of Education by 1980. After the 1980 closure of the National University, there was an explosion of 29 new universities, many started by opportunists of various kinds, although some of these have failed to enroll any students. There are currently 32 private universities in addition to the UCA. In 1988 the country's lawmakers approved army plans for the establishment of a military university.

There is no university-wide set of course requirements. Each faculty determines its own curriculum, leading to a variety of degrees and corresponding titles, such as *licenciado, ingeniero,* and *arquitecto.* A more limited set of degrees in selected specialized fields are offered by the private universities. For example, the Albert Einstein University, which opened in 1977, specializes in architecture and engineering, while the Alberto Masferrer University, founded in 1980, specializes in medicine and dentistry. Probably the largest private university is the University of New San Salvador (UNSSA), founded in 1982, which is rightist in political orientation and publishes a rightwing journal, *Análisis,* a counterweight to the left-leaning *Estudios Centroamericanos* journal of UCA. One of the better established universities is the José Matias Delgado University, also decidedly rightwing, which specializes in business and engineering.

The largest and oldest private university is the University of Central America "José Simeón Cañas," operated by the Jesuits from Spain. Founded in 1965, UCA enrolls about 6,500 students, with the largest enrollment in the faculty of economics. The university is serious about faculty research and publishes nine academic journals, including three that have provoked virulent reaction by the military and the right: *Proceso, Estudios Centroamericanos,* and *Carta a las Iglesias.* In July 1989, shortly after the extreme right Crusade for Peace and Work accused UCA authorities of collaborating with the FMLN, the university's print shop was dynamited.

In contrast to the shabby National University, the UCA—known by some as the "Princeton of Central America"—has an attractive campus with a substantial library, a computer center, and laboratory facilities. Its faculty of 100 full-time professors contrasts markedly with even one of the better smaller private universities, the Albert Einstein University, which has no full-time faculty. UCA students are of a higher social status and are conservative when compared either with the students of the National University or with their own faculty. Student and worker organizations are discouraged at the UCA.

Problems and Politics at the National University

The National University, founded in 1841, has its main campus in San Salvador and branches in Santa Ana and San Miguel. It was granted legal autonomy in 1927. However, its autonomy has been revoked by several governments since then, although it was guaranteed in the constitution of

1950 and again in that of 1983. The military closed the university in 1972, again in 1976, and between between 1980 and 1984 it was closed and occupied by troops. During the occupation the institution sustained about $20 million worth of damage to buildings, equipment, and books. The earthquake of October 1986 caused additional damage. An estimated $15 million in damaged resulted from the military's efforts to drive the FMLN out of San Salvador in November 1989.

The university remains in poor condition because of the unwillingness of governments to budget funds adequate to restore it. Government funds are necessary simply for operations, whose costs far exceed the minimal tuition and other charges paid by students. Despite these low charges, however, inability of students to meet their expenses contributes to a high rate of attrition—fewer than 30 percent of entering students stay to graduate, with the figure for medical students even lower at 20 percent. Some attrition is also due to the poor quality of student preparation at the secondary level.

Nevertheless, enrollment has grown rapidly. When the university reopened, enrollment in all post-secondary institutions in the country reached 12 percent of the relevant age group, compared to only 2 percent 20 years before. Because of its low fees and lax admission standards, most students at the National University are children of lower-status urban and rural families.

The political sympathies of most students and most faculty at the National University are no secret. The three main university organizations— the AGEUS student federation, the ADUES faculty union, and the CCTU university workers' union—are affiliated with the leftist UNTS through a coalition group called University Unity. As the university's chief administrator, René Mauricio Mejía, put it, "The University of El Salvador is seen as a potential political center and not as a center of academic studies, which is why there is a permanent campaign to destroy it through defamation, through a restrictive economic policy, a boycott against the university's efforts for seeking international aid, and a constant campaign of political aggression."[23]

The university is "a nest of subversives," in the words of former police chief Nicolás Carranza.[24] Frequently the Armed Forces and National Police station armed guards at the entrances to the campus to search anyone entering or leaving. Continual demonstrations and acts of repression contribute to the maintenance of turmoil on the campus, still in deteriorated physical shape from the earthquake, which is full of posters, banners, and leftist wall paintings. Faculty members at the university are assumed to be leftists, which inhibits any other job prospects they might have.

Fears began rising among university authorities in 1989 that under the ARENA government the campus would be occupied and officials would be replaced with those of a more rightist persuasion. In the late 1980s the rightwing Committee for the Rescue of the UES was calling for such a takeover, claiming that the university is a guerrilla training ground. The government has refused to raise the university's meager budget. Its 1989 budget of $12 million is hardly adequate to serve 70 percent of the country's 66,000 university students. The National University has also been hurt by the U.S. embassy's policy of directing all U.S. educational aid and exchange programs to the nation's private universities, while declining to release $2 million in earthquake relief aid approved by Congress.[25] The occupation and closure of the National University during the FMLN's November 1989 offensive opened the way for a conservative takeover once the campus is reopened.

The main student organization is the General Association of Salvadoran University Students (AGEUS), which is more than 50 years old and pursues traditional objectives such as the maintenance of university autonomy and the allocation of adequate government funds to the university. Operating on a more political level is the Federation of Salvadoran University Students (FEUS), founded in 1986, whose demands include an end to military conscription and support for a negotiated solution to the civil war. The most recent student organization, the Salvadoran Revolutionary Student Front (FERS), aims to reach students at all private and public schools as well as marginalized youth not attending school. It defines itself as a "patriotic popular revolutionary and democratic organization" and constitutes the student sector of the Movement for Bread, Land, Work, and Liberty (MPTL), which has mounted militant protests against the government.[26] The state of siege imposed in November 1989 and the institution of new penal codes aimed at squashing popular dissent at least temporarily silenced the student movement.

Communications Media

Under the tight control of their owners and the advertising agencies, the country's media outlets have, as a whole, served as a voice of the business sector, government, and military. This is especially true for the printed media, which is characterized by its reactionary tone and outdated production format. Beginning in the 1980s television news became increasingly aggressive and balanced, even to the extent of interviewing guerrilla commanders. Strict military control over the media and a national emergency broadcasting system (known as the *"cadena"* or chain) was instituted when a state of siege was imposed by the government in November 1989.

La Prensa Gráfica, founded in 1915, is the largest daily and counts on the most modern equipment of any of the nation's newspapers. It is owned, and staffed at the higher echelons, by members of the Dutriz family. A conservative newspaper, *La Prensa Gráfica* reproduces Armed Forces press releases as news and consistently refers to the FMLN as "terrorists." It is not, however, as stridently reactionary as its main competitor, *El Diario de Hoy*, and is commonly considered a pro-regime newspaper.

El Diario de Hoy, founded in 1936, is owned by the Altamirano family, which also has interests in coffee and cotton. A voice of the oligarchy and the extreme right wing, it supports the D'Aubuisson tendency of ARENA and has given space to extreme rightwingers to discuss the possibility that Cristiani may be too moderate. The United States Information Agency (USIA) considers it "ultraconservative." Its editorials are very strongly pro-business and opposed to government regulation of the economy or social programs. Taking advantage of its computerized facilities, Enrique Altamirano edits and even approves the daily format of the paper from his home in Miami.

Like the two other leading dailies, *El Mundo*, founded in 1968, is owned by members of the country's oligarchy, notably the coffee grower Nathan Borja. An afternoon paper, it is distinctly less conservative than the morning papers and allows its editors more independence. Denied the advertising available to its older competitors, *El Mundo* found an important source of income in the paid advertisements from opposition public organizations such as trade unions and human-rights groups, but new prohibitions by the ARENA government have limited the publication of such information. While the overall orientation of the paper is pro-business and anti-leftist, it does offer more space to critical local and international reporting.

The small *El Diario Latino*, formerly owned by Adolfo Rey Prendes, was founded in 1980 but closed down in May 1989 after owners and directors abandoned the daily newspaper. In July 1989 it reopened after having been sold to the owners of Channel 12. The Catholic Archdiocese publishes a weekly newspaper, *Orientación*, which has generally been sympathetic to the Christian Democrats. The weekly *El Salvador News-Gazette*, owned and edited by Mario Rosenthal, publishes its extreme rightwing opinions bilingually in English and Spanish.

The University Center of Documentation and Information of the University of Central America (UCA) has published since 1980 a weekly journal of news analysis and commentary called *Proceso*. It is progressive in its approach but is careful to remain scholarly and objective, criticizing the FMLN occasionally along with its much more frequent criticism of the government, the armed forces, and the political parties of the center and the right. There are many other publications of different departments and institutes of UCA, regular and occasional, some of which discuss contemporary Salvadoran reality, usually in a scholarly format. Taken together, all of the various publications emanating from UCA are among the best sources for knowledge of contemporary Salvadoran politics, economics, and society.

Radio, with its 4.3 million daily listeners, is the communications media with the most outreach. Like the printed media, however, the largest stations are owned and operated by ARENA sympathizers, although the important Radio Sonora is somewhat more open than others. Among the largest stations are La Poderosa (YSKL) and Radiocadena (YSU). The government can revoke a station's license to operate, and frequently hands down instructions on how particular issues are to be reported. Moreover, some stations are run directly by government agencies. The army runs its own station, Radio Cuscatlán. Radio broadcasters thought to be too liberal have been fired from their stations. The church radio station, call letters YSAX, was bombed several times until in 1984 a new director, Father Roberto Torruellas, who was also editor of *Orientación*, moved to a more conservative line.

An alternative source of news exists in the radio stations of the rebels, Radio Venceremos and Radio Farabundo Martí, which can be heard throughout the country daily. They provide cultural programs along with reports on political and military events, including government troop movements. The army, together with their U.S. advisers, have continually attempted to jam Radio Venceremos.

It used to be that television news was little more than a digest of official pronouncements and the latest tidbits from high society. But beginning in the mid-1980s television news programming, especially that of Channel 12, became among the best in Central America.[27] There are four commercial stations and two government stations. Despite the almost monopoly ownership of the television stations by investor Boris Ezerski, the quality and political orientation of the news programming varies because these programs are generally contracted with separate producers. The news programs of Channels 6 and 12 have provided forums for political discussion, bringing together declared enemies into polite and informative debates. The news programs have found that quality news means profits as advertisers rush to place their commercial propaganda on these popular programs. In a recent poll, 85 percent of Salvadorans with at least two years of high school said that their primary source of news was television.[28] Just five years earlier, radio had been cited as the main source of news.

The army's press office COPREFA plays a major role in formulating and controlling the news in El Salvador. All journalists have to apply to COPREFA, based in the military headquarters, for press cards; and COPREFA also arranges or denies permits for journalists to travel to conflictive areas. When three journalists were killed in a 12-hour period during the March 1989 elections, COPREFA claimed they were shot for ignoring commands by soldiers to stop for registration. COPREFA also controls news from the inside through editors who, according to Salvadoran reporters, are on the military payroll in addition to their regular pay. El Salvador continues to be a dangerous environment for journalists. Two newspapers were forced to close in the early 1980s because of bombings, and some 20 journalists have been killed covering the war.[29]

Tensions between journalists and the government have intensified with the ARENA government. The party has accused reporters of "treason-like attitudes" and of "ruining the country's image abroad." Roberto D'Aubuisson has charged that couriers for the FMLN come in and out of the country "disguised as journalists." He has roused crowds of party supporters by denouncing *"los cheles"* (white-skinned reporters) for reporting on human-rights violations.[30]

In El Salvador, as in neighboring Guatemala, it is a general and tolerated practice for journalists to receive gratuities from the sources they cover. These may be occasional or regular, so that if a reporter is assigned to education news he can expect a regular monthly payment from the Ministry of Education. Some journalists receive several of these regular payments, which are known as *mentas*. This is hardly an environment designed to encourage objective reporting.

Health and Welfare

The deteriorating health situation in El Salvador is due primarily to the war but is also the result of widespread malnutrition, the lack of access to potable water and sanitary facilities, and the reduced government commitment to public health care. Since 1980 political violence has been a leading cause of death.[31]

The war in El Salvador is being played out against a background of poverty and malnutrition. During the 1970s health indicators generally improved, reflecting both a gradual rise in per capita income and increased health-care services. Encouraged by AID and other foreign donors, the government in the late 1960s began extending health-care services. The Ministry of Health established a a network of health posts throughout the country, and medical school graduates were required to serve at these posts for one year after graduation. The ambitious health-care program was designed as a pyramid, with small health posts at the base feeding into larger referral centers. For community outreach, AID trained *guardianes de salud* (health guardians).[32]

Although this health program was a positive step forward, its effectiveness was limited by the lack of solid government commitment, its isolation from community organizations and the popular movement, and its connections in many rural areas with the government-sponsored vigilante organization ORDEN. Many health guardians were members of ORDEN. According Francisco Metzi, author of the book *People's Remedy*, "Their access to medications gave them prestige and influence in their communities. This enabled them to identify suspected subversives."[33]

Alongside the AID-sponsored system grew a more informal network of popular medical programs, which grew out of the community work of the Catholic church and popular organizations. This network emphasized the need for popular education about health-care issues. Like other components of the mass movement and progressive church work, the popular medicine systems and its community promoters became victims of the repression in the early 1980s.

The government health-care budget steadily declined—from 11 percent of total expenditures at the start of the decade to just 6 percent in 1989.[34] Government health posts are now without medicine or completely abandoned. Public hospitals are filthy, overcrowded, and short-staffed. Only the military hospitals are fully equipped and well supplied. Patients entering public hospitals are told to bring their own sheets, food, soap, toilet paper, surgical supplies, and sutures. There is waiting list of some 20,000 people for elective surgery at the Rosales Hospital.

Aside from the marked decline in government spending, the health-care situation is also still suffering from the closing of the National University from 1980 to 1984, which meant that no new doctors, nurses, dentists, or pharmacists were being trained. Today in El Salvador for every 10,000 people there are only 3.2 doctors, 2.1 nurses, and only 12 hospital beds.[35] Only 37 percent of Salvadorans have access to medical care according to a 1989 report from the Ministry of Planning. According to 1989 figures from the Ministry of Health, 75 percent of children under five years suffer from malnutrition and 43 percent of pregnant women suffer from anemia.

Clearly the war has not been good for the country's health. Aside from people getting killed and injured, food supplies get destroyed and interrupted. Water supplies get interrupted and polluted. Transportation to health delivery centers becomes difficult, and medical supplies run out. In a repopulated village in Chalatenango, health promoters reported that of all the children who had died since 1980, nearly half had been killed by the army.[36]

The war, in all of its aspects, has resulted in a number of "excess" deaths, especially among males. Between 1965 and 1985 female life expectancy at birth increased from 56 to 67 years, almost exactly the same as in the Dominican Republic. Male life expectancy in 1965 stood at 53 years in El Salvador, the same figure as in the Dominican Republic, but whereas Dominican life expectancy increased by ten years for males by 1985, it had increased only seven years, to 60, in El Salvador.[37]

Yet countering these adverse tendencies have been two striking trends. The first of these is that the FMLN has made a special effort to provide and staff health posts in the areas under their control. The other positive tendency has been the contribution of various international nongovernmental organizations in providing doctors and other health workers, funds, and supplies. There is a long honor roll of such groups with health-care outreach programs, including the Catholic Social Secretariat, the Lutheran and Mennonite churches, CONCERN, Aesculapius, and Medicins du Monde. In addition, U.S. groups such as Medical Aid for El Salvador and the National Central American Health Rights Network have provided essential supplies to villages in conflictive zones.

The efforts of international volunteers, like those of other health personnel in El Salvador who work with the urban poor or the rural poor in the conflictive zones, make them suspect in the eyes of the military as collaborators with the FMLN. They are subject to assassination, disappearance, the interdiction of travel, detention, and confiscation of property including medical supplies. Some international health workers were forced to leave the country as part of a government crackdown in late 1989 against foreigners associated with church and popular organizations.

Religion

Although the country's religion is traditionally Roman Catholicism, the constitution does not give Roman Catholicism any official standing as an established religion. In fact, the number of evangelicals in the country, primarily of the fundamentalist denominations, has been growing rapidly, and the population is now estimated to be only about 82 percent Catholic. (As elsewhere in Central America, the common use in El Salvador of the term "evangelical" refers to all non-Catholic Christians, including pentecostals, fundamentalists, and mainline historical Protestants.)

There is one Catholic archdiocese (covering San Salvador, Cuscatlán, La Libertad, and Chalatenango), six dioceses (Santa Ana, San Vicente, Santiago de María, San Miguel, Sonsonate, and Zacatecoluca) as well as a military ordinate. Archbishop Arturo Rivera y Damas and Auxiliary Bishop Gregorio Rosa Chávez are the most prominent and influential church leaders. About 60 percent of the priests in El Salvador are natives, a higher percentage than in other Central American countries.

El Salvador was strongly affected by the development of the progressive "theology of liberation" tendency within the Catholic church from the 1950s on. This tendency within the church was expressed at the 1968 Medellín Conference of Latin American bishops which called for a "preferential option for the poor." The institutional expression of this new tendency is the so-called "base community," groups of people who worship, study, and on occasion take action together. The study component often takes the form of consciousness-raising, with a progressive or even revolutionary emphasis.

The some 350 base communities that formed in El Salvador were early targets of repressive activity, with the assassination or disappearance of about 600 members between 1979 and 1989. In the face of this repression, most base communities in rural areas disintegrated. Today Christian base communities are founded mostly in the poorer communities on the periphery of San Salvador and among the repopulation communities.[38]

The persecution of Catholic clergy and laity began in the 1970s as a reaction to the increased identification of the church with the country's poor majority. The Jesuits were among the main targets of rightwing vigilante groups and the military. In March 1977 Father Rutilio Grande, a Jesuit working in Aguilares, was murdered for his commitment to the poor. Three years later Archbishop Oscar Arnulfo Romero was gunned down on March 24, 1980 while celebrating mass. The archbishop, whose political position had originally been moderate and passive, was gradually drawn into becoming the voice of the oppressed as repression grew. His weekly nationally broadcast homilies, in which he denounced terror and pleaded for social justice, made him a hero to many Salvadorans but also a target of the rightwing extremists.

Archbishop Rivera y Damas was appointed to replace Romero and immediately pulled the church back from the prophetic, committed posture of Romero, attempting to maintain a more moderate, centrist role for the church, both politically and spiritually. The preaching of liberation theology was not encouraged.

Rivera y Damas has been more moderate and careful, not to mention a great deal less charismatic, than Archbishop Romero. He has toned down the outspokenness of the church's newspaper and its radio broadcasts. The archbishop has, however, been a key figure in mediating between government and guerrillas and has worked to bring the more conservative provincial bishops around to his position in favor of a peaceful settlement. In July 1988 the archbishop launched a National Debate for Peace among nearly five-dozen popular organizations which has proven to be a major voice calling for a negotiated peace.

The main social arm of the church is the Social Secretariat of the Archdiocese (SSA), which has been operating since 1981. The SSA is an agency of the archdiocese's Social Ministry Secretariat. It is responsible for the social-assistance programs of the archdiocese but also frequently administers programs in other areas of the country. The SSA receives international aid for health, agriculture, nutrition, and other humanitarian-assistance programs for the displaced population and other disadvantaged Salvadorans. The SSA and the ecumenical social-service organization Diaconía have coordinated a food program that brought together Lutherans, Baptists, Mennonites, and the emergency food program of Catholic Relief Services. Two U.S. health-care organizations, CONCERN and Aesculapius International Medicine, work under the auspices of the social secretariat. Another important social institution is the national Caritas organization, which is administered by a board appointed by the National Bishops' Conference. Caritas distributes U.S. food aid from Catholic Relief Services as well as managing other assistance programs on a local level.

The archdiocese also operates a Caritas program that has a national as well as archdiocesan character. COAR (Oscar Arnulfo Romero Community), an orphanage created in 1980 by priests from the Diocese of Cleveland, is another church assistance organization associated with the Social Secretariat of the Archdiocese. FUNPROCOOP (Cooperative Development Foundation) is a Salvadoran nongovernmental organization closely linked to the SSA and the Catholic church. FUNPROCOOP, which receives mostly European funds, was created in 1968 by the archdiocese to encourage the development of rural cooperatives and to assist community development projects. Another social service organization associated with the Catholic church is FUCRIDES, a development organization based in Sonsonate. FUCRIDES also has links to the Christian Democratic Party.

Church-Military Tensions Escalate

With the March 1989 electoral victory of ARENA, relations between the Catholic church and the armed forces sunk to the lowest point since the 1980 assassination of Romero. Both the army and ARENA have frequently charged that clerics and church organizations are linked to the FMLN, incensing the church hierarchy.[39] Among the targets of this red-baiting have been Tutela Legal, the legal-aid office of the Catholic church which monitors human-rights violations and which the army accuses of being a guerrilla front. The other is the University of Central America (UCA), the Jesuit-run university which is the major serious source of research and publication on the condition of the country. Col. Orlando Zepeda charged that the 1989 attacks of the urban guerrillas were organized at the UCA. The church hierarchy, in turn, became increasingly critical of the hardline policies of the army and the government, all of which leads many observers to believe that a new church-state showdown is in the making.

ARENA and the army, however, are not without their allies within the church. In their efforts to associate the church with the FMLN, they are aided by a small conservative sector of bishops and clerics. As evidence, they point to the recently published *The Popular Church Was Born in El Salvador*, a book by the rightwing Monsignor Fredy Delgado which accuses church leaders of embracing Marxist theory.[40]

Tensions between the church and the state reached a new high in November 1989 when the FMLN launched its offensive in San Salvador. The military reacted by arresting religious activists, searching churches and church-sponsored refuges, and repeating charges that the church was supporting the guerrillas. The threats and violence against the church culminated in the November 16 massacre by the military of six Jesuits, their housekeeper, and her daughter. Immediately following the massacre Attorney General Eduardo Colorado sent a letter to the Pope asking him to withdraw from El Salvador all bishops who were "fomenting violence."

Evangelical Churches Show New Dynamism

Of all the evangelical missions and churches founded in El Salvador, nearly 50 percent have been opened in the past ten years. Since 1978 the annual rate of growth has ranged from 15 to 22 percent. Today about 18 percent of the Salvadorans are evangelicals. The country has over 3,300 evangelical churches operated by some 79 evangelical denominations and sects.[41]

The Assemblies of God is the largest evangelical denomination, followed by the Church of Apostles and Prophets, Church of God, and Central American Mission. Most evangelical churches are branches or associates of U.S. pentecostal and fundamentalist church organizations. The main exception to this is the country's second-largest church, the pentecostal Church of Apostles and Prophets, which is an indigenous institution. Three Guatemalan evangelical churches have also penetrated El Salvador, including Prince of Peace, Elim, and Shaddai.

Although the surge in evangelical growth is a recent phenomenon, Protestant missionaries began proselytizing in El Salvador nearly a century ago. Unlike other Central American countries, however, where evangelical missionaries began working first with English and Creole-speaking people living on the Atlantic coast, there has never been a strong English-speaking ministry in El Salvador. Protestant missionaries have been working with with Spanish-speaking congregations in El Salvador since the 1890s. Early evangelical missionaries belonged to the Central American Mission, the California Yearly Meeting of Friends (Quakers, which had a base in Guatemala), the Seventh Day Adventist church, the American Baptist church, and independent pentecostal sects – all from the United States. It was not, however, until the 1950s that the evangelical missionaries began making a large impact. Of the evangelical churches now established in El Salvador, only 5 percent existed before 1950.[42]

The pace of evangelical growth has dramatically increased since 1978 with the Assemblies of God leading the way with its aggressive proselytizing and church-building campaigns. Other pentecostal churches – including Church of God, Church of Apostles and Prophets, and Prince of Peace – have also experienced sharp increases in members. Central American Mission, the largest non-pentecostal fundamentalist church, has not experienced the rapid growth enjoyed by the pentecostals. One exception has been the steady advance of the socially-committed Lutheran church. Other traditional Protestant denominations with churches in El Salvador are the Baptist and Episcopalian churches.

In the last ten years, the number of evangelicals has almost tripled. Evangelical organizations like the Salvadoran Evangelical Fraternity

(CONESAL) say that ambitious pastor training and evangelization campaigns explain this increase. But the spread of evangelical faith in El Salvador is also attributable to the internal political/economic crisis and the increased interest of U.S. evangelical organizations in the country. Beset by political violence and economic crisis, many Salvadorans have searched for refuge in a religious community that offers an escape from the political turmoil, emotional bonding, and hope for better days to come.

The Salvadoran evangelical movement did not rise independently from the crisis conditions but is largely a product of the increased U.S. evangelical presence. Televangelists such as Jimmy Swaggart and Pat Robertson have traveled to El Salvador to preach before massive crowds in the national stadium. They have been joined by an array of independent sects including Maranatha, Gospel Outreach/El Verbo, Chapel Hill Harvester, and Evangelistic Faith Mission.

Another factor in the evangelical boom is the presence of transnational interdenominational evangelical organizations like Youth with a Mission and Campus Crusade for Christ. Evangelical humanitarian assistance agencies like World Relief, World Vision, 700 Club, Manna International, and Paralife International have contributed to this surge in evangelicalism. While they do not have a direct presence in the country, evangelical relief agencies such as World Concern and MAP International also bolster the evangelical movement by channeling relief supplies through conservative evangelical organizations like CESAD and Manna Bible Institute.

Evangelical growth has also been fueled by the deepening dissatisfaction among middle- and upper-class Catholics over the influence within the Catholic church of Christian base communities and other advocates of the theology of liberation. Evangelical ministers say they are rapidly making inroads in the upper-class Escalón section of San Salvador.

Asked to describe their politics, most evangelical representatives say that they are neutral — that they are aligned with neither the right nor the left. Unlike the openly politicized activity of many pentecostal evangelicals in the United States, most evangelicals in El Salvador maintain a less direct but equally conservative political approach. Proclaiming their political neutrality all the while, the sermons of many evangelical pastors make repeated references to anticommunism, capitalist ethics, and their own pro-U.S. sympathies. Pastors commonly encourage support of authorities while discouraging social-justice activism.

While the vast majority of Salvadoran evangelicals belong to pentecostal churches where conservative theology mixes easily with conservative politics, there does exist a significant sector of more liberal churches. The

Lutheran church, the Episcopal church, and sectors of the Baptist church, for example, have offered important support to repopulating and repatriating refugees and lent assistance to community organizing efforts that are often subject to harassment and violence by the military.

Lutheran Bishop Medardo Gómez was forced to flee El Salvador after receiving a series of death threats in November 1989. He later returned to the country escorted by a group of U.S. clerics and said: "I am not a criminal. I am not a terrorist. I am a pastor, and our work is to worry about the poor and is not inspired by any social ideology." A January 1990 press conference in the United States sponsored by Catholic, Lutheran, Baptist, and Episcopalian bishops noted that in November and December 1989 some 50 Salvadorans working for church organizations had been arrested.

These and other evangelical churches, mostly mainline nonpentecostal ones, regard social assistance and community development activities as part of practicing your faith — not simply as a a way to open the door for evangelism. They generally try to maintain their independence from AID and Salvadoran government programs. Because of the efforts of this small but influential sector of the evangelical community, ecumenism has become an important social force in El Salvador, especially in comparison with the neighboring countries of Honduras and Guatemala.

Nongovernmental Organizations

During the 1980s there was a sharp increase in the social-service, relief, and development operations of nongovernmental organizations (NGOs) in El Salvador. These NGOs, both local and foreign, are sharply divided between those that receive funds from the U.S. government (mainly through the Agency for International Development) and those that have tried to maintain an independent posture. The former are usually U.S.-based NGOs while the latter are commonly associated with Catholic and Protestant churches (See Religion) or are part of the popular movement (repopulation groups, women's organizations, etc.). Support for this more independent sector of NGOs comes largely from European agencies and churches.[43]

Because of the direct U.S. involvement in the unpopular war, to work or not work with the U.S. Agency for International Development (AID) is a major issue for NGOs in El Salvador. Since 1980 AID has greatly expanded its work with NGOs in El Salvador; and the agency has sought to involve private organizations in a three-pronged strategy: 1) pacification (political demobilization and control) of the population, 2) political and economic stabilization, and 3) private-sector support.

Three-fourths of AID funding for NGOs in El Salvador goes to organizations dedicated to private-sector solutions of the country's economic and social problems.[44] Most of this aid flows to FUSADES (Salvadoran Foundation for Economic and Social Development), which was established by AID to do the following: strengthen other private-sector organizations; promote nontraditional exports (light-assembly industries and winter vegetable/fruit production); pressure the government for investment incentives, exemptions, and lower taxes; and promote foreign investment. AID and FUSADES say that these "reforms" will lead to economic growth, the benefits of which will trickle down to the impoverished majority.

Another Salvadoran NGO that receives AID support is the Asociación Pro-Superación Juvenil, the local affiliate of Junior Achievement. This group, which has received $4 million in AID funds, is dedicated to promoting the practices and principles of capitalism among Salvadoran teenagers. Through its Youth Entrepreneurs program, the association offers a course in which students start their own business, sell stock, and then liquidate their holdings. Yet another business-oriented NGO is the International Executive Service Corps (IESC) which has offered free business consultation to the ultra-right *El Diario de Hoy* daily newspaper.

Not all NGOs that receive AID funds get the money through the local AID mission. Some NGOs receive grants and contracts through the AID mission in San Salvador, but these same NGOs and others may also receive grants through the Washington, Latin American regional, and Central American regional offices of AID. In many cases, such as with Foster Parents Plan and Sister Cities, these grants are specifically targeted for programs in El Salvador. NGOs may get funding from the regional AID office (ROCAP) in Guatemala City for programs that take place in more than one Central American country, as is the case for National Rural Electric Cooperative Association, and Agricultural Cooperative Development International. Several NGOs, like the American Institute of Free Labor Development (AIFLD) and the Cooperative Housing Foundation, receive general funding from AID for their regional and worldwide programs.

To Accept or Reject AID Funding

If AID had its way, there would be many more NGOs working with AID and the government in El Salvador. AID considers NGOs—both

U.S. and indigenous ones – to be the preferred instruments for its political-economic strategies for the following reasons:

* They are considered to be more efficient and less corrupt than government agencies.
* It is easier for NGOs to work in many communities than it is for the government, the military, or AID itself because of the suspected political objectives of the latter institutions and the easier time private organizations have in building community confidence.
* NGOs bring additional resources and personnel into the country.
* NGOs, because of their religious or humanitarian character, can serve to legitimize U.S. military and economic presence.
* The use of NGOs as intermediaries corresponds to AID's new commitment to involve the private sector in implementing U.S. foreign-policy objectives.

Despite AID's intense interest in working with NGOs, the agency has been repeatedly frustrated by the refusal of many NGOs to accept U.S. government money for programs in El Salvador. Salvadoran government regulations that make it difficult for local currency to be directly transferred to NGOs have also hindered these plans. To overcome this second obstacle AID is pressuring the government to change its statutes and has arranged a deal whereby a certain amount of local currency will be handed back to AID, which in turn will pass it on to NGOs. The lack of interest of NGOs, however, remains the principal obstacle to having more private organizations work with AID and the government.

It was in 1983 – the year that AID and the government kicked off the national pacification plan in San Vicente – that the agency began looking hard for NGOs to participate in its plan. AID funds were used to pay for the trips of numerous NGO representatives to El Salvador to explore the possibility of opening programs. While there are NGOs that do not have any objections to cooperating with AID in less politicized circumstances (in neighboring Guatemala and Honduras, for instance), few are willing to risk their reputations by working with AID in the more politicized El Salvador.

Many NGOs also stay away from the country because of the violence, reasoning that they should not risk their personnel when an organization such as the Peace Corps is unwilling to reopen its program there. (Before 1979 El Salvador hosted one of the largest Latin American programs of Peace Corps.) Some NGOs, like World Relief, Project Hope, Technoserve, and International Rescue Committee, do not feel that AID funding compromises their independence and humanitarian or development objectives. World Relief, for example, is so closely tied to AID that it has used the agency's address as its own and even refers reporters to AID for questions about its work. But there have been cases when AID-funded NGOs, like Save the Children and OEF International, have declined to accept AID money for certain projects considered to be too closely linked to U.S. political and military objectives.

In other countries, AID may have an easier time making a convincing case that it has no political or military objectives. That case is harder to make in El Salvador where AID funds are used directly to support civic-action programs, pay for the military's United to Reconstruct pacification campaign, and cover over 40 percent of the government's budget. The fact that the United States is such a direct party to civil war in El Salvador also makes it difficult for some NGOs to associate themselves with AID.

It is not publicly known how many NGOs have been approached by AID about working in El Salvador. Among those that have declined AID funds for its Health and Jobs for Displaced Families project in El Salvador are: Catholic Relief Services (which does receive U.S. PL480 Title II food aid for other projects), World Vision, the Mennonite Central Committee, and the U.S. Methodist, Presbyterian, Lutheran, and Episcopal churches. AID's search for NGOs has even reached the point of approaching private organizations known to be hostile to U.S. foreign policy in the region.

AID has brought on board two highly politicized private organizations: the elite Catholic organization Knights of Malta and a fanatically pro-U.S. group called Family Foundation of America. In the past, AID has been reluctant about funding organizations whose purposes are so obviously political. AID's funding of Knights of Malta and Family Foundation of America, both of which work closely with the military, could be considered one more indication of the mainly political nature of AID's own mission in El Salvador and the degree to which it has lowered its criteria to find groups willing to accept its money.

Besides the concern about being politically connected to AID, an additional concern for some NGOs is that AID's main interest is neither humanitarian nor developmental in nature. More than just being politically tainted, critics say that AID money is morally corrupt. They feel that it is impossible to separate the military-aid funds that continue an unjust war and the economic-aid money that supposedly is for humanitarian purposes.

Although social-service and development NGOs in El Salvador administer generally the same kind of projects, such as productive projects for displaced families, there are marked differences between them. One major difference is that the more independent NGOs tend to work with and serve already existing community organizations, while those closer to the government supplant, divide, or avoid existing popular organizations.

Not only are there serious issues about who NGOs work with but also about the direction of their project aid. In El Salvador, as elsewhere in the third world, NGOs and foreign donors are channeling an increasing percentage of their assistance to what they call productive projects. Donors and NGOs express concern that their assistance be used to create income and jobs. The development philosophy espoused by AID, and currently in vogue among the NGO community, places more emphasis on private initiative and calls for development aid to build businesses. This has meant moving away from such priorities as the formation of cooperatives, *campesino* training, community education, and meeting basic needs.

Although such a development strategy does stress production rather than relief and dependency, there are questions about its political effects and about its appropriateness to a country at war. Some NGOs are concerned that the current interest in building businesses has the result of rewarding private initiative and competitiveness, rather than encouraging collective solutions to collective problems. Creating a new entrepreneurial class among the poor is not a solution to either community or national underdevelopment.

Questions about economic development are inextricably linked to political issues. A common complaint of NGOs and popular organizations is that there can be no economic development and forward progress in socioeconomic conditions in the context of a civil war. They say that peace must be the foundation for any meaningful development activity. Without peace, conditions of the poor majority only worsen. As one NGO representative put it: "A realistic goal in the short term is that the poor can return to the same level of misery that they lived in before the war." Another said, "We're not here to solve the problems but to provide limited support. As U.S. NGOs, we have decided that our primary purpose is to understand what is happening around the country and to educate others about that reality."

Repression and Deportation

Just as the relationship between AID and NGOs is a major issue in El Salvador, so too is the relationship of NGOs with the national government and military. Most NGOs proclaim their independence and neutrality, but their projects often take place in a context defined by the military through its various security and development plans. Those NGOs that assist projects with an independent character often have a difficult time getting their staff and supplies to the project sites. They are also subject to official and extra-official repression and harassment.

NGO and church workers, particularly those working with the displaced, are often victims of military harassment and intimidation. One of the major forms of this harassment is requiring that these workers obtain appropriate military permission to enter certain areas of the country. In the late 1980s, the military has expanded the area where special permission is required. There has been considerable and perhaps deliberate confusion about the documents to needed to travel outside the capital; and in many cases, NGO and church workers are often prohibited by local military commanders from entering communities even when they have the appropriate permission from military authorities in San Salvador or department capitals. The workers of many organizations collaborating with independent or church-sponsored resettlement efforts have been threatened and detained by the military.

The question about NGO and church relationships with community and popular organizations like *campesino* associations and squatters groups is a particularly sensitive one in El Salvador, where many such organizations have been victims of military and rightwing repression. Official pressure, as well as the reluctance of NGOs themselves to associate with politically active groups, has meant that there is little direct association between NGOs and popular organizations. Instead of working with pre-existing community groups, NGOs and foreign agencies like AID often create new community directorates and entirely new organizations that they control.

There exists a high level of popular organizing in El Salvador despite the oppressive economic realities and long years of political repression. Many of these organizations — ranging from crafts cooperatives to unions and squatter groups — receive foreign financial support from the United States and Europe. Although these groups may receive most of their funds from outside El Salvador, they often are highly self-determined organizations with their own development and organizing priorities and political agenda.

The repression and harassment against NGOs, church workers, and internationals working in El Salvador sharpened in 1989, particularly after the FMLN's November 1989 offensive. Numerous foreigners were arrested and forced to leave the country. Some, like Jennifer Casolo of the Christian Education Seminars, were even charged with harboring arms for the FMLN. In December 1989 the Salvadoran Air Force dropped flyers throughout the country addressed to "Salvadoran

Patriots," advising them: "You have the plain and legitimate right to defend your life and property. If to do that you have to kill terrorists of the FMLN as well as their international allies, then do it."

One of the U.S. citizens forced to leave El Salvador was Josephine Beecher who provided health services for refugees in Usulután. She said: "I came in the first place to work with the poor and displaced, but there's no space for the most basic humanitarian work anymore. I'm not talking about basic social-service work, like child care and medical care, the kind of things the Rotary Club or the Junior League might do at home."[45]

Women and Feminism

The continuation of the war and the deepening of the economic crisis have had a particularly severe impact on Salvadoran women. During the 1980s the percentage of female-headed households has risen dramatically and more women have been forced to seek work while at the same time caring for their families. But unemployment among women is some 20 percent higher than male unemployment, forcing many Salvadoran women to eke out a living in the country's rapidly expanding informal sector of markets and street vendors.[46]

Traditional exploitation and oppression occurring in the context of the home and the family, including marital violence, unrecognized and uncompensated domestic work, and treatment as second-class human beings, are facts of life in El Salvador. Although these generally are women's lot everywhere, they may, in many respects, be worse in El Salvador. For example, landowners have traditionally taken sexual advantage of peasant women while similar abuse of girls working as maids is quite common.

In the countryside fathers often marry off their daughters at puberty, which has meant that child-bearing begins early and large numbers of children per individual woman are the rule. According to the last general census (1971), one-third of 14-year-old females had already experienced at least one pregnancy. The requirement of virginity at marriage is not merely an aspect of traditional Hispanic culture, but has also characterized the indigenous communities. In the department of Cuscatlán, for example, it has been customary for a girls' parents to beat her on the night before a betrothal to make her confess to any past sexual indiscretions; if she confessed she was deemed not marriageable.

Modern Salvadoran women are increasingly demanding that their rights be respected and, as a result, have gained a certain amount of territory in middle-class occupations, constituting about 30 percent of the country's physicians and attorneys, over 30 percent of university professors, and about half of dentists and high school teachers.[47] Women in business organizations, however, are subject to all the forms of discrimination that are a familiar experience in other countries. In addition, some manual occupations are legally closed to women, considered too dangerous or threatening to health. Nevertheless, women are in the manual labor force in great numbers, working in factories and retail trade. Of course, "protective" legislation very easily becomes discriminatory. Immediately after Article 110 of the Labor Code, which prohibits employers from requiring pregnant women to do heavy work that would endanger their health, comes Article 111, which provides that an employer can switch a pregnant woman out of a position dealing with the public. Nevertheless, Article 112 gives a new mother the right to return to the job she held before becoming pregnant.

The legal status of women has improved considerably in recent years. Article 3 of the 1983 constitution stipulates the equality of all people before the law and prohibits restrictions based on differences of gender. In 1983 the government ratified the International Convention to Eliminate All Forms of Discrimination Against Women. Article 123 of the Labor Code mandates equal pay for equal work within a single enterprise. Needless to say, work traditionally identified as "women's work" is on a lower pay scale than the kind of work traditionally identified as men's. Law enforcement officials also generally ignore complaints by women of inequality of treatment, or even of domestic violence. Moreover, there is enough ambiguity in the phrasing of the law that, for example, female agricultural workers earn a lower wage than males. Despite the updating of Salvadoran laws in some respects, in other respects they remain bound by the older model of gender roles. According to Article 182 of the Civil Code "the husband owes protection to his wife, and the wife obedience to the husband."

The Labor Code takes account of the special problems of pregnancy but not of child-care requirements; a few collective labor contracts, however, do include provision for nurseries at places of work. The problem of sexual harassment on the job has not even been recognized in public debate or law as a problem needing attention.[48]

State family-planning programs were first introduced in 1968. Family-planning methods are used reportedly by about one-third of women of child-bearing age. The pill is the most commonly used method. Abortions are not permitted in publicly-funded hospitals. Although the Catholic church opposes artificial methods of birth control, the government's position in favor of family planning is very strong, causing some women complain that at government-run hospitals and public health centers they feel under too much pressure to limit family size. It has even been reported that hospital personnel are given a quota of sterilizations to perform. Certainly a lot of pressure is brought to bear on women who go to hospitals to give birth, and one-half of the women using contraception report sterilization as the method.[49] The state family-planning program is sometimes criticized by the left as another imperialist counterinsurgency strategy. Nevertheless, abortion, according to one report, is the most common cause of death among women of child-bearing age.[50] Another study revealed that one-third of all beds in the gynecological wards of public hospitals are occupied by women suffering from serious complications from badly performed abortions.[51]

To some extent the hardships of the war have had a different effect on Salvadoran women than on men. To be sure, men are being killed in the fighting and by political assassinations in much larger numbers than women, to the point that male life expectancy has increased only by seven years during a period in which female life expectancy increased by ten years, much more than any differential that might be expected to exist under normal circumstances. Nevertheless, it should not be thought that any special gentility toward the fair sex inhibits the military or the death squads; female activists and FMLN sympathizers are also tortured and assassinated, and run the additional likelihood of rape.

The forced recruitment of young men for military service has been adopted as a women's issue by working-class women and has been the subject of protest by organizations of mothers. Because of women's traditional role of homemaker, the problems of food shortages and increases in the cost of living are also seen as women's issues. Moreover, the increase in widowhood, together with the loss of sons to the war, mean that more women face the prospect of lack of family support, especially as they grow older. These are not really new problems, but exaggerate the traditional problem of abandonment of common-law spouses which has always existed in the country.

Other legal provisions derive from antiquated conceptions of the special status of women. Thus the law contemplates greater penalties for rape if the victim is a virgin, lesser if she is a prostitute. Moreover, prosecution for sexual offenses occurs only with the consent of the victim; that is, the victim may "forgive" the offender (or, in other words, be intimidated by him into not pressing charges).

Women's Organizing Expands

Responding to these and other problems, a variety of women's organizations have emerged since the mid-1980s.[52] These groups have filled a space left vacant by repression of earlier attempts to organize women. For the most part, they are situated at the heart of the popular movement. In addition to addressing the common economic and political problems faced by Salvadorans, these women's organizations also target gender-specific issues.[53] International Women's Day was celebrated for the first time with marches in San Salvador and San Vicente. Another demonstration of the deepening strength and unity of women's organizations came shortly after the ARENA government announced its new economic program and seven women's groups organized a protest around the theme "Empty Shopping Baskets."

The Association of Salvadoran Women (ADEMUSA) works primarily with base communities and domestics and has played a major role in the campaign against forced recruitment. The Association of Salvadoran Indigenous Women (AMIS) aims to promote the values of the country's native people and the use of traditional medicinal plants. The Association of Salvadoran Women (AMS) is a strong peasant organization of committees from more than one hundred rural communities, including those in conflictive areas. The Women's Committee of FENASTRAS (COFENASTRAS) focuses on consciousness-raising among the women in this strong and combative labor confederation and also provides child care and medical services.

The National Coordinator of Salvadoran Women (CONAMUS) is closely linked to the labor movement, including, for example, the women of the ANDES teachers' union. It aims to coordinate the various groups working on women's issues in El Salvador, while establishing relations with foreign women's organizations. The Movement of Salvadoran Women (MSM), also associated with the labor movement, includes members of the Union of Unemployed Workers (COFEDYDES) and the Pro-Development Association for Women and Children. MSM helped formed the National Cipotes Movement (Youth Movement). The Institute for Research, Training, and Development of Women (IMU) provides training, research, and communications assistance to women's organizations and sponsors the Center of Legal Assistance for Salvadoran Women (CALMUS).

The Salvadoran Women for Peace (ORMUSA) works on peace and justice issues and sponsors income-generating projects and consciousness-raising education for women in rural cooperatives. The Unity of Women, University of El Salvador (MUES) brings together women workers, students, and professors, has sponsored a workshop on domestic violence, and is promoting a new women's studies programs. UNICEF has taken an increased interest in improving the condition of women in El Salvador and is sponsoring the Casa de Mujer for victims of violence against women.

Historically, the most important women's organization has been the Association of Women in El Salvador (AMES), which was formed in the late 1970s and is closely associated with the FMLN and FDR. It organizes around a wide range of issues of interest to women in Salvadoran refugee camps in Honduras and in the controlled zones. In 1987 AMES became part of the Salvadoran Women's Union (UMS), which is a coalition of the five revolutionary women's groups associated with the FMLN.

The Association of Salvadoran Women (ASMUSA) has representatives in Nicaragua, Mexico, and Costa Rica, but its main activities are to raise funds and publicize the situation in El Salvador. Within the country, ASMUSA is active in organizing classes, nurseries, and workshops especially in the zones controlled by the FMLN. The Association of Progressive Women of El Salvador (AMPES) has continuity of membership with a previous organization, the Fraternity of Salvadoran Women (FMS), which disbanded under political repression in 1969. The FMS was set up with the guidance of the Communist Party of El Salvador. The AMPES today emphasizes political and labor-union work, operating openly in the FMLN-controlled zones but clandestinely outside them, in an auxiliary role to the forces of the FMLN.

In the controlled zones, and among the FMLN combatants themselves, attempts are being made to improve the traditional position of women, although *machista* attitudes remain strong. The all-woman Sylvia Battalion was formed in December of 1981 by AMPES and fought effectively in the region of the Guazapa Volcano. There are numerous women commanders within the FMLN, although there are no female members in the five-person FMLN directorate. According to AMES:

> The revolutionary process can be measured by observing the extent of women's participation. It is impossible to speak of a true revolution if women continue to be subjugated and marginalized. In a true revolution, there are advances by women in all areas. The revolutionary process that is now in progress in our country has as one of tis goals the abolition of social inequality.[54]

On the right, there are three women's organizations associated with ARENA: Crusade for Peace and Work, Salvadoran Feminine Front, and the Women's Civic Association (which receives U.S. government funds through the National Endowment for Democracy). The Pro-Solidarity Committee is an organization formed by the wives of army colonels.

Native Peoples

Like other sectors of Salvadoran society, the Amerindian population is also organized. The demands of the native population reflect, for the most part, the concerns of the entire popular movement. But the new Amerindian groups which emerged in the 1980s are also struggling to protect their communities from cultural extinction. Typical of the rising cultural and ethnic consciousness in the country, on October 12, 1989 the organized native community led a protest about the historical inaccuracy of Christopher Columbus Day celebration and the tradition of racism and exploitation that day signifies.

El Salvador was never a center of Amerindian civilization, but when the Spanish conquistador Pedro de Alvarado led his expedition into what is now El Salvador he did find a sizable native population. The group first encountered by the Spanish conquistadors were the Pipils living in communities south and west of the Río Lempa. These were Nahuatl-speaking Indians related to Aztecs who had migrated from Mexico in the 11th century. Resistance by the Pipils kept the Spanish from colonizing the territory until 1539, when the native rebellions were finally crushed.

In the country's northwest lived the Pokoman Indians, the original settlers of El Salvador and closely related to the the Mayan people then living Honduras, Guatemala, and Yucatán. Also living in El Salvador at the time of the conquest were the Lenca Indians, who lived in the area to the north and east of the Río Lempa.[55]

There are no reliable figures on the percentage of El Salvador's population that is currently Indian. The figures range downward from 20 to 6 percent.[56] What is certain is that the Indian population of El Salvador is not very visible, a circumstance that can be traced back to the *matanza* of 1932. The repression of the popular insurrection was a genocidal act aimed specifically at El Salvador's Indian population. In the belief that Indians were the backbone of the rural rebellion, Gen. Maximiliano Hernández Martínez specifically ordered his troops to kill anyone obviously Indian, as indicated by their clothing style and other outward features. As the word spread about what was happening, Indians hastened to adopt outward signs of belonging to the majority *mestizo*. Indian dress was dropped, and hair was cut. Only Spanish was spoken in public.[57]

Still spoken in El Salvador are two indigenous languages — Nahuatl (also known as Pipil) and Lenca — although the number Indians speaking Nahuatl as their first language is rapidly dwindling. During the 1980s there has been a revival of Indian identity promoted by two groups: ANIS (National Salvadoran Association of Native People) and the Salvadoran Association of Democratic Indigenous People (ASID). ANIS was closely associated with the American Institute for Free Labor Development (AIFLD) in the early 1980s. Frustrated with the Christian Democrats and disgusted with the political control exercised by AIFLD, ASID split off from ANIS in 1985 to join the UNTS popular alliance. There is also a government-affiliated organization called MAIS, which promotes traditional Indian cultural activities through the mass media and government-sponsored events.

Some of the most successful efforts to retain and promote Indian culture are happening in refugee camps outside the country and in areas controlled by the FMLN. One focus is the revival of traditional crafts, such as weaving and basketmaking. Activity in traditional crafts had dwindled, not only with the ethnocide of 1932, but also with the availability of cheap factory-made products. Supported by nongovernmental organizations and church groups, Indian refugees have formed cooperatives and found markets for their crafts in Western Europe and the United States. In Nicaragua, one Salvadoran weaver said that Indians were using their time in exile to "rescue our lost culture."[58]

Since 1985 ANIS has sponsored an annual festival to promote Indian culture and enable Indians to share experiences. The war has complicated the holding of the festival and people's ability to attend it. The military used the 1989 festival as a shield to penetrate FMLN territory, knowing that the FMLN would not counterattack for fear of endangering the lives of participants in the festival.

Refugees and the Displaced

At least a quarter of the population has fled the country or been internally displaced as a result of the civil war. Estimates of the number of those displaced from their homes but still living in the country range from 200,000 to 500,000.[59] Most of the internally displaced are rural families fleeing the war but they also include the thousands of families displaced by the 1986 earthquake and most recently those displaced by fighting and bombardment in San Salvador.

Salvadoran refugees have fled principally to the United States, Mexico, and other Central American countries. As many as 750,000 Salvadorans have emigrated, mostly illegally, to the United States since the war broke out in 1979. Up to 250,000 have found new homes in Mexico, and some 50,000 to 100,000 Salvadorans are now living elsewhere in Central America because of the war. The largest concentration of Salvadoran refugees within Central America has been in Honduras where some 39,000 have found refuge in United Nations camps. Only a small portion of those Salvadorans living outside their country have been officially treated as refugees. Joint UN and host government programs have established refugee programs in the other Central American countries and in Mexico, with the largest program being in Honduras.

Salvadorans in the United States

Counting those who came to the United States before the beginning of the civil war, there are some one million Salvadorans living in the United States. The principal centers of Salvadoran residents in the United States are Los Angeles, Washington DC, Houston, and San Francisco. According to a study by Segundo Montes at the University of Central America, three-quarters of those Salvadorans living in the United States arrived in the country after 1979, and almost half immigrated after January 1, 1982 and are therefore not eligible for amnesty under the most recent immigration law. Based on his survey, Montes reported that 46 percent of Salvadoran said they would like to return to El Salvador.[60]

About 160,000 Salvadoran illegal immigrants have applied for amnesty under the provisions of the law; between 3,000 and 4,000 a year apply for political asylum.[61] The Immigration and Naturalization Service (INS) and the State Department are unsympathetic to Salvadoran requests for political asylum, following the U.S. government rule which, despite the letter and spirit of applicable law, takes the view that only political refugees from leftwing and communist governments are legitimate. In 1988, for example, the INS approved 68 percent of the requests for political asylum from Nicaraguans but only 4 percent from Salvadorans.

In one ruling, the State Department advised the INS that María Teresa Tula, a leader of the human-rights group COMADRES, did not have a "well-founded fear of political persecution." In fact, the State Department claimed that as a leftist, she was likely to persecute others.[62] Tula left El Salvador after her husband had been tortured and killed, and after she had been arrested, beaten, tortured, and raped. Even when the INS entertains petitions for asylum, applicants typically go through a long unsuccessful process in which they are continually preyed on by shysters, who only go through the motions of giving them effective representation.

Although most undocumented Salvadoran immigrants to the United States come through Mexico, many Salvadorans settle in Mexico, where they constitute half of Mexico's illegal immigrants. Subject to petty extortion from Mexican police and officials, these refugees living in Mexico are commonly forced to find work under miserable conditions for much lower pay than a Mexican worker would accept.

A Displaced Nation

Migration and displacement, while having dramatically increased during the 1980s, have long been part of the Salvadoran society's adaptation to landlessness and repression. In the 1950s and 1960s the ruthless expansion of agroexport (cotton and sugar) production displaced thousands of rural families. Estate owners pushed the sharecroppers off their *latifundios* and began to rely more on seasonal wage labor. Distorted land-use and tenure patterns have meant that an ever-increasing number of rural Salvadorans grow up without a place to call their own.

The number of homeless and landless Salvadoran peasants rose dramatically as a result of the tensions between El Salvador and Honduras which resulted in the 1969 war. The decision by the Honduran government to expel tens of thousands of Salvadoran *campesinos* living in their country caused a sharp rise in the landless population in El Salvador.

Homelessness and landlessness have deep historical roots in El Salvador. But the numbers of displaced really began to escalate in the late 1970s as a result of the repression by the military government of General Romero. The outbreak of the civil war in 1979-1980 resulted in yet another wave of refugees and displaced families seeking to escape the army's rural counterinsurgency campaign. The counterinsurgency war – complete with scorched-earth tactics, aerial bombing, and forced relocations – has caused a massive displacement of the Salvadoran population. A major influx of internal refugees resulted from the initiation of the National Plan in 1983. Another jump in the displaced population came in the wake of the military's Operation Phoenix against guerrilla-controlled areas of the Guazapa volcano. Finally, the 1986 earthquake that shook San Salvador displaced over 10,000 families.

The Catholic church was the first nongovernmental organization to come to the aid of displaced population. In 1980 the church began channeling Caritas food assistance to the displaced as well as opening up church grounds as places of refuge. Another early and major source of aid for displaced families has been Diaconía, an ecumenical grouping that includes the Social Secretariat of the Archdiocese, the Lutheran church of El Salvador, Emmanuel Baptist church, the Episcopal church, and several other nongovernmental organizations (NGOs).

The government's response to the growing numbers of displaced began in 1981 with the creations of the National Commission to Aid the Displaced (CONADES), an agency founded with funds from the U.S. Agency for International Development (AID). Over the decade CON-ADES worked hand-in-hand with CONARA, another government agency funded by AID to coordinate the military's civic-action programs. AID has also sought out NGOs to carry out its relief and resettlement programs for the displaced. In many cases, NGOs spurned AID's offers of funding, feeling that their independence and integrity as humanitarian organizations would be compromised if they accepted funds from the U.S. government — one of the major parties in the civil war.

In 1985 AID did succeed in drawing two major NGOs — World Relief and Project Hope — into its plans to relocate and care for displaced communities. Failing to involve either the archdiocesan Caritas organization or Catholic Relief Services, AID did succeed in contracting CESAD, an alliance of evangelical churches, to assist displaced persons in areas authorized by the government and military. Other NGOs drawn into AID's program for the displaced population were Knights of Malta and Family Foundation of America. (See Nongovernmental Organizations)

By the mid-1980s the problem of the displaced population had clearly become a crisis. Initially, it was thought that the war would be over in a matter of years. But as it persisted, so did the problem of the displaced. Providing for the basic needs of the displaced was becoming an increasingly heavy burden — and there was no end in sight. AID and other agencies dealing with the displaced were concerned that the number of people "on the dole" was growing without any long-term solutions on the horizon. There was also mounting concern in official circles about incipient popular organizing among displaced families demanding to return home.

The idea of resettling displaced families in "secured" villages and farms was one that had first been tried during the implementation the National Plan in 1983-1985. However the army's inability to maintain constant military security in towns in conflictive areas and to maintain volunteer civil-defense patrols in those communities doomed this early attempt. Subsequent AID and military resettlement programs also proved either unworkable, inadequate, or unacceptable.

Repopulation and Repatriation

Since 1985 the official (AID, government, and military) response to the crisis of internal refugees has been largely shaped by the initiative of independent NGOs, churches, and the displaced population itself. Tired of waiting for government permission to repopulate areas from which they had fled years before, groups of displaced families began returning on their own. An innovative resettlement program was sponsored in 1986 in the town of Tenancingo by the Catholic church and FUNDASAL, a Salvadoran NGO that sponsors low-income housing programs. The program attempted to create a nonmilitarized zone in the abandoned town where displaced families could resettle. The Tenancingo experiment created some political space for other repopulation efforts. By the end of the decade, however, the nonmilitarized status of Tenancingo was lost, and the town had army-run civil-defense units and an ARENA mayor.

Two popular organizations—the Christian Committee of the Displaced (CRIPDES) and the National Repopulation Coordinator (CNR)—were in the forefront of the repopulation movement in the late 1980s. After four major repopulations in 1986-1987, the military clamped down, refusing to allow any more independent community repopulations. Nonetheless, the repopulation movement has continued as individual families have steadily trickled back to their former homes and other previously abandoned areas.

Joining this resettlement movement have been thousands of Salvadorans who had been living as refugees in Honduras. Like the internally displaced, the refugees in Honduras took the initiative in formulating and then carrying out plans to return to their former homes. Over 6,500 refugees returned from Honduras between October 1987 and November 1988, mainly as part of three church-sponsored repatriations. Most of those returning refugees came from the Mesa Grande camp. By mid-1989 the over 10,000 refugees living in the San Antonio and Colomoncagua camps were also petitioning to return to their former communities.

The new ARENA government resisted, however, insisting that the repatriations be gradual and sponsored by the government, rather than by the churches or independent NGOs like CNR or PADECOES (Patronato for Communal Development in El Salvador) as preferred by the refugees. Facing the possibility of more large repatriations from Honduras, the ARENA government in 1989 claimed that the male refugees were really FMLN militants who planned "terrorist actions" upon their return to El Salvador.

The massive dislocations that resulted in November 1989 from the FMLN offensive and the army's harsh response further aggravated the crisis of the displaced in El Salvador. At least 50,000 Salvadorans were displaced in the last two months of 1989, mainly by indiscriminate military bombing of poor neighborhoods. The intensified fighting of late 1989 also created a new group of displaced—those U.S. citizens and wealthy Salvadorans who left for the United States when the conflict reached the wealthy enclaves of San Salvador.

Ecology and Environmentalism

El Salvador is a spectacularly beautiful land of lakes and volcanoes which also boasts some of the world's longest uninterrupted beaches.[63] The native people knew it as Cuscatlán—Land of the Jewel. For all the beauty still found here, El Salvador the country in Central America with the most severely degraded environment. Erosion, which affects at least 50 percent of the country, has created a national agricultural crisis.[64] The quetzal is extinct in El Salvador as are most of the formerly abundant species of cats and monkeys that once made this country their home. El Salvador also has the distinction of being the region's only wildlife importer.[65] In the upper-class neighborhoods of San Salvador, turtle eggs, iguana, armadillos, and mangrove clams are among the items on sale for the curious and the hungry.

There is also a human side to the ecological devastation. When torrential rains caused the hills of Monte Bello to give way, more than a thousand squatters and displaced people were buried under 40 feet of mud. As much of half the land on large estates has been cleared for pasture, but peasant families have to scrounge to feed their families from tiny parcels of mountainside land. Only one-tenth of the rural population has easy access to clean drinking water, and seepage of sewage and wastes is quickly contaminating the groundwater in San Salvador. Along with Guatemala, El Salvador is the country most contaminated by pesticides. High concentrations of DDT have been found in cow's milk, mother's milk, and beef.[66]

The tropical forests that once covered the country have been cut down to made room for agroexport production and subsistence agriculture of the large peasant population. Primary forests cover only 3 percent of the national territory. Together with secondary growth, natural vegetation covers only 7 percent. Severe erosion causes an annual topsoil loss of 20 percent.[67] According to the United Nations' Food and Agricultural Organization, El Salvador is undergoing a process of desertification.

Coastal savannahs and stands of old-growth ebony, cedar, mahogany, and granadilla have been lost in the onslaught of an advancing agroexport economy. As their habitat disappeared, so did the country's howler monkeys, anteaters, and white-lipped peccaries.[68]

Probably the second major environmental problem after deforestation and soil erosion is the buildup of toxic pesticides, which have poisoned thousands of workers and accumulated in soil, the water table, livestock and other elements in the food chain. Environmental pollution, according to the Agency for International Development, is "a problem that now permeates almost every facet of Salvadoran life."[69]

During the 1970s cases of pesticide poisoning averaged between 1,000 and 2,000 a year nationwide. Salvadoran environmentalists say that 50 children died from pesticide contamination in one San Salvador hospital alone.[70] There are laws governing pesticide use, but they are not enforced. Every year there are massive fish kills in the Gulf of Fonseca as rains wash pesticides from the cotton fields into the sea.[71] In the urban areas, there are problems with smog, pollution of water supplies by industrial effluents, and improper disposal of human waste. It has been estimated that only 10 percent of the rural population has access to safe drinking water, and that only 15 percent of rural residents and 38 percent of urban dwellers are served by sewage-disposal systems.

El Salvador's fishing and shrimping industries, the latter an important earner of foreign exchange, have been seriously affected, not only from pesticide runoff but also from silting. Silting has also combined with other factors to choke to death almost 3,000 acres of mangroves.

The war has contributed in various ways to the degradation of the environment. Bombing by the Salvadoran Air Force, which has dropped over 3,000 tons of bombs across the country, has set off fires that destroyed wilderness and cultivable land, and contributed to floods and landslides. Napalm and white phosphorus, as well as the infamous "Daisy Cutter" bomb which explodes above the ground, have been used — all of which tend to cause fires. The Cerro Nejapa, once an important wildlife and forest reserve, has lost its original forest cover as a result of fires caused by bombing.[72] Such war-related destruction caused one community to respond:

> We, the people who inhabit the town of Perquín and surrounding areas, are very worried by the grave damage caused by the devastating forest fires provoked by the bombardment and indiscriminate mortar attacks, as well as by soldiers in their patrols and operations. The fires are accelerating the destruction of the *patrimonio* [inherited resources] of this zone: forests, logging areas, crops of coffee, and basic grains. By deforesting great areas, the fires and bombardments have noticeably affected the rain

cycle. The duration of the rainy season has diminished in recent years, and the levels of the creeks and rivers have dropped.

The army has said that it is burning the mountains as part of its operations against the guerrillas. But in practice, the fires clearly do not hurt the guerrillas, but rather hurt us, the civilian population.[73]

Environmental consciousness is on the rise among all sectors in El Salvador. Business groups have sponsored TV programs and announcements explaining how the water cycle works, while the daily paper *La Prensa Gráfica* has run a campaign supporting reforestation. Sixteen organizations with memberships of mostly professionals have formed the Salvadoran Ecological Unity Coalition. For the most part, however, these environmental organizations avoid connections with the popular movement.

The government, through its Department of National Parks and Wildlife and other agencies, has begun some conservation projects, especially since it has become clear that international financing for such projects is available. With only 2 percent of the country with any significant remaining forest cover, little of El Salvador is regarded as suitable for preservation in parks.[74] The government has set aside about 50,000 acres for reserves and parks but no timetable has been set. Currently, only six protected areas, covering 15,000 acres, have been established.

At the Laguna Jocatal, a wildlife-restoration project has a good chance of saving the most important wetlands area.[75] The Trifinio Development Project, a project combining economic development and conservation in a 7584-square kilometer zone along the borders of Guatemala, Honduras and El Salvador, has secured funding from the Inter-American Development Bank and other agencies. But Salvadoran environmentalists are concerned that economic-development projects scheduled for the tri-country program have taking priority over environmental considerations. There is also rising concern that the world-renowned Montecristo Park will be threatened by the agricultural, mining, and timber development projects of the nearby Trifinio Project.[76]

This situation has been made worse by the purely exploitative attitude of the ruling groups toward the country's resource endowment, and a relatively heavy industrial development, resulting in the unregulated dumping of industrial waste. Also bearing responsibility for industrial pollution and careless use of agrochemicals are the foreign investors who can do business in El Salvador without many of the environmental constraints they would confront at home.

Chapter 5

Foreign Influence

U.S. Foreign Policy

The State Department outlined the main principles and features of U.S. foreign policy in El Salvador in its January 1989 statement "El Salvador: The Battle for Democracy," making the following observations:[1]

* The U.S. government supports the process of democratic transition in El Salvador. The most recent example of this policy's success was the peaceful transfer of power after the March 1989 elections.

* The chief threat to democratic transition is the FMLN, which is a Marxist-Leninist coalition guided and financed by Cuba, Nicaragua, and the Soviet Union and determined to seize power by military means. The FMLN is characterized as a terrorist organization.

* There is a large centrist political base in El Salvador, which is on attack from both political extremes. These extremes are marginal elements which are relevant only because of their use of violence.

* Human-rights violations have steadily diminished from the early 1980s, largely because of increased professionalism of the security forces and the lack of government/army support for rightwing extremists.

* U.S. military aid is necessary to permit the Salvadoran armed forces to protect the fragile democratic institutions against the FMLN terrorists. The success of these local armed forces in repelling and isolating the FMLN military obviates any need for the introduction of U.S. combat troops.

* U.S. economic aid is necessary to stabilize the economy. This economic stabilization is accomplished through balance-of-payments assistance and through programs to promote private-sector investment. Other smaller economic-aid programs address the basic needs of the poor through food distribution,

health and education programs, low-income housing projects, and care for the displaced. Economic aid also directly supports the democratization process through support for elections, the judicial system, and nongovernmental democratic organizations.

These claims notwithstanding, U.S. foreign policy had begun to seriously unravel by the end of the decade. All of Washington's justifications for continuing to support the counterinsurgency project in El Salvador suddenly seemed obviously flawed. Human-rights violations were increasing – a situation brought to international attention by the October 1989 bombing of the FENASTRAS union office and the November 1989 murder of the Jesuits. The FMLN offensive exposed the myth long propagated by the State Department that the guerrilla army had little popular support and lacked military strength.

The U.S. contention that El Salvador was a nascent democracy in which a centrist civilian government exercised control of the country's military forces no longer seemed credible. Rumors of military coups, increased friction between the government and church groups, and the imposition of a state of siege belied U.S. claims that El Salvador had been democratized. Despite the injection of nearly $3 billion in economic aid, the economy had not been stabilized and conditions for most Salvadorans had not improved. Instead the economy was in shambles and there was little real hope for economic recovery.

The U.S. foreign policy – predicated on the assumption that the FMLN was an insignificant political and military force – seemed after ten years to have exhausted all its alternatives. No matter how much military aid and training was lavished on the Salvadoran army and police, they proved unable to gain an upper hand in the war. None of a wide variety of military tactics – from aerial bombings and death-squad terror to civic-action programs and psychological operations – seemed to work in countering the advance of the FMLN and the popular movement. The U.S. political strategy had also stalled when the Christian Democrats were booted out of office by a disgusted populace and the new ARENA government, having no chance of developing the popular support needed to turn the tide of the war, was elected. Invasion by U.S. troops remained a possibility, but a remote one given the likely failure of this option and the international repudiation such an action would generate.

Washington's medium and long-term strategies for El Salvador had all been found wanting. By early 1990 the Bush administration's foreign policy in El Salvador seemed limited to short-term strategizing designed to weather new congressional challenges and to fortify the embattled ARENA government. It clung to badly worn and discredited formulas and appeared incapable of seriously reevaluating and revising its foreign policy in El Salvador.

From Carter to Bush

Shortly before President Carter left office, he authorized military aid for El Salvador, thereby beginning a decade of U.S. commitment to the counterinsurgency war against the FMLN. During the 1980s over $4 billion in U.S. economic and military aid backed this commitment. Although the aid levels of the 1980s were unprecedented, U.S. support for military-controlled regimes in El Salvador was nothing new.

During the Alliance for Progress era of the 1960s the United States had backed economic and military-aid programs designed to modernize the country and block the rise of a leftist alternative. The U.S. Agency for International Development (AID) reported to Congress in the mid-1960s that El Salvador was continuing on its "course of steady progress" and praised the military government as "a model for other Alliance countries." In its 1967 annual budget presentation, AID asserted: "El Salvador has been pushing social reform and economic development on a broad front" and "has taken a leading role in the Central American Common Market and fostered a good climate for foreign investment." Military aid was used to establish a civil-affairs program within the armed forces. According to one U.S. military adviser, the U.S. military aid in the 1960s resulted in "a high degree of expertness and a strengthening of corporate loyalty" within the Salvadoran army.[2]

In the late 1970s military aid was cut off from the hardline regime of Gen. Carlos Humberto Romero as a consequence of the Carter administration's human-rights policy. Some $8 million in annual economic aid, nonetheless, continued to flow to the military government and the 18 U.S. military advisers assigned to the Salvadoran army remained in the country.[3] In 1978 the *New York Times* reported that the U.S. embassy was still "closely identified with the military government."[4] Once it became apparent that the destabilized military government was being seriously challenged by a left-of-center opposition, Washington renewed its direct military aid to El Salvador.

During the early 1980s presidential requests for increasing military aid proved a contentious issue in the U.S. Congress. In the wake of the killings of two U.S. agrarian-reform advisers, four religious workers, an archbishop, and tens of thousands of Salvadorans, Congress made some effort to hold onto the reins of El Salvador policy. From 1979 to mid-1984 Congress required that the president semi-annually certify that human-rights abuses were declining, the land reform was continuing, and efforts were undertaken to achieve a peaceful settlement.[5]

The 1984 election of Duarte and the release of the recommendations of the National Bipartisan Commission on Central America (Kissinger Commission) created a solid bipartisan consensus on El Salvador. With a civilian government and an economic-stabilization plan in place, El Salvador became a non-issue in Congress, where attention had switched to the contra war against Nicaragua. Duarte's election was a major success for the U.S. counterinsurgency strategy. In the view of the State Department, the election demonstrated that there was indeed a political center in El Salvador that was worth defending.

Duarte was elected on a platform of peace and reforms. But neither dialogue nor reforms were on the agenda of the Reagan administration. Uncomfortable with the reformist element in the counterinsurgency plan for El Salvador, the Reagan administration soon dropped its insistence on the full implementation of the agrarian reform. Instead, it began to place new emphasis on projects aimed at supporting the private sector. The war against the FMLN, however, continued to be the overriding priority of Washington. In its second term, the Reagan administration counted on bipartisan support for a prolonged war of attrition aimed at wearing down and isolating the FMLN. Elections, not negotiations, were promoted as the only permissible solution to the civil war. These policies were continued by the Bush administration. But by the end of the 1980s the failures and contradictions of U.S. foreign policy in El Salvador had become more evident.

A Ten-Year Scorecard

After a decade of U.S. military and economic intervention in El Salvador, Washington could only point to one real achievement. Its intervention in the civil war had kept the FMLN-FDR out of power, albeit at a high cost in Salvadoran lives. On the economic side, the U.S. economic-stabilization program was successful only in that it kept a bankrupt government afloat. It failed, however, to spark the promised economic growth.

At the start of 1990 the United States had little to show for its long and costly involvement in El Salvador. The 1980 reforms, originally justified as necessary to move the country from backward oligarchic structure to a modern economy, were in the process of being dismantled by the ARENA government with the support of the U.S. embassy. The economic-aid programs which had as their stated purpose the alleviation of the deteriorating conditions of the country's poor majority turned into military-controlled pacification programs. Large amounts of aid were lost to widespread government corruption during the Duarte years. Military aid proved critical in stopping the military advances of the FMLN but failed to fashion a self-motivated army which could depend on popular support and was committed to fighting an unconventional war.

Perhaps the greatest failure of U.S. foreign policy was its apparent inability to recognize and respond to the class nature of the conflict. The 1980 reforms had represented a superficial but still meaningful attempt to address the war's underlying causes. Despite persistent rhetoric about its commitment to improve socioeconomic conditions, U.S. policy had, in practice, allied itself with the rich. The continued support for the military after the Jesuit killings and Washington's failure to insist that those murders be properly investigated highlighted U.S. complicity in the dirty war.[6]

After a decade of intervention Washington continued to justify its support for the counterinsurgency war with the same foreign policy myths that U.S. intervention was bolstering a political center, protecting civilians against terrorism, and strengthening the transition to democracy.[7] But frustration was growing in Congress with the failure of U.S. policy to bring the war to an end, and in late 1990 the lawmakers cut U.S. military aid to El Salvador by 50 percent. The aid cut, which would be revoked if the FMLN launched another large offensive, sent a clear signal to the Salvadoran army that it could no longer count on steady U.S. backing for its program of militarism and repression. As Salvadorans begin to look to a future without war, they also will have to face the long-term consequences of this intervention. El Salvador has become extremely dependent of U.S. economic aid — which approached $1 million a day in the 1980s. The eventual absence of this stabilization aid will be profoundly destabilizing. The country has also grown dependent on large injections of U.S. food aid and will face serious food shortages if this aid is also cut. Lasting peace in El Salvador will also be threatened by the future of a 55,000-member professional army and the mountains of weaponry and aircraft that the United States may leave behind.[8]

U.S. Trade and Investment

The United States dominates the country's foreign trade and investment. About 70 percent of the country's exports go to the United States and 40 percent of its imports come from the United States.[9] With $95 million in direct foreign investment in El Salvador, the United States accounts for 48 percent of total foreign investment in the country.[10]

The U.S. exports to El Salvador consist largely of grain, animal fats and vegetable oils, fertilizer, chemicals, pharmaceuticals, electrical machinery, and paper products. The United States supplies virtually all the country's imported food and is the main supplier of intermediate and capital goods for its industrial sector. Exports to the United States are primarily coffee, shrimp, sugar, textiles, and electrical capacitors.

The major U.S. investors in El Salvador, in order of economic significance, are Esso Standard Oil, Kimberly Clark, AVX Ceramics, Crown Zellerbach, Texaco Caribbean, Chevron Oil, and Foremost-McKesson. Other U.S. corporations with substantial investments are: National Cash Register, Phelps Dodge, Cargill, and Minnesota Mining and Manufacturing.[11] Of the $196 million in direct foreign investment registered, the United States accounts for about half. Panama and Japan are the next largest investors after the United States, followed by Canada. The Japanese have substantial investment in the textile industry; Bayer of Canada dominates the agrochemical industry; and Shell Petroleum is also a major presence.

The main sectors of U.S. investment are the petroleum industry, manufacturing, and services. Direct U.S. investment was sparked in the 1960s by the opening up of the Central American Common Market and the subsequent formation of import-substitution industries, mainly in the food-processing sector. Transnational corporations also came to El Salvador in the 1970s to establish *maquiladora*-type export-processing plants, mostly in textiles and electronics. There is no substantial U.S. investment in the agricultural sector, although large firms like General Foods, Coca-Cola, and Proctor & Gamble do buy Salvadoran coffee. Through the Salvadoran Foundation for Social and Economic Development (FUSADES) and the Latin American Agribusiness Development Corporation (LAAD), AID subsidizes U.S. private investment in the production and processing of nontraditional agroexports. Except for melon production, this development strategy has failed to generate significant export income. In 1980 the Bank of America left the country after the military-civilian junta nationalized banking, while Citibank maintains offices within the country.

In recent years the only economic sector in which direct U.S. investment has increased has been in services. McDonald's is one of several U.S. fastfood firms operating in the country, the luxury hotels are owned by U.S. firms, Taca Airlines is largely U.S. owned, and U.S. advertising and consulting firms do an active business in El Salvador. AID-funded infrastructure-repair projects and its development-assistance programs have also brought U.S. firms to the country.

As part of an effort to increase foreign investment, AID pressured the Salvadoran government to pass the 1986 Export Promotion Law and the 1988 Foreign Investment Development and Guarantee Law, both of which give preferential tax treatment to new foreign investors. AID is also funding the expansion of the San Bartolo Free Trade Zone and the creation of a new privately owned industrial zone for export-processing factories.

U.S. Economic Aid

Between $300 and $320 million in U.S. economic assistance enters El Salvador each year through the AID Mission in San Salvador. About two-thirds of this annual allotment arrives in the form of Economic Assistance Funds (ESF), with the balance split between Development Assistance and PL480 food aid. This aid exceeds the Salvadoran government's own contribution to its budget. The large injection of direct AID assistance is complemented by other sizable foreign-aid programs. These include those of the U.S. Department of Agriculture's Commodity Credit Corporation (CCC), the Overseas Private Investment Corporation (OPIC), Trade Investment Insurance Program of the Export-Import Bank (Eximbank), as well as millions of dollars channeled through AID's regional and Washington offices for labor programs, disaster preparedness, business strengthening, and a variety of other programs. In addition, hundreds of millions of dollars have been directed to El Salvador in the last ten years through the Inter-American Development Bank and the World Bank.

In describing U.S. assistance programs, there is the immediate difficulty in defining what is truly "economic" and what should be better counted as military or political aid. In its reports on U.S. economic aid in El Salvador, the Arms Control and Foreign Policy Caucus of the U.S. Congress has rejected State Department statements that most U.S. aid to El Salvador is economic. Instead, the Arms Control Caucus has more correctly defined most AID assistance (about 75 percent) as "war-related."[12]

Seeking Stability with Dollars

Economic stabilization has been one of the chief goals of U.S. economic aid. It has also been one of the most successful elements of AID's program in war-torn El Salvador. Economic stabilization refers basically to the effort to keep the government and the economy afloat by alleviating the country's foreign-exchange shortage and resulting balance-of-payments crisis. By pumping about a million dollars a day into the country, AID relieves the government of the debt-servicing pressures and dollar shortages that plague other third world nations. During the 1980s El Salvador has ranked among the top half-dozen countries receiving ESF and Title I stabilization aid.

Without this stabilization aid El Salvador would have faced the kind of economic bankruptcy confronting Nicaragua – which, in contrast, has been virtually cut off from all Western bilateral and multilateral aid. From the start AID has defined stabilization aid only as a necessary first step toward economic recovery and growth. But contrary to AID projections, this stabilization assistance has not provided the foundation for the economic progress. Instead, the country has grown increasingly dependent on the injections of stabilization funds and has failed even to match pre-war levels of economic activity. Sharp declines in export income in recent years threaten the artificial economic stability that AID's massive stabilization program has managed to achieve.[13]

AID for Pacification

Political stabilization and pacification (or population control) represent another major thrust of economic-assistance programming in El Salvador. In the context of a civil war, the "development" objectives of the Agency for International Development have been largely interpreted according to the imperatives of the U.S. counterinsurgency project. Economic-aid programs are designed to complement the strictly military aspects of counterinsurgency. As it did in Vietnam, AID funds and manages this "other war."[14]

While striving to keep the economy stable, AID has also played a leading role in seeking to establish a pro-U.S. political stability in the country. The U.S. government calls this political focus of economic aid "democratization." Recognizing that a key ingredient of counterinsurgency is the existence of a government capable of maintaining a wide base of national and international support, the U.S. government lent its support to the establishment of a Christian Democratic government that could claim centrist and moderate credentials. It also financed an elaborate electoral system to give credibility to U.S. assertions that El Salvador is a democratic republic fighting off a challenge by anti-democratic leftwing terrorists.

The economic reforms announced by the military-civilian junta in March 1980 constituted a major component of the political stabilization program of the early 1980s. According to AID, the agrarian-reform program was "a political imperative to help prevent political collapse, strike a blow to the left, and help prevent radicalization of the rural population." Accompanying the land-distribution program was a rural organizing campaign by the AID-funded American Institute for Free Labor Development (AIFLD). The cooperatives, rural associations, and labor coalitions sponsored by AIFLD formed the main organized popular base for the Christian Democratic government. After Duarte won the presidential election in 1984, AID support for economic reformism slackened, leaving the reform sector without adequate financial and technical support.

Although initial support for popular reforms diminished, AID did not lose sight of the importance of winning Salvadoran hearts and minds for the counterinsurgency project. Rather than addressing the structural injustices of the society, however, AID chose after 1983 to stress programs aimed at controlling the rural population through pacification strategies. Several new government agencies were created for the express purpose of pacifying the rising displaced population and the communities in conflictive zones. These AID-funded agencies included the National Commission for Aid to the Displaced (CONADES) and the National Commission for the Restoration of Areas (CONARA).

The military-controlled CONARA served as the main channel for AID pacification aid. As an AID evaluation of CONARA explained: "CONARA seeks to challenge the guerrilla presence not through military strategies but by creating positive images of the government in the minds of the population."[15] AID funds have flowed through CONARA to support the military's civic-action programs, National Plan, United to Reconstruct (UPR) program, the Chilatenango '88 program, Municipalities in Action, and the Plan Oriente '89 of the ARENA government. Local currency generated from the sales of ESF dollars and Title I food has footed the bill for CONARA and the other pacification agencies.

Yet another aspect of political stabilization is the "institution-building" support AID and the Department of Justice have offered to variety of governmental and nongovernmental institutions in El Salvador. Most of this aid is administered by AID's Office of Democratic Initiatives. To refurbish the democratic image of the government, AID in 1984 launched several projects to strengthen the country's judicial system by offering training courses and through the creation of a Special Investigative Unit (SIU) and a Judicial Protection Unit. As part of its democratization program AID also finances the Revisory Commission on Salvadoran Legislation, which works with the National Assembly in reviewing and revising laws, regulations, and procedures of the country's judicial system.

After six years of funding Washington had little to show for this judicial project: human-rights abuses by security forces were still not being investigated or prosecuted and the judicial system remained hostage to military and political control. The program had not addressed the fundamental weakness of the judicial system, namely its lack of independence. Instead, military detectives and other members of the security forces were being hired and trained to investigate human-rights abuses and protect judges and witnesses. A 1989 report by the Lawyers Committee for Human Rights, *Underwriting Justice: AID and El Salvador's Judicial Reform Program*, concluded that the U.S.-initiated project had failed to rectify the inability of the country's judicial system to prosecute human-rights cases.[16] Another project of the Office of Democratic Initiatives is the governmental Human Rights Commission (CDH), which looks the other way at human-rights violations by the security forces while acting as arm of the military high command in its condemnation of the FMLN.

Institution-building also extends to private organizations. As part of its democratization program, AID has worked through AIFLD to create anti-leftist peasant and labor associations. To fortify the private sector, a phalanx of business promotion and pressure groups have been created through the AID-sponsored Salvadoran Foundation for Social and Economic Development (FUSADES). In addition, AID works with numerous local and U.S. nongovernmental organizations to carry out its various pacification projects. (See Nongovernmental Organizations)

Using Aid to Leverage Reforms

In 1980, when U.S. military and economic aid began flowing into El Salvador, the Salvadoran government and military had little alternative but to accede to U.S. policy demands. As an integral part of the counterinsurgency project foisted on the country by Washington, the military-civilian junta announced a series of economic reforms, rewrote the constitution, and established an election schedule.

Throughout the 1980s the U.S. embassy continued to use its aid package as leverage for desired policy changes. But the nature of the "reforms" proposed by AID markedly changed over the course of the decade. Although the earlier reforms were explicitly designed to improve the lot of the poor and support a centrist political alternative, AID's "policy dialogues" with the government during more recent years increasingly turned to measures designed to promote the business sector and support IMF-type structural adjustment.

Among the policy changes or reforms advocated by AID in the late 1980s were increased government credit to the private sector, reduced public spending, legislation for a new investment law and export promotion law, the privatization of state-owned enterprises, increased interest rates, liberalization of international trade, and devaluation – all of which impact most severely on the poor.

Nowhere has this change of policy priorities been so evident and shocking as in the agrarian-reform program. Rather than using its aid package to insist on the full implementation of the program, AID quietly backed away from its former commitment to agrarian reform. Instead of demanding that the agrarian-reform sector receive adequate credit and technical assistance, AID now stipulates that its development assistance go to commercially successful agribusinesses and to those areas of the agricultural sector "where comparative advantage exists."[17]

In line with ARENA's own bias towards privatization and against cooperative development, AID dropped its agrarian-reform projects. Instead, it announced its intention to support a privately run land-sales bank and supported legislation allowing the government to sell off agrarian-reform cooperatives to individual *campesinos*. To facilitate this privatization process, AID encouraged the reform cooperatives to enter into agribusiness projects with former owners or other private investors.[18]

AID now dismisses the 1980 reforms as economically unsound and defines development almost exclusively in terms of increased exports and new private investment. A small amount of the AID budget is still allocated to social services such as health, education, and low-income housing. But even here, the aid is often directed through the private sector. Education funds go to such groups as FUSADES and the Junior Achievement, a group sponsoring high-school instruction in the principles of capitalism. FUSADES, which was established in 1982 with AID funds, is the standard-bearer of AID's private-enterprise development program. With a staff of nearly a hundred and a dozen branch organizations, FUSADES is the country's main center for economic planning. Tens of millions of AID funds have been channeled to FUSADES.[19]

U.S. Military Aid

Creating a Client Military

During the first years of the war in El Salvador anti-intervention activists in the United States sought to spark public and congressional opposition to the war by likening stepped up U.S. involvement in El Salvador to the experience in Vietnam. There were, of course, many parallels. Both were wars of counterinsurgency in countries of little economic interest to the United States. The guerrilla opposition in both cases espoused socialist solutions, and neither government enjoyed wide public support.

Many of the counterinsurgency programs implemented—agrarian reform, election campaigns, extensive use of food aid, nation building strategies, etc.—also bore a close resemblance.

As the civil war in El Salvador intensified, however, the differences between the two cases became more obvious. Some 55,000 U.S. troops died on Vietnamese soil while only seven U.S. military personnel have died in El Salvador.[20] The lack of major direct military intervention in El Salvador has kept it a "small war" in U.S. military terms and has kept military aid to El Salvador from ever becoming a prominent public concern in the United States. If asked, most U.S. citizens would oppose military aid to El Salvador, but Washington has not asked for public approval of U.S. support for this dirty war. And without large-scale intervention of U.S. troops, there has been only small-scale public outcry over the significant military role that Washington does play in continuing the war.

Still, after a decade of war, the Vietnam analogy is being increasingly alluded to, mostly in terms of the United States having wandered into a quagmire with no honorable way to extricate itself. After ten years of military aid and intervention, there are voices in the State Department and the Pentagon claiming to see "the light at the end of the tunnel." But military experts are already beginning to think about the El Salvador war in the same way they did the one in Vietnam—as a lesson of what not to do in "small wars" in the third world. In 1988 a team of U.S. Army colonels produced an extensive report entitled *American Military Policy in Small Wars: The Case of El Salvador*, which called the El Salvador counterinsurgency war "a fertile ground for teaching Americans" how to avoid similar mistakes in future low-intensity conflicts elsewhere in the world.[21]

Facts and Fiction of Military Assistance

U.S. assistance to El Salvador does not fit easily into the two major aid categories: military and economic. Most economic aid is war-related, even food aid and development programs. Even using the Pentagon's own limited definition of military aid, this category of assistance is quite substantial. Since 1980 over $1 billion in U.S. military aid has been used to keep the Salvadoran armed forces trained, equipped, and on the battlefield. This does not include the costs of maintaining U.S. advisers in the country, nor the various logistical and intelligence services provided by the U.S. Southern Command, the CIA, Defense Intelligence Agency (DIA), or National Security Council (NSC).

Although not officially designated as military aid, the United States also provides support and training for Salvadoran security forces. Congress terminated AID's controversial international police-training program in 1974, but special congressional waivers have allowed Washington to sponsor several police-assistance and training programs in El Salvador. Through AID and the Justice Department, programs train and supply special criminal and judicial police units and prison police. Since 1983 the country's police forces have received training as part of the State Department's Anti-Terrorism Assistance (ATA) program.[22] Beginning in 1985 the ATA program was complemented by a much larger program designed to combat urban "terrorism." As part of the U.S. government's counterterrorist assistance to El Salvador, three special units of the Salvadoran security forces were trained: Special Antiterrorist Force, Liberator, and Lightning Battalion.[23]

The lack of clarity about the full extent of U.S. military commitment to El Salvador is best illustrated by Washington's claim that there have been only 55 U.S. military advisers in the country at any one time. Even U.S. military sources place that figure closer to 150,[24] while Salvadoran military sources place the figure at 300. In addition, Salvadoran military sources estimate that for each U.S. military adviser there is at least one other U.S. adviser connected to the CIA, DIA, or NSC working in intelligence or security operations.[25] A major recipient of covert U.S. aid is the National Directorate of Intelligence (DNI), which is a large intelligence and special operations center financed by the CIA.[26]

Within the country, the contingent of U.S. military advisers is coordinated by the Military Advisory and Assistance Group (MILGROUP). An Operations and Training Team (OPATT) is assigned to each Salvadoran brigade. Officially, they do not engage in combat themselves, but sometimes it becomes clear that the official story disguises the truth. A 1988 recommendation for awarding medals to two Marines was turned down by a review board at U.S. Southern Command when it was determined that the Marines had organized and led a counterattack against a guerrilla unit which had attacked the 6th Infantry Brigade in Usulután.[27] More than advisers, U.S. officers have provided intelligence to the Salvadoran Air Force allowing them to pinpoint targets for aerial bombardment.[28]

Initially, the large injection of U.S. military aid in the early 1980s was approved in the belief that the Salvadoran army with adequate U.S. support could easily crush the incipient guerrilla movement. By 1983, however, it became clear that a longer term and better planned commitment was needed to defeat the well-established guerrilla forces. It was that year when U.S. advisers began paying closer attention to the implementation of a broad counterinsurgency strategy. Psychological operations (Psyops) teams were formed, an air-war strategy put in place, elite hunter battalions trained, a civic-action and nation-building campaign designed, and the U.S. commitment of aid and advisers expanded. To win the war, the United States stepped in to direct the war, restructure the army, train the troops, and financially back a long-term war of attrition against the FMLN.

Although the level of military aid increased dramatically in the 1980s, the Salvadoran military and police already had a long history of being aided and trained by Washington. Between 1950 and 1980 the Salvadoran military received $16.8 million in military aid and had over 2100 of its officers trained at U.S. military schools.[29] During the 1980s congressional sponsors of military aid to El Salvador often cited the need to professionalize the Salvadoran military. It was, in fact, the Pentagon which for over three decades had been providing the country's officer corps with "professional" training in such courses as Urban Counterinsurgency, Basic Officer Preparation, and Basic Combat and Counterinsurgency. In addition, AID, through its Office of Public Safety, had trained (from 1957 to 1974) 448 police officers through U.S. courses designed to "develop the managerial and operational skills and effectiveness."[30]

Military-aid requests in the 1980s were regularly couched in language about the necessity of defending the country's fragile democracy against a communist conspiracy and to allow the country to rebuild its economy in the face of guerrilla terrorism. An emergency grant of $5.7 million in military aid requested by President Carter in late 1979 set off the present era of U.S. military intervention in El Salvador. Called the "decisive battle for Central America" by the Reagan administration, within a few years the counterinsurgency war in El Salvador was supported annually by over $80 million in direct military aid.

The Bush administration backed its request for a continued high level of aid on the grounds that "U.S. security assistance contributes to regional stability. It also promotes professionalism, respect for human rights, self-sufficiency, and deference to civilian leadership." According to the administration, U.S. military aid is needed because "the guerrillas continue to reject conciliation that would be keyed to elections." Not only is the aid needed, but the Pentagon says it has also proved successful. "The armed forces have become increasingly successful in countering ever-changing guerrilla tactics." Military aid in 1988 and 1989 was "aimed principally at sustainment," while 1990 aid is necessary for "the replacement and reconditioning of essential equipment, particularly helicopters."[31]

A Field Test for Low-Intensity Conflict Doctrine

Since 1983 the predominant military doctrine applied in El Salvador has been what its advocates call Low-Intensity Conflict (LIC). Defined from the perspective of the United States, the two main characteristics of LIC are the limited involvement of U.S. military personnel (therefore "low intensity") and the coordination of a broad range of elements in the counterrevolutionary offensive, including: economic aid, food assistance, civic-action programs, psychological operations, electoral campaigns, military terror, and private relief activities.

Once having discovered that the guerrilla insurgency could not be quickly erased, U.S. military strategists came to accept the war as a prolonged low-intensity conflict. This long-range war would be fought on two fronts. Politically, a civilian government would work to create a sense of national unity and patriotism through economic reforms, while military/civic action and Psyops programs would seek to reduce popular support for the guerrillas in the conflictive zones. Militarily, the well-supplied Salvadoran military, relying on its logistical advantage and superior fire power, would wear down the FMLN.

Dissatisfaction with the progress of the war has surfaced within the U.S. military. The 1988 report *American Military Policy in Small Wars* by a team of U.S. Army colonels offered a devastating critique of the war.[32] Once again, the United States found itself in a tunnel with no light at the end: "By most estimates," noted the authors, "the war in El Salvador is stuck; unhappily the United States finds itself stuck with the war."

Unlike the rightist critique of the war strategy, the colonels did not advocate a higher-intensity war but rather stressed that a low-intensity conflict strategy integrating political and economic reforms was the only possible way to fight "small wars." Military victory requires "first redressing the grievances of the Salvadoran people." But typical of other counterinsurgency strategists, they never specified the nature of the "genuine reforms" needed nor addressed the real obstacles preventing the implementation of such preemptive social reforms. Instead of advocating reforms that would address the country's structural injustices, the colonels called for better coordination of current pacification strategies sponsored by AID, the Salvadoran government, and the Civil Affairs Division of the Salvadoran army.

For the U.S. colonels, U.S. military aid and training are inappropriate, misdirected, and narrowly conceived. "Almost instinctively," they said, "Americans take a rich man's approach to the war." Seemingly unlimited supplies of U.S. technology — aircraft, artillery, antitank weapons — reinforced the Salvadoran armed forces' bias toward conventional warfare while keeping them immobile, isolated from the people, overly reliant on mass firepower. "Despite professed American intentions, the Salvadorans today are using a conventional army and conventional tactics to fight an unconventional war." By 1988 U.S. military aid had "reached the point of diminishing returns."

The *Small Wars* report also lamented the absence of a coherent U.S. approach to the war. With no consensus at home and the lack of a total U.S. commitment to win the war, the authors claimed that counterinsurgency has floundered and the war remains stalemated. While they agree with the decision in Washington not to "gringo-ize the war" through more direct U.S. intervention, the colonels noted that "avoiding American casualties...became the preeminent goal" of U.S. military advisers. But even without direct U.S. combat intervention, the war is, at its heart, a gringo war. As the report states: "Terminating American support for El Salvador with guerrillas still in the field will result in the armed forces' defeat and the collapse of the Government of El Salvador." Furthermore:

> Avoiding direct combat in "small wars" does not necessarily translate into greater latitude in determining how and when the United States might extricate itself. Although the United States has wisely kept the Salvadoran war "theirs" to fight, the years of American involvement have made that conflict in a political sense "our war."

Like Vietnam, the U.S. military entered El Salvador full of Yankee confidence. As the determination of the guerrillas and the structural problems of the country became more evident, initial optimism turned to cynicism and helplessness. Now the problem is how to escape the quagmire. But as the colonels observed: "Withdrawal without credible evidence of success will result in embarrassment, diminished credibility, and sacrifice of important interests."

In late 1989, after the high-profile murder of the Jesuits, voices were again heard in Congress demanding that U.S. military aid be conditioned on the prosecution of human-rights violators within the military. But short of direct U.S. military intervention, the United States was dependent on the Salvadoran military to fight the war. It could demand that some elements within the army be scapegoated for human-rights violations but had to be careful not to threaten the stability and tenuous unity of military institutions unless it was prepared for a FMLN victory.

Addressing the issue of U.S. dependence on the Salvadoran military, Col. Robert Herrick, former head of a U.S. Army think tank monitoring the war, observed: "It's the same mistake we made in Vietnam. Military aid is easy; all you have to do is give the bucks, and all they have to do is take them. But we got ourselves into a position where we have no leverage, so we have been acquiescing for years in corruption and methods of operations we don't believe in, all because of the *realpolitik* of winning the war."[33] The *realpolitik* of U.S. military policy in El Salvador has, however, been more than simply handing out dollars and passing around U.S. arms. Washington has played a central role in directing this dirty war in which popular organizations, churches, universities, and indeed the Salvadoran people themselves are regarded as justifiable targets in a counterinsurgency war. Neither congressionally imposed human-rights conditioning of U.S. aid nor presidential proclamations about U.S. commitments to democratic rule can alter the fact that it is the United States that provides the guns, dictates the counterinsurgency strategy, and trains the soldiers in El Salvador. A central actor is this third world tragedy, the U.S. government cannot wash its hands of the blood of the Salvadoran people.

Other Foreign Interests

Outside of the United States and Central America itself, West Germany is El Salvador's principal export market. In some years it has rivaled the United States itself, purchasing goods valued at between $100 and $200 million. Purchasing over $10 million worth of goods annually are Canada, Japan, and Spain. The distribution of imports is somewhat different. Outside of Central America and the United States, principal suppliers are Japan, West Germany, the United Kingdom, Italy, the Netherlands, and Canada.[34] Apart from the United States, the most significant countries in terms of government-to-government aid and technical assistance are West Germany, Great Britain, Israel, and Canada. For Canada and the West Europeans, the general pattern was for a cessation of government aid during the periods of notorious civil-rights violations under the Romero government of the late 1970s and during the "death squad" years of the early 1980s. With the transition to civilian government, these countries, like the United States, resumed aid.

In late 1989 the European Economic Community (EEC), Spain, and West Germany cut off economic aid to the ARENA government in response to increased human-rights violations. Rather than channel aid to the displaced and other war victims through the Cristiani government, most foreign governments, with the principle exception being the United States, directed their aid to nongovernmental organizations working outside the government's own network.

The fact that conservative leaders held power in all three countries — Kohl in West Germany, Thatcher in Britain, and Mulroney in Canada — made it easier for their policies to work in parallel with that of the United

States during most of the 1980s, although the legislative opposition in all three countries demonstrated a sensitivity to human-rights questions in El Salvador.

West German foreign aid is channeled through the nongovernmental sector; public money is given to the foundations operated by the political parties and the churches. The principal emphases of West German funding have been rural development, food production, and technical assistance. Although leftwing Salvadoran leaders have visited Bonn to lobby against these aid programs, where they found support in the small opposition Green Party, the more compelling arguments were those of Duarte, like Kohl a member of the international Christian Democratic movement. The $40 million-plus provided to El Salvador by West Germany during the first half of the 1980s made West Germany El Salvador's second largest source of development assistance.[35]

The Thatcher government in Great Britain has made a point of supporting Reagan's policies wherever possible. Arms sales had been halted under the Romero government, and British representatives in international financial institutions declined to support Salvadoran requests for funding. These policies were reversed when the decision was made to support the Duarte government. British aid has taken the form of offering training for Salvadoran soldiers at British bases in Belize, scholarships for Salvadoran students in Britain, and a grant for civilian purchases from Britain.[36] The money amounts involved in British aid have not been substantial, however.

Canada has traditionally traded with El Salvador and invested there (the Montreal-based International Power Company, which furnished San Salvador with electricity, was one of the last power systems in Central America to be nationalized, in 1977).[37] Canada has been one of the destinations of refugees from El Salvador.

In search of an international role, Canada became committed to a program of aid and technical assistance to developing countries during the 1960s. In 1981, however, bilateral assistance to El Salvador was discontinued in response to human-rights violations and out of concern for the safety of Canadian field workers. Although some Canadian money continued to reach El Salvador from multilateral institutions, the Canadians joined in Western European efforts to block credit to El Salvador following the rape and murder of the four U.S. churchwomen in 1980. Canada also supported efforts in the United Nations to condemn El Salvador's human-rights record and demand an end to U.S. military assistance. However, the Canadian government resumed aid with the establishment of the Duarte government, at a level of about $6 million Canadian annually.[38]

Israel's relations with El Salvador are built on a tradition of good relations that started with El Salvador's favorable vote for the establishment of the state of Israel. Israel has offered technical assistance in fields such as agricultural development, where Israeli experience was extensive and often unique, and capital requirements were not great.

Israel became El Salvador's second most important arms supplier after the United States during the early 1970s, and its largest supplier when the Carter administration discontinued arms sales to El Salvador in 1977. During this latter period, Israeli technicians installed a computerized system that enabled the Salvadoran army to track surges in telephone and utility use, useful in locating insurgent operations. Israel has also supplied police trainers to El Salvador, a role legally prohibited the U.S. government, and during the early 1980s placed more than a hundred military advisers in the country. El Salvador has reciprocated by moving its embassy in Israel to Jerusalem, a recognition of that disputed city as Israel's capital which most countries have refused to make.[39]

Reference Notes

Introduction

1. Joaquín Villalobos, "Popular Insurrection: Desire or Reality?" *Latin American Perspectives*, Summer 1989.
2. Quoted in Kenneth J. Grieb, "The United States and the Rise of General Maximiliano Hernández Martínez," *Journal of Latin American Studies*, November 1971, p. 152.
3. Communication with Americas Watch, January 23, 1990.
4. Segundo Montes, Florentín Meléndez, and Edgar Palacios, *Los Derechos Económicos, Sociales, y Culturales en El Salvador* (San Salvador: IDHUCA, May 1988).
5. Housing figures from FUSADES, cited in *Proceso*, August 30, 1989.
6. Brook Larmer, "Papering Over the Economic Divide," *Christian Science Monitor*, October 21, 1988.
7. *New York Times*, October 16, 1988, citing AID figures.
8. Segundo Montes, *Estructura de Clases y Comportamiento de las Fuerzas Sociales* (San Salvador: IDHUCA, 1988).

Chapter One

1. Total votes by election: 1982: 1,551,687; 1984: 1,419,493; 1985: 1,101,606; 1988: 1,083,812; and 1989: 1,003,153. *Proceso*, April 5, 1989.
2. *Proceso*, April 12, 1989.
3. Philip L. Russell, *El Salvador in Crisis* (Austin: Colorado River Press, 1984), p. 90.
4. Ibid., p. 91.
5. ARENA won 19 additional seats in the Assembly while the PDC lost 11, and ARENA gained control of 178 municipalities while the PDC lost 174.

6. Lindsey Gruson, "The Right's New Face," *New York Times*, March 21, 1989.

7. Raúl Marín, "Una Ofensiva Anunciada," *Pensamiento Propio*, December 1989.

8. Sara Miles and Bob Ostertag, "D'Aubuisson's New ARENA," *NACLA Report on the Americas*, July 1989, p. 15.

9. Quoted by Alexander Cockburn in "Beat the Devil," *The Nation*, May 15, 1989.

10. *Facing Reality in El Salvador: Cristiani's First 100 Days* (Philadelphia: NARMIC/American Friends Service Committee, November 1989), p. 10.

11. "El Salvador Notes: April 1989," (AFSC).

12. According to José Antonio Morales Erlich, cited in Gianni Beretta and Camino Lagos, "ARENA United in Purpose," *Regionews*, July 1, 1989.

13. *Central America Report*, October 27, 1989.

14. *Latin American News Update*, January 1990.

15. Beretta and Lagos, *Regionews*, op. cit.

16. *Facing Reality in El Salvador*, op. cit., p. 13.

17. *Proceso*, May 17, 1989.

18. Raúl Marín, "La Ultraderecha Contra Todos," *Pensamiento Propio*, December 1988.

19. Morris J. Blachman and Kenneth E. Sharpe, "Things Fall Apart: Trouble Ahead in El Salvador," *World Policy Journal*, Winter 1988-1989, p. 118.

20. Miles and Ostertag, *NACLA Report on the Americas*, op. cit., p. 24.

21. Gianni Beretta, "Todos Contra ARENA," *Pensamiento Propio*, August 1989.

22. Thomas P. Anderson, "El Salvador," in Richard F. Staar, ed., *Yearbook on International Communist Affairs* (Stanford: Hoover Institution Press, 1981), p. 72.

23. Marc Shaffer, "Rubén Zamora: The Opposition has to Get Together," *The Progressive*, July 1989.

24. Joaquín Villalobos, "Popular Insurrection: Desire or Reality?" *Latin American Perspectives*, Summer 1989.

25. "El Salvador: Presidential Election News Notes," *Update* (Central American Historical Institute), November 21, 1988.

26. Ibid.

27. Interview by Terry Karl with Salvador Samoya, "Negotiations or Total War," *World Policy Journal,* Spring 1989, p.331.

28. *Central America Report,* March 17, 1989.

29. *Central America Report,* October 20, 1989.

30. Jack Calhoun, "U.S. Firms Engineered Elections," *Guardian,* April 12, 1989.

31. Villalobos, *Latin American Perspectives,* op. cit.

32. Tom Barry and Debra Preusch, *El Salvador: The Other War* (Albuquerque: Resource Center, 1986).

33. This program aims to extend local government structures in conflictive or formerly conflictive areas which can direct and coordinate resources made available through CONARA and other AID-financed pacification efforts. As of 1988, AID had trained over 250 local governmental officials and had organized a National Association of Municipalities (COMURES) and the Salvadoran Municipal Development Institute (ISDEM), both of which are now under ARENA control.

34. Interview by Debra Preusch with AID Mission official in San Salvador, September 17, 1987.

35. Allan Austin, Luis Flores, and Donald Stout, *CONARA Impact Evaluation* (Research Triangle Institute, AID Contract PDC-0000-I-00-6169-00), September 20, 1988.

36. See interview by Terry Karl with Salvador Samoya, *World Policy Journal,* op. cit., p. 345.

37. "El Poder de Doble Cara," (FMLN internal document, 1987) as cited in *NACLA Report on the Americas,* September 1989.

38. Sara Miles and Bob Ostertag, "FMLN New Thinking," *NACLA Report on the Americas,* September 1989, p. 22.

39. James A. Morris, *Honduras: Caudillo Politics and Military Rulers* (Boulder, CO: Westview Press, 1984); Thomas P. Anderson, *The War of the Dispossessed: Honduras and El Salvador 1969* (Lincoln: University of Nebraska Press, 1986).

40. The Contadora Group first met in January 1983 on the Panamanian island of Contadora and included representatives from Mexico, Panama, Venezuela, and Colombia. A Contadora Support Group, formed in July 1985, included Brazil, Argentina, Uruguay, and Peru. The main thrust of Contadora was to formulate an agreement that would limit foreign intervention in Central America—whether it be from the United States or Cuba. When it became clear that

Nicaragua supported the Contadora peace process and would sign
an agreement, Washington sought to undermine the process. El
Salvador, under U.S. pressure, backed away from the Contadora
process. In June 1986 El Salvador's foreign minister called for the
Contadora peace process to be set aside, saying: "We urgently
need to resort to more active and dynamic forums. We are leaving
the forum of complacency to turn to a more demanding forum."
Soon, the Contadora process slowed to a standstill. For the best
description and analysis of the Contadora peace process, see the
following: Jim Morrell and William Goodfellow, "Contadora:
Under the Gun," *International Policy Report*, May 1986 and
"Contadora Will Continue" *International Policy Report*, June 27,
1986.

41. Sara Miles and Bob Ostertag, "Rethinking War, Rethinking
    Peace," *NACLA Report on the Americas*, September 1989.

42. *Central America Report*, September 1, 1989.

43. President Cristiani went into the San Isidro Coronado summit of
    December 10, 1989 intent on condemning Nicaragua for having
    allegedly supplied arms to the FMLN. On the defensive because of
    reports that a Nicaraguan plane carrying arms had been shot down
    in El Salvador, President Ortega signed the accord condemning
    "the armed and terrorist actions of the irregular forces of the
    region" and calling for the FMLN to lay down its arms apparently
    in an effort to keep the regional peace talks alive.

44. Amnesty International, *El Salvador: Death Squads — A Government
    Strategy* (New York, October 1988).

45. Americas Watch, *Nightmare Revisited: 1987-1988* (New York, 1988).

46. Cited in Human Rights Watch and Lawyers Committee for Human
    Rights, *The Reagan Administration's Record on Human Rights*
    (New York, 1989).

47. Ibid.

48. Americas Watch, *The Civilian Toll: 1986-1987* (New York, 1987).

49. Edward S. Herman, "Disinformation as News Fit to Print," *Covert
    Action Information Bulletin*, Winter 1988.

50. Walt Spencer, "Herbert Ernesto Anaya Sanabria: 1954-1987,"
    Links (National Central America Health Rights Network), Winter
    1987.

51. Americas Watch, *Nightmare Revisited: 1987-1988* (New York, 1988).

52. Ibid.

53. Ibid.

54. Victoria Sanford, "Of Death Squads and Depopulation," *Bulletin of Municipal Foreign Policy,* Winter 1988-1989.

55. U.S. Department of State, *Country Reports on Human Rights Practices for 1988* (Washington, February 1989), pp. 564-565.

56. Lindsey Gruson, "Tension Rise in Salvador After Arrests," *New York Times,* January 15, 1989.

Chapter Two

1. ARENA placed first in the Constituent Assembly elections, and Roberto D'Aubuisson was elected as the Assembly president. Acting to prevent the probable selection of D'Aubuisson as the country's provisional president, the U.S. embassy and the army, which was dependent on U.S. aid, pressured the Assembly to choose instead Alvaro Magaña, a little-known banker from a wealthy coffee family.

2. U.S. military advisers have described the pre-1980 Salvadoran armed forces as "a militia of 11,000 that had no mission" which "acted historically as a blight on the political system." While the army claims now to have about 50,000 men, the FMLN say that number is inflated, the real number being 36,000 to 38,000.

3. The proclaimed number of civil-defense members also appears inflated, given the self-acknowledged failure of the army to organize the population in conflictive areas to take up arms or to establish paramilitary groups.

4. Figures from the Ministry of Treasury, cited in Alexander Segovia, "Límites y Dilemas de la Política Económica en un País en Guerra: El Caso de El Salvador," *Realidad Económico-Social,* November-December 1988.

5. *Central America Report,* February 8, 1985.

6. The United States has attempted unsuccessfully to reform the officer corps, while also attempting to develop a cadre of noncommissioned officers which are regarded as essential for small unit operations. But the concept of noncommissioned officers is alien to the military establishment, which "consists of the commissioned officer elite above and short-service peasant conscripts below." Only 10 percent of the noncommissioned officers trained in the United States reenlist for another term. Ltc. A. J. Bacevich, Ltc. James Hallums, Ltc. Richard White, and Ltc. Thomas Young, John F. Kennedy National Security Fellows, "American Military Policy in Small Wars:

The Case of El Salvador," Paper presented at the John F. Kennedy School of Government, March 22, 1988.

7. Ibid.

8. Douglas Farah, "Younger Generation Takes Command," *Washington Post*, November 9, 1988.

9. The tension between the Army and the Air Force almost broke out in open conflict in May 1989 over bids to replace outgoing Defense Minister Vides Casanova. Gen. Juan Rafael Bustillo, commander of the Air Force, was the choice of the hard line within ARENA while the U.S. embassy and the officer corps were leaning toward Col. René Emilio Ponce. A temporary solution to the dispute was reached with the appointment of Gen. Rafael Humberto Larios. *Proceso*, May 31, 1989; *Washington Post*, May 28, 1989.

10. Bacevich, et al., op. cit.

11. "El Salvador Notes: September 1989," (AFSC).

12. Morris J. Blachman and Kenneth E. Sharpe, "Things Fall Apart: Trouble Ahead in El Salvador," *World Policy Journal*, Winter 1988-1989, p. 11.

13. Joaquín Villalobos, "El Estado Actual de la Guerra y sus Perspectivas," *Estudios Centroamericanos*, March 1986.

14. *Alert!* (Committee in Solidarity with the People of El Salvador), January 1989.

15. This discussion on military corruption draws largely from an excellent article by Joel Millman, "El Salvador's Army: A Force Unto Itself," *New York Times*, December 10, 1989.

16. Ibid.

17. *El Boletín* (ACEN-SIAG), August 18, 1986.

18. Allan Austin, Luis Flores, and Donald Stout, *CONARA Impact Evaluation* (Research Triangle Institute, AID Contract PDC-0000-I-00-6169-00), September 20, 1988.

19. *Estudios Centroamericanos*, March 1986.

20. Douglas Farah, "Younger Generation Takes Command," *Washington Post*, November 9, 1988.

21. Another death squad associated with ORDEN was Regalado's Armed Forces (FAR), run by Dr. Antonio Regalado who turned a Boy Scout troop into a death squad. The FAR and other death squads were coordinated by ANSESAL, which was directed by military intelligence specialist D'Aubuisson. Later, Regalado was selected by D'Aubuisson to run the special protection unit which

had its headquarters in the Constituent Assembly building. Regalado was fingered by a fellow collaborator as the man who shot Archbishop Romero. Douglas Farah and Tom Gibb, "Confessions of an Assassin," *Mother Jones*, January 1989.

22. Allan Nairn, "Behind the Death Squads," *The Progressive*, May 1984. Also see Jim Naureckas, "Death Squad Strategy was Made in U.S.A.," *In These Times*, January 13-19, 1988; and Michael McClintock, *The American Connection: State Terror and Popular Resistance in El Salvador* (London: Zed Books, 1985).

23. See interview with Col. Juan Orlando Zepeda in Max Manwarring and Court Prisk, eds., *El Salvador at War: An Oral History* (Washington: National Defense University Press, 1988), pp. 310-314.

24. Chris Norton, "Spectre of Terror in El Salvador," *Christian Science Monitor*, April 21, 1989.

25. Villalobos, *Estudios Centroamericanos*, op. cit.

26. *NACLA Report on the Americas*, September 1989, p. 19.

27. Kenneth Freed, "Weekend Warriors Aid Salvador Rebels' Strategy," *Los Angeles Times*, November 2, 1988.

28. According to the FMLN platform of 1981, the revolutionary democratic government, after defeating the military-civilian junta representative of the oligarchy and reformist plans of the United States, would establish along with the working class, the *campesinos*, the "advanced" middle classes, democratic parties, and honest army officials a "democracy for the popular masses." Among the political measures taken would be the disarmament and dissolution of all the security and defense forces, the abolition of the three state organisms, and the restructuring of "municipal power," which was to be converted into a real organ of popular power. A sole Popular Army would be created and the new government would break the economic, political, and military dependence on the United States, establish relations with socialist countries, and be incorporated into the Movement of Nonaligned Nations. "Special Report: A New FMLN Project," *Central America Report*, September 22, 1989.

29. Joaquín Villalobos, "A Democratic Revolution for El Salvador," *Foreign Policy*, Spring 1989; Joaquín Villalobos, "Popular Insurrection: Desire or Reality?" *Latin American Perspectives*, Summer 1989; Villalobos, *Estudios Centroamericanos*, op. cit.

30. *Foreign Policy*, Spring 1989.

31. *Central America Report*, September 22, 1989.

32. *Foreign Policy*, op. cit.

33. Ibid.

34. Fermán Cienfuegos, *Veredas de la Audacia* (San Salvador: Ediciones Roque Dalton, 1989). Cited in *NACLA Report on the Americas*, September 1989.

35. *Foreign Policy*, op. cit.

36. Ibid.

37. *Estudios Centroamericanos*, March 1986.

38. Ibid.

39. Raúl Marín, "Signs of Insurrection Ignored," *Regionews*, December 1, 1989.

40. *Regionews*, December 14, 1989.

41. Rubén Zamora, "For Salvador, Democracy Before Peace," *New York Times*, January 24, 1990.

Chapter Three

1. For this analysis of the economy, the author relied extensively on the monthly reports circulated by the American Friends Service Committee ("El Salvador Notes") and two UCA publications: *Proceso* and *Realidad Económico-Social*.

2. Alexander Segovia, "Límites y Dilemas de la Política Económica en un País en Guerra," *Realidad Económico-Social*, November-December 1988; Segundo Montes, Florentín Meléndez, and Edgar Palacios, *Los Derechos Económicos, Sociales, y Culturales en El Salvador* (San Salvador: IDHUCA, 1988), p. 165.

3. *Proceso*, December 6, 1989.

4. Sen. Mark Hatfield, Rep. Jim Leach, and Rep. George Miller, *Bankrolling Failure: United States Policy in El Salvador and the Urgent Need for Reform: A Report to the Arms Control and Foreign Policy Caucus* (November 1987).

5. Segundo Montes, "La Crisis Social Agudizada por la Crisis Política Salvadoreña, la Migración a los Estados Unidos," *Estudios Centroamericanos*, October 1987.

6. "El Salvador Notes: April 1989," (AFSC).

7. *Realidad Económico-Social*, November-December 1988.

8. *Situación Actual y Perspectivas de la Economía y la Integración*, CEPAL, June 9, 1989.

9. The only major new construction projects scheduled are those related to the military (new Armed Forces Pension Fund building) or to U.S. government projects (new U.S. embassy compound and new buildings for the AID-funded FUSADES and the industrial training center of the Salesians).

10. El Salvador's 3 to 4 percent budget deficit/national-income ratio falls safely under the 5 percent maximum recommended by the International Monetary Fund (IMF).

11. *Proceso*, May 10, 1989.

12. Lindsey Gruson, "Who Stands to Gain by the Right Wing's Election Triumph," *New York Times*, March 22, 1989.

13. *Proceso*, April 19, 1989.

14. Ibid.

15. Segundo Montes, et al., *Los Derechos Económicos,* op. cit., p. 8.

16. Budget allocations to the ministries of health and education dropped from 27 percent of the total budget in 1983 to 23 percent during the 1984-1988 period. *Coyuntura Económica*, July-August 1989.

17. U.S. Agency for International Development, *Congressional Presentation FY1989* (Washington, 1988).

18. *Proceso*, April 26, 1989.

19. *Facing Reality in El Salvador. Cristiani's First 100 Days* (Philadelphia: NARMIC/AFSC, November 1989), p. 11.

20. *El Salvador: Agricultural Situation Report* (Washington: Foreign Agricultural Service/U.S. Department of Agriculture, March 31, 1989).

21. William C. Thiesenhusen, "How Agriculture has Effected Social Change in El Salvador," Paper prepared for delivery at the University of Wisconsin, February 2, 1984.

22. *El Salvador: Agricultural Situation Report* op. cit.

23. Kenneth Freed, "Bad Times for Salvador Coffee Growers," *Los Angeles Times*, February 21, 1989; *Centroamérica/USA*, November-December 1988. It is estimated that if the quota system is not renewed, it will mean an annual 20 percent loss of coffee income for countries like El Salvador and Nicaragua which have marketed most of their coffee through the controlled international market.

24. *El Salvador: Agricultural Situation Report* op. cit., p. 7; Rachel Garst and Tom Barry, *Feeding the Crisis: U.S. Food Aid and Farm Policy*

in Central America (Lincoln: University of Nebraska Press, forthcoming);

25. Garst and Barry, *Feeding the Crisis*, op. cit.; Jonathan Kandell, "Conservatives' Victory in El Salvador Signals End to Land Reform," *Wall Street Journal*, March 22, 1989.

26. *El Salvador: Agricultural Situation Report* op. cit., p.19.

27. *Proceso*, September 13, 1989.

28. Ibid.

29. Kandell, *Wall Street Journal*, op. cit.

30. See "Reforma Agraria," *Coyuntura Económica* (Instituto de Investigaciones Económicas, UES), January-February 1989.

31. The government's monitoring agency PERA found in 1987 that 9.9 percent of agricultural lands of the Phase I estates were not being cultivated and that forest lands and pasture were largely underutilized, resulting in a total of 47.4 percent of the estates being uncultivated or underutilized. *Proceso*, March 15, 1989.

32. Ibid.

33. Under Phase II, parcels of land between 100 and 500 hectares were to be redistributed, equivalent to about 24 percent of the country's primary cropland. Political pressure led to an increase in the lower limit to 250 hectares. This was clarified in the 1983 constitution, which established a limit of 245 hectares (605 acres) that an individual could own, with the state allowed to expropriate without compensation any excess. However, landowners were given a three-year period to dispose of this land by themselves. There was thus no obstacle to the legal subdivision of an estate, on paper, among members of the same family, so it is unclear how many of the original 640 properties that were eligible at the time of passage of the revised version of Phase II could actually be expropriated. Nevertheless, on December 3, 1987 the Assembly passed laws to implement Phase II, providing for the evaluation and negotiation of properties, determination of the price and form of payment to the former owners, and selection of the beneficiaries. Control by ARENA of the legislature and the presidency make it now unlikely, however, that Phase II will in fact be implemented.

34. Under Phase III, renters or sharecroppers could receive title to the land they worked up to a maximum of 7 hectares (17.3 acres). By the cut-off date for filing petitions of June 30, 1984, 63,640 persons had filed claims, representing more than 300,000 family members. Phase III affects many small landowners who have rented out part

of their land, and the legislation is strongly resented by them. Many landowners have filed protests and many claims have been contested and become bogged down in legal processes, which are usually decided in favor of the landowner. Moreover, resistance to Phase III has taken extra-legal channels, with violence and forced eviction of potential beneficiaries.

35. "Parcelación o Colectivación: Dilema de la Reforma Agraria en El Salvador," *Realidad Económico-Social*, September-October 1988; These figures come from the "VII Evaluación del Proceso de Reforma Agraria" (PERA).

36. Kandell, *Wall Street Journal*, op. cit.

37. Calculated from data given in *Realidad Económico-Social*, September-October, 1988, pp. 355-356.

38. U.S. Department of Commerce, *Foreign Economic Trends and Their Implications for the United States*, pp. 4-5; U.S. Embassy, San Salvador, "Investment Climate Survey;" *Encyclopedia of the Third World 1987*, p. 640.

39. *IDB Annual Report* (Inter-American Development Bank, 1987).

40. Interview by Tom Barry with Carlos Palacios, director of PRIDEX, February 1989.

41. "Los Industriales Desprotegidos Frente al Ajuste," *Proceso*, August 23, 1989.

Chapter Four

1. Important sources on the popular movement include: Segundo Montes, *Estructura de Clases y Comportamiento de las Fuerzas Sociales* (San Salvador: IDHUCA, 1988) and *Problemática Urbana, Movimiento Popular y Democracia en el Area Metropolitana de San Salvador, 1986-1988*, Documento de Trabajo (San Salvador: Coordinación Universitaria de Investigación Científica, UES, September-October 1988).

2. *Problemática Urbana*, op. cit., p. 127.

3. Ibid., citing *Proceso*, No. 327.

4. Mike Zielinski, "An Explosion of Popular Organizing," *Frontline*, August 29, 1988.

5. *Proceso*, November 1, 1989.

6. Mary Jo McConahay, "No Political Space Left," *Pacific News Service*, November 20, 1989.

7. *El Salvador: Critical Choices — A Special Report by the National Labor Committee in Support of Democracy and Human Rights in El Salvador*, June 1989.

8. Segundo Montes, "Levantamientos Campesinos en El Salvador," *Realidad Económico-Social*, January-February 1988.

9. The best history of the labor movement is found in: William Bollinger, "El Salvador," in Gerald Greenfield and Sheldon Maran, eds., *Latin American Labor Organizations* (Westport, CT: Greenwood Press, 1987).

10. *A Critique of the Americas Watch Report on Labor Rights in El Salvador* (AFL-CIO/AIFLD, June 10, 1988).

11. *Washington Post*, May 7, 1988.

12. For the best detailed breakdown of union federations see: Segundo Montes, *Estructura de Clases*, op. cit.

13. U.S. Embassy, San Salvador, *Foreign Labor Trends: El Salvador 1984-1987* (Washington: U.S. Department of Labor, 1988); Also see *A Critique of the Americas Watch Report*, op. cit.

14. *Proceso*, January 25, 1989.

15. In August 1989 the CGT (which is associated regionally with the Christian Democratic CLAT confederation) "froze" its relationship with UNOC because of its joint declarations with UNTS. *Facing Reality in El Salvador: Cristiani's First 100 Days* (Philadelphia: NARMIC/AFSC, November 1989).

16. Americas Watch, *Labor Rights in El Salvador* (New York, 1988).

17. *Decisions of the 14th World Congress*, ICFTU, March 14-18, 1988.

18. Americas Watch, "Petition before the U.S. Trade Representative on Labor Rights in El Salvador," March 1989.

19. *Critical Choices*, op. cit., p. 8; *Washington Report on the Hemisphere*, June 7, 1989; David Slaney, "Thinking Globally: Labor Rights Legislation and El Salvador," *Dollars & Sense*, May 1989.

20. Thirty percent of the National University's buildings were left unusable because of the damage caused by the military occupation. Another 20 percent were severely damaged by the 1986 earthquake. Continued military attacks, such as the 1989 bombing of the Biology Building, keep the campus in ruins.

21. *The Advancement and Placement of Students from Central America*, P.I.E.R. Workshop Report, 1987 (Washington: National Association of Foreign Student Affairs, 1987); *CIA World Factbook 1988*.

22. *Central America Report*, June 16, 1989.

23. *El Mundo*, March 17, 1988; *Central America Report*, July 15, 1988.

24. *Peace Brigades International Informe*, January 1989.

25. *Central America Report*, July 28, 1989.

26. Interviews with AGEUS and FEUS leaders by Tom Barry, February 1989; *Alert!* (CISPES), September 1988.

27. Lindsey Gruson, "Salvador TV Dares to Tell the News," *New York Times*, September 27, 1988.

28. U.S. Embassy, San Salvador, *Country Data: El Salvador*, January 1, 1989.

29. Mary Jo McConahay, "Open Season Resumes in El Salvador," *Pacific News Service*, March 20, 1989; Notimex, December 1, 1989 (through Latin America Data Base).

30. Ibid.

31. Richard Garfield, Dr.PH, and Pedro Rodriguez, MD, "Health and Health Services in Central America," *JAMA Journal of the American Medical Association*, August 16, 1985.

32. Antonio Dajer, "The Complicated Path to Simple Medicine: Interview with Francisco Metzi," *Links* (NCAHRN), Summer 1989.

33. Ibid.

34. "A Ten Year War on Health," *Links* (NCAHRN), Spring 1989.

35. Figures from Ministry of Planning, cited in *Proceso*, August 30, 1989.

36. Alan Myers and Adrienne Epstein, "Passage to Chalatenango," *Links* (NCAHRN), Winter 1988-1989.

37. *World Development Report 1987*.

38. *Central America Report* (London), Summer 1989.

39. Colum Lynch, "Salvadoran Church, State Tensions Rise," *Washington Post*, June 24, 1989.

40. Ana Arana, "Salvador Church Relations with Military Grow Tense" *Miami Herald*, May 21, 1989.

41. *Directory and Analysis: Private Organizations with U.S. Connections – El Salvador* (Albuquerque: Resource Center, 1988).

42. Clifton L. Holland, ed., *World Christianity: Central America and the Caribbean* (MARC/World Vision International, 1981).

43. For a more complete treatment of NGOs in El Salvador see: *Directory and Analysis: Private Organizations with U.S. Connections – El Salvador*, op. cit.

44. Data on AID funding to NGOs supplied to Resource Center by AID in communications of September 12, 1987 and April 5, 1988. For a complete breakdown see: *Directory and Analysis: Private Organizations with U.S. Connections — El Salvador*, op. cit., p. 7.

45. Mary Jo McConahay, "El Salvador's War: Human Rights Abuses on the Rise," *Pacific News Service*, November 24, 1989.

46. *Diagnóstico de la Situación de la Mujer Centroamericana* (CEPAL, September 1988).

47. U.S. Department of State, *Submission to the Senate Foreign Relations Committee on Human Rights in El Salvador* (Washington, 1985).

48. Alda Facio Montejo, "La Mujer en el Derecho Salvadoreño," paper prepared for the United Nations Children's Fund, San Salvador, December 1988; Margaret L. Popkin, "Los Derechos de la Mujer en el Campo Laboral," (San Salvador: IDHUCA, December 1988).

49. Marilyn Thomson, *Women of El Salvador: The Price of Freedom* (London: Zed Books, 1986), pp. 36-38.

50. "Gathering Strength," (London: El Salvador and Guatemala Human Rights Committees).

51. Thomson, *Women of El Salvador*, op. cit., p. 27, which cites: T. Monreal, et al., "Abortos Hospitalizados en El Salvador," *Salud Pública en México*, May-June 1977, pp. 387-95.

52. For an overview of women's issues and organizing in El Salvador, see: New America Press, eds., *A Dream Compels Us: Voices of Salvadoran Women* (Boston: South End Press, 1989).

53. *Guide to Salvadoran Women's Organizations* (Global Exchange, 1989); Interviews by Tom Barry (Resource Center) with various women's organizations, February 1989.

54. Cited in *A Dream Compels Us*, op. cit., p. 9.

55. Jenny Pearce, *Promised Land: Peasant Rebellion in Chalatenango El Salvador* (London: Latin American Bureau, 1986), pp. 12-17.

56. Indians are not a census category, and definitions are arbitrary. The highest figure, of 20 percent, was cited by Helen Schooley in *Conflict in Central America* (Longman, 1987). Many other estimates refer back to to to estimates made in authoritative works of 40 years ago. The *CIA World Factbook 1988* reports 10 percent, and *Encyclopedia of the Third World 1987* gives 6 percent.

57. Theodore MacDonald, "El Salvador's Indians," *Cultural Survival Quarterly*, Vol. 6, No. 1, Winter 1982; Thomas P. Anderson, *Matanza* (Lincoln: University of Nebraska Press, 1971), p. 17; Richard N. Adams, *Cultural Surveys of Panama, Nicaragua, Guatemala, El Salvador and Honduras* (Detroit: Ethridge, 1957), p. 504.

58. Judy Branfman, "Politics Affect Fiber Arts Development," *Cultural Survival Quarterly*, Vol. 11, No. 1, 1987.

59. United Nations High Commission on Refugees, Information Paper, International Conference on Central American Refugees (CIREFCA), Guatemala City, May 29, 1989; *Central America Bulletin*, December 1988; U.S. Government Accounting Office, *Central America: Conditions of Refugees and Displaced Persons* (Washington, March 1989).

60. Segundo Montes, *El Salvador 1987: Salvadoreños Refugiados en los Estados Unidos* (San Salvador: Instituto de Investigaciones, UCA, 1987); Zita Arocha, "Study Pegs Salvadorans in U.S. at 1 million," *Washington Post*, September 23, 1988.

61. Robert Pear, "A Letter from Duarte Urges U.S. to Temporarily Accept Refugees," *New York Times*, September 11, 1988.

62. Ken Silverstein, "Blaming the Victim: State Department Tries to Rid U.S. of Human Rights Activists," *In These Times*, May 18, 1988.

63. H. Jeffrey Leonard, *Natural Resources and Economic Development in Central America* (New Brunswick: Transaction Books, 1987), p. 21.

64. Because of the exceptionally high quality of the volcanic soil in El Salvador, much of the cropping is on hillsides. As erosion becomes more severe, the country's food production and agroexport systems are increasingly endangered.

65. Leonard, *Natural Resources*, op. cit., p. 155.

66. Ibid.

67. Bill Hall and Daniel Faber, "El Salvador: Ecology of Conflict," *Earth Island Journal*, Summer 1989.

68. Ibid., citing Howard E. Daugherty, *Man-Induced Ecologic Change in El Salvador* (Ph.D. dissertation, University of California, Los Angeles, 1969) and Ernesto López, *Ecological Impacts of Cotton Cultivation in El Salvador: Example of Jiquilisco* (York University, April 1977).

69. AID, *El Salvador Environmental Profile* (Tucson: Arid Lands Information Center, University of Arizona, 1982), p. viii.

70. Hall and Faber, *Earth Island Journal*, op. cit.

71. Bill Hall, "Central America's Environmental Time Bomb" *San Francisco Bay Guardian*, April 27, 1988.

72. Hall and Faber, *Earth Island Journal*, op. cit.

73. A paid announcement published in *El Mundo*, February 24, 1988, cited in Bill Weinberg, *War on the Land: The Politics of Ecology and the Ecology of Politics in Central America* (unpublished manuscript).

74. Leonard, op. cit., p. 119.

75. Hall and Faber, *Earth Island Journal*, op. cit.

76. Ibid.

Chapter Five

1. U.S. Department of State, "El Salvador: The Battle for Democracy," *Department of State Bulletin*, January 1989.

2. Robert Elam, *Appeal to Arms: The Army and Politics in El Salvador* (Ph.D dissertation, University of New Mexico, 1969).

3. Philip l. Russell, *El Salvador in Crisis* (Austin: Colorado River Press, 1984), p. 120.

4. *New York Times*, May 8, 1978.

5. K. Larry Storrs, "El Salvador: New Challenges for U.S. Policy," *CRS Review*, February 1989.

6. For a provocative discussion of the regional implications of a strong and uncontrolled Salvadoran military, see: Ltc. A. J. Bacevich, Ltc. James Hallums, Ltc. Richard White, and Ltc. Thomas Young, John F. Kennedy National Security Fellows, "American Military Policy in Small Wars: The Case of El Salvador," Paper presented at the John F. Kennedy School of Government, March 22, 1988.

7. *Department of State Bulletin*, op. cit.

8. For further discussion of U.S. foreign policy, see: Sam Dillon, "Dateline El Salvador: Crisis Renewed," *Foreign Policy*, Winter 1988-1989; Ricardo Stein, "Civil War, Reform, and Reaction in El Salvador," in *Crisis in Central America* (Boulder: Westview, 1988); Chris Norton, "U.S. Salvador Policy: Spell It Unsalvageable," *In These Times*, February 1989.

9. U.S. Embassy, San Salvador, *Foreign Economic Trends and their Implication for the United States: El Salvador* (Washington: U.S. Department of Commerce, March 1989; CEPAL, *Current Situation and Economic Perspectives*, June 19, 1989.

10. U.S. Embassy, San Salvador, "Update of Investment Climate," July 13, 1988.

11. Ibid.

12. Sen. Mark Hatfield, Rep. Jim Leach, and Rep. George Miller, *U.S. Aid to El Salvador: An Evaluation of the Past, A Proposal for the Future* (February 1985) and *Bankrolling Failure: United States Policy in El Salvador and the Urgent Need for Reform: A Report to the Arms Control and Foreign Policy Caucus* (November 1987).

13. For a more thorough treatment of AID's stabilization strategy see: Tom Barry and Debra Preusch, *The Soft War: Uses and Abuses of U.S. Economic Aid in Central America* (New York: Grove Press, 1988).

14. The term "other war" was first used by officials of the Johnson administration to describe the nonmilitary aspects of the Vietnam war which were managed by AID, military/civic action teams, and NGOs. See: Barry and Preusch, *The Soft War*, op. cit.

15. Allan Austin, Luis Flores, and Donald Stout, *CONARA Impact Evaluation* (Research Triangle Institute, AID Contract PDC-0000-I-00-6169-00), September 20, 1988.

16. Lawyers Committee for Human Rights, *Underwriting Injustice: AID and El Salvador's Judicial Reform Program* (April 1989).

17. U.S. Agency for International Development, *Congressional Presentation FY1987, Latin America and the Caribbean* (Washington, 1986).

18. U.S. Agency for International Development, *Congressional Presentation FY1989, Latin America and the Caribbean* (Washington, 1988).

19. AID stated in its *Congressional Presentation FY1989*, "Thus, while ESF, PL480 Title I, and Section 416 are provided mainly through government channels, the private sector is the main beneficiary." This happens in three principle ways: 1) private-sector benefits from infusion of ESF dollars into the economy allowing buyers of these dollars to import luxury and intermediary goods, 2) local currency generated from sales of U.S. food (PL480 and Section 416) and ESF dollars on the local market is channeled to private-sector organizations like FUSADES, and 3) AID uses its ESF and PL480 programs as leverage to obligate the government to support the private sector.

20. Kevin Whittacker, El Salvador Desk Officer, U.S. Department of State, January 25, 1990.

21. Bacevich, et. al., "The Case of El Salvador," op. cit.

22. Lionel Gómez, former director of the Agrarian Reform Institute (ISTA), informed Sen. Tom Harkin that at least six of the 18 Salvadoran officers being trained by the Anti-Terrorism program had death-squad links. *In These Times*, August 20, 1986.

23. Barry and Preusch, *The Soft War*, op. cit., pp. 181-183; *Underwriting Justice* (Lawyers Committee for Human Rights, April 1989).

24. Ibid.

25. *NACLA Report on the Americas*, July 1989.

26. According to Col. Juan Orlando Zepeda, former director of military intelligence: "The DNI receives most of its aid from the Central Intelligence Agency. The CIA provides some support to the C-2 [Intelligence Division of Combined General Staff], such as direct training. But the whole product, the handling of sources, such as communications, traffic analysis, and equipment, is handed over to the DNI." Max G. Manwarring and Court Prisk, eds., *El Salvador at War: An Oral History* (Washington: National Defense University Press, 1988).

27. Alfonso Chardy, "Two U.S. Advisors Played Role in Salvador Battle," *Miami Herald*, January 19, 1989.

28. Frank Smyth, "Caught with their Pants Down," *Village Voice*, December 5, 1989, reported monitoring radio conversations in which the U.S. military command center in San Salvador instructed the Salvadoran Air Force to "hit" an area several blocks "north of the church."

29. U.S. Department of Defense, *Congressional Presentation for Security Assistance Programs FY1982* (Washington, 1981); U.S. Department of Defense, *Foreign Military Sales and Military Assistance Facts as of September 1981* (Washington, 1982).

30. Cynthia Arnson, "Background Information on the Security Forces in El Salvador and U.S. Military Assistance," Institute for Policy Studies, March 1980.

31. U.S. Department of Defense, *Congressional Presentation for Security Assistance Programs FY1990* (Washington, 1989).

32. Bacevich, et al., "The Case of El Salvador," op. cit.; For discussion of this report, see William Bollinger, "Villalobos on Popular Insurrection," *Latin American Perspectives*, Summer 1989.

33. Joel Millman, "El Salvador's Army: A Force Unto Itself," *New York Times Magazine*, December 10, 1989.

34. *Direction of Trade Statistics Yearbook, 1988* (International Monetary Fund), pp. 170-171.

35. *Geographical Distribution of Financial Flows to Developing Countries* (Paris: OCED, 1988); Esperanza Durán, *European Interests in Latin America* (London: Royal Institute of International Affairs, 1985).

36. Duncan Campbell and Patrick Forbes, "Cover Blown on the UK's Support to El Salvador," *New Statesman*, May 17, 1985; *The Thatcher Years: Britain and Latin America* (London, Latin America Bureau, 1988).

37. *NACLA Report on the Americas*, March-April 1980.

38. Tim Dramin, "Canadian Foreign Policy and El Salvador," *Central America Update*, October 1981; "Taking Sides: Canadian Aid to El Salvador," Latin American Working Group, August 1987; *Annual Report 1986-1987* (CIDA).

39. Milton Jamail and Margo Gutiérrez, "A Special Relationship," *NACLA Report on the Americas*, March-April 1987, pp. 14-15; Jane Hunter, *Israeli Foreign Policy: South Africa and Central America* (Boston: South End Press, 1987), p. 100.

Statistics

Population

Population:	5,389,000 (1988)[1]
Urban Population:	47.7% (1987)[2]
Population Density:	652 per sq. mi. (1988)[1]
Annual Growth Rate:	2.4% (1988)[1]
Literacy:	65%[3]
Ethnic Composition:[4]	
Mestizo:	92%
Indian:	6%
White:	2%
Religion:	
Catholic:	81% (1987)[4]
Protestant:	18% (1988)[5]

Health

Life Expectancy at Birth:	58.8 years (1988)[1]
Infant Mortality per 1,000 Live Births:	86 (1988)[1]

Economy

GDP:	$4,440 million (1987)[2]
Per Capita GDP:	$900 (1987)[2]
Income Distribution (1980):[6]	
Poorest 20% of population:	2.0% of income
30% Below the Mean:	10.0% of income
30% Above the Mean:	22.0% of income
Richest 20%:	66.0% of income
Rural Population in Absolute Poverty:	70%[7]

(Absolute poverty is the inability to afford food providing minimum nutritional requirements.)

Land Distribution:[7]
1% of farms comprise 71% of farmland
41% of farms comprise 10% of farmland

External Public Debt:	
1970:	$88 million[8]
1989:	$1,825 million[9]

Trade Balance:	-$520 million (1989)[9]
Debt Servicing as % of Exports:	19.0% (1987)[1]
External Debt as % of GNP:	29.0% (1987)[1]
Property & Income Taxes as % of Current Revenues:	23.1% (1987)[2]
Labor Force by Sector (1988):[10]	
Agriculture:	34%
Services:	24%
Commerce:	18%
Manufacturing:	17%
Unemployment (1988):[11]	
Urban:	50%
Rural:	71%
Top Agriculture Products (1988):[10]	
Coffee:	90.2%
Shrimp:	5.1%
Sugar:	4.4%
Cotton:	0.2%

U.S. Economic Aid[12]
(millions of dollars)

	1946-1979	1980-1988	1989	1990*	1991**
Development					
Assistance	123.4	584.2	62.3	67.8	64.1
ESF	0	1,372.7	109.9	180.0	180.0
PL480	36.7	377.6	48.8	39.8	39.8
Peace Corps	12.3	0.4	0	0	0
Total	172.4	2,334.9	302.0	287.6	283.9

U.S. Military Aid[12]
(millions of dollars)

	1946-1979	1980-1988	1989	1990*	1991**
MAP	5.0	733.8	80.0	0	0
FMS	3.5	107.1	0	97.0	1.4
IMET	5.8	11.3	1.4	1.6	85.0
Total	14.3	852.2	81.4	98.6	86.4

*Estimated

**Requested. One half of the $85 million in military aid will be withheld unless the FMLN withdraws from negotiating process.

Sources

1) Congressional Presentation FY1990, Annex III, Latin America and the Caribbean, U.S. Agency for International Development; 2) Economic and Social Progress in Latin America; 1988 Report, Inter-American Development Bank; 3) CIA World Factbook 1988; 4) Encyclopedia of the Third World 1987; 5) Directory and Analysis: Private Organizations with U.S. Connections—El Salvador, Resource Center, 1988; 6) CEPAL Review, April 1984; 7) Tom Barry, Roots of Rebellion: Land and Hunger in Central America, Resource Center, 1987; 8) World Development Report 1988, World Bank; 9) CEPAL, Notas sobre la

Economía y el Desarrollo, December 1989, preliminary figures; 10) U.S. Department of Agriculture, "El Salvador: Agricultural Situation Report," March 31, 1989, citing Central Reserve Bank of El Salvador figures; 11) Salvadoran Ministry of Planning; 12) U.S. Overseas Loans and Grants: Obligations and Loan Authorizations July 1, 1945-September 30, 1983, U.S. Agency for International Development, Office of Planning and Budgeting; U.S. Overseas Loans and Grants: Obligations and Loan Authorizations July 1, 1945-September 30, 1987, U.S. Agency for International Development, Office of Planning and Budgeting; Fiscal Year 1990 Summary Tables, U.S. Agency for International Development.

Chronology

1525	Area of El Salvador conquered by Pedro de Alvarado, becomes part of Captaincy-General of Guatemala.
1700	San Salvador second most important city of region.
1786	El Salvador raised to status of intendency, equal to Honduras and Nicaragua.
1811	First Central American pro-independence revolt, led by Salvadorans.
1821	Declaration of independence of Central America; the United Provinces of Central America continues to exist until 1838.
1822	Revolt against attempt by Mexican emperor Augustín Iturbide to dominate Central America.
1838	Independence of El Salvador, but pro-Conservative interventions from Guatemala and pro-Liberal interventions from Honduras continue; inter-party conflict, assassinations, revolutions.
1886	Stability under Conservative rule for next 45 years. Communal lands privatized. Coffee becomes dominant crop, and coffee oligarchy consolidates into "14 families."
1913	Presidency alternates between Meléndez and Quiñónez families until 1927.
1922	Formation of the National Guard.
1924	Formation of the Regional Federation of Salvadoran Workers.
1930	Formation of the Communist Party of El Salvador (PCS).
1931	
Mar.	First honest elections; no clear popular winner; Congress elects Arturo Araujo, who begins reformist government.
	Depression wipes out market for coffee.
	Popular agitation led by PCS under charismatic Augustín Farabundo Martí.
Dec.	Coup led by Minister of War Gen. Maximiliano Hernández Martínez. His dictatorship continues until 1944.
	Martí organizes revolt but is captured first. Revolt occurs, especially among Indian peasants, easily put down.
	Up to 30,000 peasants rounded up and massacred in the matanza. Martí and PCS leadership publicly executed, PCS outlawed.
	Union organizing outlawed until 1944.
1944	Hernández Martínez overthrown by sit-down strike (Fallen Arms Strike).
	Salvadoran Trade Union Reorganizing Committee (CROSS) builds underground union movement.
1945	Gen. Salvador Castañeda Castro elected president.

	Major strike by Railway Workers Union.
1948	Revolt by reformist junior officers.
1950	New constitution promulgated.

Government party (PRUD) organized.

Presidential elections won by PRUD's Lt. Col. Oscar Osorio. Over next six years, unions are legalized, social security, public housing, and electric power projects are begun.

1952	CROSS outlawed; increased anticommunism.
* 1956	Lt. Col. José María Lemus of PRUD becomes president after rigged elections. Repressive rule, repudiated by Osorio.
1960	Coup by reformist officers.

Leftwing parties legalized.

| 1961 | Conservative counter-coup led by Lt. Col. Julio Rivera. New government Party of National Conciliation (PCN, renamed from PRUD) wins all seats in Constituent Assembly. |

Foundation of National Democratic Organization (ORDEN), a rural paramilitary network of informers and enforcers, by Gen. José Alberto Medrano of military intelligence.

Formation of Christian Democratic Party (PDC).

| 1962 | Rivera elected president on pro-Alliance for Progress platform. Opposition parties boycott elections. |

New constitution adopted.

| 1964 | Opposition PDC and Party of Renovating Action (PAR) win over 40 percent of votes in honest election for Legislative Assembly. |

José Napoleón Duarte of PDC elected mayor of San Salvador.

Formation of Federation of Christian Campesinos (FECCAS).

| 1965 | Formation of the National Revolutionary Movement (MNR). |

American Institute for Free Labor Development (AIFLD) begins educational seminars for farmworkers.

1967	Col. Fidel Sánchez Hernández of PCN elected president.
1968	Formation of the Salvadoran Communal Union (UCS).
* 1969	"Soccer War" with Honduras over mistreatment of Salvadorans in Honduras and related issues lasts four days.

Formation of UNO and the Nationalist Democratic Union (UDN).

1970	Formation of Popular Liberation Forces (FPL).
1971	Formation of People's Revolutionary Army (ERP).
1972	Duarte and Guillermo Manuel Ungo of UNO apparently elected president and vice president, but results altered by electoral commission; Col. Arturo Molina of PCN elected by Legislative Assembly. Nixon administration declines to use influence to assist Duarte.

Revolt led by reformist younger officers put down with 200 deaths. Duarte arrested, tortured, exiled.

| 1974 | Fraudulent legislative elections, all PCN candidates win. |

Formation of Unified Popular Action Front (FAPU).

| 1975 | Murder of Roque Dalton. |

Formation of second mass organization, Popular Revolutionary Bloc (BPR), linked to FPL.

	Formation of Armed Forces of National Resistance (FARN), linked to FAPU.
1976	President Molina attempts moderate land reform, abandoned when landowners threaten armed resistance.
	Formation of the Salvadoran Institute of Agrarian Transformation (ISTA).
1977	Monsignor Oscar Arnulfo Romero becomes Archbishop of El Salvador.
	Assassination of Jesuit Father Rutilio Grande by a death squad apparently sponsored by security forces, the first of seven priests killed in next two years.
	Gen. Carlos Humberto Romero elected president in fraudulent election; over 200 peaceful protesters killed. Catholic church boycotts inauguration.
	Assassinations of several prominent government figures, including Foreign Minister Mauricio Borgonovo Pohl, by guerrillas.
1978	Third popular organization formed: People's League of February 28 (LP-28), linked with ERP, favoring more direct action than FAPU and BPR.
1979	Escalating violence: kidnappings, assassinations, building seizures, and hostage-taking by guerrillas; repression and killings by government forces. Over 600 political killings during year. Shafik Handal of PCS says armed revolt now necessary.
Oct.	General Romero overthrown by junior officers. First junta formed, including Guillermo Ungo and Lt. Cols. Majano and Gutiérrez. Progressive cabinet; Col. José García Defense Minister.
	United States begins increase in military and economic assistance.
1980	
Jan.	First junta and cabinet resign, charging military noncooperation; Ungo goes into exile. Second junta formed, with Majano, Gutiérrez, and Christian Democrats.
	Formation of Revolutionary Coordinator of Masses (CRM).
Feb.	Banks nationalized and land reform decreed. Death-squad killings escalate.
	Archbishop Romero writes letter to President Carter requesting halt of aid.
Mar.	Archbishop Romero assassinated while saying mass.
	Third junta formed with Duarte a member.
May	Coup organized by Roberto D'Aubuisson fails. D'Aubuisson organizes Secret Anticommunist Army to coordinate death-squad activities.
	Formation of the Farabundo Martí National Liberation Front (FMLN) to coordinate guerrillas; formation of the Democratic Revolutionary Front (FDR) to coordinate leftist political opposition, which links up with FMLN; six FDR leaders killed.
	Attempt by U.S. Ambassador Robert White to negotiate peaceful settlement.
	Gutiérrez narrowly elected commander-in-chief by officers over more progressive Majano. War escalates.
	Military occupy National University campus.
Dec.	Four U.S. churchwomen raped and killed; U.S. military aid cut off.
	Third junta disbanded; Duarte becomes provisional president.
1981	Reagan takes office; U.S. military aid resumes.
	FMLN launches "final offensive."
	Head of land-reform institute and two U.S. advisors assassinated.
	D'Aubuisson organizes Nationalist Republican Alliance (ARENA).

1982

Mar.   Elections for Constituent Assembly, boycotted by left. Rightwing majority,
         though PDC largest single party.

         Four Dutch journalists killed.

         Alvaro Magaña elected president after United States blocks D'Aubuisson, who
         becomes president of Assembly.

         Foreign Ministers of Costa Rica, El Salvador, and Honduras form the Central
         American Democratic Community.

1983   Military insubordination forces García to resign as Defense Minister, replaced by
         U.S. protege Eugenio Vides Casanova.

         Salvador Cayetano Carpio suicide in Managua.

         Massacre at Las Hojas.

         Contadora group meets for first time to develop dialogue and negotiation in
         Central America; parties to the peace accords include Costa Rica, El Salvador,
         Guatemala, Honduras, and Nicaragua.

         New constitution promulgated.

         Cumulative total of political killings reaches 45,000.

1984   Kissinger Commission report: fight, but win hearts and minds.

         Presidential elections: Duarte beats D'Aubuisson in May run-offs, inaugurated in
         June.

         Duarte attempts peace talks with FMLN without prior consultation with the
         United States, but FMLN power-sharing demands are unacceptable to army
         and the United States.

         Nicaragua agrees to sign Contadora treaty, but Costa Rica, El Salvador, and
         Honduras refuse to sign.

1985   PDC success in municipal elections credited to peace overtures.

         Four U.S. marines killed by FMLN in San Salvador restaurant.

         Duarte's daughter kidnapped, released in exchange for guerrilla prisoners.

1986   New military strategy to clear and hold areas one by one is unsuccessful.

         Formation of the National Unity of Salvadoran Workers (UNTS).

         New round of peace talks sabotaged by military violation of ground rules.

         Third revised Contadora treaty presented, Costa Rica, El Salvador, and
         Honduras refuse to sign.

Oct.   Disastrous earthquake in San Salvador: 1,500 killed, 10,000 families displaced,
         $1.5 billion damage.

         PDC passes taxes on wealthy.

1987

Feb.   Costa Rica President Arias takes leadership role in regional peace initiatives,
         meets with representatives from El Salvador, Guatemala and Honduras in
         Esquipulas, Guatemala.

Aug.   Presidents of Costa Rica, El Salvador, Guatemala, Honduras, and Nicaragua sign
         Esquipulas II peace accord. Duarte tries to make parallels between Nicaraguan
         contras and Salvadoran rebel groups.

Oct.   Formation of National Reconciliation Commission, as required in peace plan;
         FMLN-government talks begin.

         Duarte proposes amnesty for political prisoners; Herbert Anaya of
         nongovernmental Human Rights Commission speaks out against the amnesty

and is killed in death-squad fashion. Some political parties withdraw from the National Reconciliation Commission and FMLN talks are broken off as a result.

Duarte bows and kisses the U.S. flag during a visit to the United States.

Guillermo Ungo and Rubén Zamora return from exile to enter overt political activity; Zamora kisses the Salvadoran flag.

Mass repatriation of refugees from the Mesa Grande camps in Honduras.

1988   Tensions increase with prospect of presidential elections in El Salvador and U.S.

Death-squad killings rise; FMLN increases military actions, sabotage, assassinations (especially of local officials).

Col. René Emilio Ponce replaces Gen. Adolfo Blandón as army chief of staff.

PDC and ARENA split over presidential candidacies.

Honduras requests a UN peacekeeping force to patrol its borders with El Salvador and Nicaragua.

Catholic church initiates National Debate for Peace; over 60 organizations participate.

1989

Jan.   FMLN offers to participate in elections if they are postponed six months, dropping demand for prior participation in government and new military force.

Pressure from new Bush administration induces PDC and ARENA to send representatives to Mexico discussions: FMLN asks reduction in size of military, civilian control, prosecution of assassins; rejected by army.

Feb.   Esquipulas peace talks held in Costa Del Sol, La Paz, El Salvador after four postponements. On the same day as the peace summit, Salvadoran military forces attack a FMLN field hospital, raping the female doctor and paramedics, and killing them and the wounded guerrilla combatants.

Mar.   Presidential elections won by Alfredo Cristiani (ARENA), 53 percent, to 37 percent for PDC, and only 3.2 percent for Ungo (Democratic Convergence). FMLN ambiguous: calls for boycott, or spoiling ballot, or voting for Ungo. Turnout low.

New Cristiani administration pro-free market, privatization. Split between "total war" and "hearts and minds" strategies.

Sep.   New FMLN offer of truce if U.S. stops military aid; new talks in Mexico.

Oct.   FMLN calls off talks with government after the bombing of FENASTRAS, the country's largest labor federation.

Nov.   FMLN launches major military offensive.

Six Jesuit priests of the University of Central America, including the rector, are assassinated by the army.

1990

May   Series of U.N.-mediated peace talks begin.

Oct.   United States cuts military aid by 50 percent.

Sources for the chronology include: El Salvador Election Factbook (Washington: Institute for the Comparative Study of Political Systems, 1967); Thomas P. Anderson, Politics in Central America (New York: Praeger, 1982); Conflict in Central America (1987); Jan K. Black, Sentinels of Empire (Westport, CT: Greenwood Press, 1986); Crisis in Central America (Boulder: Westview, 1988); Labor Organizations in Latin America, Gerald Greenfield and Sheldon Maran, editors (Greenwood Press, 1987); Central America Report, 3 March 1989; Central America Bulletin, April 1989.

Bibliography

The following periodicals are useful source of information and analysis on El Salvador:

Alert!: Focus on Central America, Committee in Solidarity with the People of El Salvador (Washington, DC), monthly, English.

Central America Report, Inforpress Centroamericana (Guatemala City), weekly, English.

El Salvador Notes, American Friends Service Committee (Philadelphia), irregular, English.

Pensamiento Propio, Coordinadora Regional de Investigaciones Económicas y Sociales (Managua), monthly, Spanish.

Proceso, Centro Universitario de Documentación e Información, Universidad Centroamericana (San Salvador), weekly, Spanish.

Realidad Económico-Social, Universidad Centroamericana (San Salvador), bimonthly, Spanish.

Regionews from Managua, Coordinadora Regional de Investigaciones Económicas y Sociales (Managua), weekly, English.

The following are recommended articles appearing in journals:

Morris J. Blackman and Kenneth E. Sharpe, "Things Fall Apart: Trouble Ahead in El Salvador," *World Policy Journal*, Winter 1988.

Bill Hall and Daniel Faber, "El Salvador: Ecology of Conflict," *Earth Island Journal*, Summer 1989.

Sara Miles and Bob Ostertag, "D'Aubuisson's New ARENA," *NACLA Report on the Americas*, July 1989.

— — —, "FMLN New Thinking," *NACLA Report on the Americas*, September 1989.

Interview by Terry Karl with Salvador Samoya, "Negotiations or Total War," *World Policy Journal*, Spring 1989.

Joaquín Villalobos, "A Democratic Revolution for El Salvador," *Foreign Policy*, Spring 1989.

— — —, "El Estado Actual de la Guerra y sus Perspectivas," *Estudios Centroamericanos*, March 1986.

— — —, "Popular Insurrection: Desire or Reality?" *Latin American Perspectives*, Summer 1989.

The following reports and books contain valuable background on many issues important to understanding El Salvador:

Americas Watch, *The Civilian Toll: 1986-1987* (New York, 1987).

— — —, *Labor Rights in El Salvador* (New York, 1988).

— — —, *Nightmare Revisited: 1987-1988* (New York, 1988).

Amnesty International, *El Salvador: Death Squads — A Government Strategy* (New York, 1988).

Ltc. A. J. Bacevich, Ltc. James Hallums, Ltc. Richard White, and Ltc. Thomas Young, John F. Kennedy National Security Fellows, "American Military Policy in Small Wars: The Case of El Salvador," Paper presented at the John F. Kennedy School of Government, March 22, 1988.

Tom Barry, *Roots of Rebellion: Land and Hunger in Central America* (Boston: South End Press, 1987).

Tom Barry and Debra Preusch, *El Salvador: The Other War* (Resource Center, 1986).

— — —, *The Soft War: Uses and Abuses of U.S. Economic Aid in Central America* (New York: Grove Press, 1988).

Centro América 1988: Análisis Económicos y Políticos sobre la Región (Guatemala: Inforpress Centroamericana, 1988).

Directory and Analysis: Private Organizations with U.S. Connections — El Salvador (Albuquerque: Resource Center, 1988).

William H. Durham, *Scarcity and Survival in Central America* (Stanford, CA: Stanford University Press, 1979).

El Salvador: Critical Choices — A Special Report by the National Labor Committee in Support of Democracy and Human Rights in El Salvador (1989).

El Salvador Notes 1989 (Philadelphia: NARMIC/American Friends Service Committee, 1989).

El Salvador Update: Counterterrorism in Action (Los Angeles: El Rescate Human Rights Department, 1987). Based on the findings of a research team to El Salvador in May 1986 investigating U.S. assistance to the Salvadoran police.

Michael McClintock, *The American Connection, Vol. 1: State Terror and Popular Resistance in El Salvador* (London: Zed Books, 1985).

Max G. Manwarring and Court Prisk, eds., *El Salvador at War: An Oral History* (National Defense University Press, 1988).

Segundo Montes, *Estructura de Clases y Comportamiento de las Fuerzas Sociales* (San Salvador: IDHUCA, 1988).

Problemática Urbana, Movimiento Popular y Democracia en el Area Metropolitana de San Salvador, 1986-1988, Documento de Trabajo (San Salvador: Coordinación Universitaria de Investigación Científica, UES, September-October 1988).

Philip L. Russell, *El Salvador in Crisis* (Austin: Colorado River Press, 1984).

For More Information

Resources

Central America Resource Center
P.O. Box 2327
Austin, TX 78768

El Salvador Media Project
2886 Mission Street
San Francisco, CA 94110

University of Central America/El Salvador Proceso
Centro de Distribución
Apartado Postal (01) 575
San Salvador, El Salvador

Environmental Project on Central America (EPOCA)
Earth Island Institute
300 Broadway #28
San Francisco, CA 94133

Peace and Justice

American Friends Service Committee/El Salvador Notes
1501 Cherry Street
Philadelphia, PA 19102

Central America Refugee Center (CARECEN)
1801 Columbia Road, Suite 103
Washington, DC 20009

Committee in Solidarity with the People of El Salvador (CISPES)/Alert!
P.O. Box 12056
Washington, DC 20005

Global Exchange/Salvadoran Women
2940 16th Street, Room 307
San Francisco, CA 94103

International Labor Rights Education and Research Fund
110 Maryland Avenue NE, Box 68
Washington, DC 20002

MADRE
121 West 27th Street, Room 301
New York, NY 10001

National Agenda for Peace in El Salvador
P.O. Box 192, Cardinal Station
Washington, DC 20064

Neighbor to Neighbor
2601 Mission Street
San Francisco, CA 94110

Peace Brigades International
Apartado Postal 3003, Correo Central
San Salvador, El Salvador

Human Rights

Americas Watch
1522 K Street NW, Suite 910
Washington DC 20005

Amnesty International
322 8th Avenue
New York, NY 10001

COMADRES
945 G Street NW
Washington, DC 20001

Comisión para la Defensa de los Derechos Humanos en Centroamérica (CODEHUCA)
Apartado Postal 189
Paseo de los Estudiantes
San José, Costa Rica

National Labor Committee in Support of Human Rights in El Salvador
15 Union Square West
New York, NY 10003

National Central America Health Rights Network (NCAHRN)/Links
P.O. Box 202
New York, NY 10276

Aid

Aesculapius International Medicine
11 John Street, 9th Floor
New York, NY 10038

Concern
P.O. Box 1790
Santa Ana, CA 92702

Mennonite Central Committee
21 South 12th Street
Akron, PA 17501

New El Salvador Today Foundation (NEST)
P.O. Box 411436
San Francisco, CA 94141

Salvadoran Medical Relief Fund
P.O. Box 1194
Salinas, CA 93902

SHARE Foundation
P.O. Box 16, Cardinal Station
Washington, DC 20064

Tours

Center for Global Education
Augsburg College
731 21st Avenue South
Minneapolis, MN 55454

Cristianos por la Paz en El Salvador (CRISPAZ)
701 S. Zarzamora
San Antonio, TX 78207

Business/Official

Embassy of El Salvador
2308 California Street NW
Washington, DC 20008

Embassy of the United States in El Salvador
APO Miami, FL 34023

Fundación Salvadoreña para el Desarrollo Económico y Social (FUSADES)
Apartado Postal 01-278
San Salvador, El Salvador

U.S. State Department
Citizen's Emergency Center/Travel Information
Main State Building
Washington DC 20520
(202) 647-5225

Country Guides

If you really want to know Central America — get the whole set!

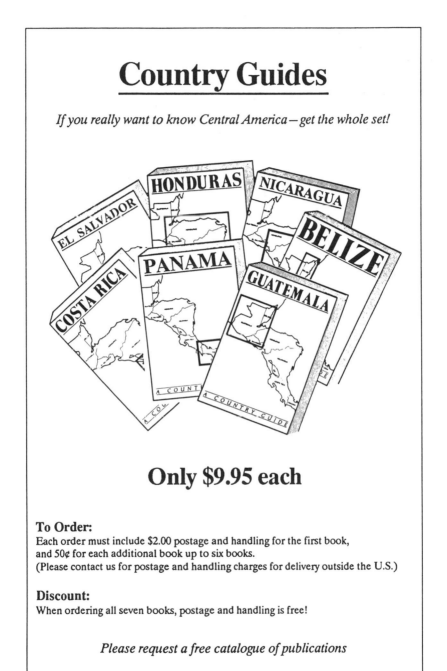

Only $9.95 each

To Order:
Each order must include $2.00 postage and handling for the first book,
and 50¢ for each additional book up to six books.
(Please contact us for postage and handling charges for delivery outside the U.S.)

Discount:
When ordering all seven books, postage and handling is free!

Please request a free catalogue of publications

The Resource Center
Box 4506 * Albuquerque, New Mexico * 87196

Also Available